The Recreation and Entertainment Industries:
An Information Sourcebook
SECOND EDITION

The Recreation and Entertainment Industries

AN INFORMATION SOURCEBOOK

second edition

by
NORMAN F. CLARKE

McFarland & Company, Inc., Publishers
Jefferson, North Carolina, and London

Library of Congress Cataloguing-in-Publication Data

Clarke, Norman F.
    The recreation and entertainment industries : an informa-
tion sourcebook / by Norman F. Clarke.— 2d ed.
       p.   cm.
    Includes index.
    ISBN 0-7864-0797-2 (softcover : 50# alkaline paper)
    1. Leisure industry — United States — Bibliography.
2. Leisure industry — Canada — Bibliography.   3. Leisure
industry — Great Britain — Bibliography.   4. Leisure
industry — United States — Directories.   5. Leisure industry — Canada — Directories.   6. Leisure industry — Great
Britain — Directories.   I. Title.
Z7164.L53 C57   2000
[GV188.3.U6]
016.3384'779 — dc21   00-41892

British Library cataloguing data are available

Manufactured in the United States of America

McFarland & Company, Inc., Publishers
  Box 611, Jefferson, North Carolina 28640
   www.mcfarlandpub.com

Contents

Introduction   1

1. **The Fitness Industry**   5
   Fitness Centers (NAICS 71394)

2. **The Skiing Industry**   12
   Skiing Facilities (NAICS 71392)

3. **The Skating Industry**   18
   Ice or Roller Skating Facilities (NAICS 71394)

4. **The Bowling Industry**   23
   Bowling Centers (NAICS 71395)

5. **The Racquet Sports Industry**   28
   Handball, Racquetball, Squash, or Tennis Facilities
      (NAICS 71394)

6. **The Golf Industry**   34
   Golf Courses or Country Clubs (NAICS 71391)
   Miniature Golf Courses or Driving Ranges
      (NAICS 71399)

7. **The Membership Club Industry**   43
   Private Membership Clubs (NAICS 71399)

8. **The Sporting Goods Industry**   49
   Sporting and Athletic Goods Manufacturing
      (NAICS 33992)
   Sporting and Recreational Goods and Supplies

Contents

Wholesale (NAICS 42191)
Sporting Goods Stores (NAICS 45111)
Used Sporting Goods Stores (NAICS 45331)
Recreational Goods Rental (NAICS 532292)

9. **The Recreational Vehicle Industry**   64
Motor Home Manufacturing (NAICS 336213)
Travel Trailer or Camper Manufacturing
(NAICS 336214)
Motorcycle, Bicycle, and Parts Manufacturing
(NAICS 336991)
ATV, Go-cart, Golf Cart, or Snowmobile
Manufacturing (NAICS 336999)
Recreational Vehicle Dealers (NAICS 44121)
Motorcycle Dealers (NAICS 441221)
Powered Golf Cart or Snowmobile Dealers
(NAICS 441229)
Recreational Vehicle Renting or Leasing
(NAICS 53212)
Bicycle or Motorcycle Repair (NAICS 81149)

10. **The Boat Industry**   73
Boat Builders (NAICS 336612)
Boat Dealers (NAICS 41222)
Boat Wholesalers (NAICS 42191)
Marinas (NAICS 71393)
Boat Repairers (NAICS 81149)

11. **The Home Amusement Industry**   82
Doll, Toy, or Game Manufacturing (NAICS 33993)
Toy and Hobby Goods and Supplies Wholesale
(NAICS 42192)
Hobby, Toy, and Games Stores (NAICS 45112)
Used Toy or Games Stores (NAICS 45331)
Electronic Game Publishing (NAICS 51121)

12. **The Gift Industry**   94
Artistic Glassware Manufacturing (NAICS 327212)

Costume Jewelry and Novelty Manufacturing
  (NAICS 339914)
Gift, Novelty, and Souvenir Stores (NAICS 45322)
Greeting Card Publishers (NAICS 511191)

13. **The Amateur Photography Industry**   100
  Photographic Film Manufacturing (NAICS 325992)
  Photographic Equipment Manufacturing
    (NAICS 333315)
  Digital Camera Manufacturing (NAICS 334419)
  Photographic Equipment and Supplies Wholesale
    (NAICS 42141)
  Video Camera Wholesalers (NAICS 42162)
  Camera and Photographic Supplies Stores
    (NAICS 44313)
  One-Hour Photofinishing (NAICS 812922)

14. **The Musical Instrument Industry**   105
  Musical Instrument Manufacturing (NAICS 339992)
  Musical Instrument Wholesale (NAICS 42199)
  Musical Instrument and Supplies Stores
    (NAICS 45114)
  Musical Instrument Rental (NAICS 532299)
  Musical Instrument Repair Shops (NAICS 81149)

15. **The Recreation/Entertainment School Industry**   110
  Fine Arts Schools (NAICS 61161)
  Sports and Recreation Schools (NAICS 61162)

16. **The Entertainment Agency Industry**   115
  Booking Agencies (NAICS 512199)
  Casting Agencies and Registries (NAICS 56131)
  Agents or Managers for Athletes or Entertainers
    (NAICS 71141)

17. **Show Business**   120
  Theatre Companies and Dinner Theaters

(NAICS 71111)
Dance Companies (NAICS 71112)
Other Performing Arts Companies (71119)

18. **The Motion Picture Industry**   129
Motion Picture, Television, or Video Production
(NAICS 51211)
Motion Picture or Video Distribution
(NAICS 51212)
Motion Picture Theaters (NAICS 512131)
Drive-in Motion Picture Theaters (NAICS 512132)
Teleproduction and Other Postproduction Services
(NAICS 512191)
Motion Picture and Video Processing Services
(NAICS 512199)
Videotape Rental Stores (NAICS 53223)

19. **The Music Industry**   143
Prerecorded Disc, Tape, and Record Reproducing
(NAICS 334612)
Prerecorded Tape, Disc, and Record Stores
(NAICS 45122)
Music Video Production and Distribution
(NAICS 51211)
Sound Recording, Production, and Distribution
(NAICS 5122)
Music Publishing (NAICS 51223)
Musical Groups (NAICS 71113)

20. **The Professional Sports Industry**   156
Sports Teams and Clubs (NAICS 711211)

21. **The Professional Racing Industry**   164
Race Tracks (NAICS 711212)

22. **The Professional Tournament Industry**   171
Spectator Sports (NAICS 711219)

Promoters of Sports Events (NAICS 7113)

23. The Public Amusement Industry   179
Promoters of Performing Arts Events (NAICS 7113)
Private Tourist Attractions (NAICS 71219)
Amusements, Theme Parks, and Arcades
   (NAICS 7131)

24. The Gambling Industry   190
Casinos (NAICS 71321)
Other Gambling Establishments (NAICS 71329)

25. The Nightclub Industry   197
Non-Alcoholic Night Clubs (NAICS 71399)
Drinking Places (NAICS 72241)

26. The Tourist Lodging Industry   205
Traveler Accommodations (NAICS 7211)
Casino Hotels (NAICS 72112)
Bed-and-Breakfast Inns (NAICS 721191)
Tourist Homes (NAICS 721199)

27. The Campground Industry   217
Hostels (NAICS 721199)
RV Parks and Campgrounds (NAICS 721211)

28. The Vacation Camp Industry   224
Recreational and Vacation Camps (NAICS 721214)

29. The Tour Industry   229
Scenic and Sightseeing Transportation, Land
   (NAICS 48711)
Scenic and Sightseeing Transportation, Water
   (NAICS 48721)
Scenic and Sightseeing Transportation, Aerial
   (NAICS 48799)
Tour Operators (NAICS 56152)
Guide Services (NAICS 71399)

30. The Travel Agency Industry   239
    Travel Agencies (NAICS 56151)
    Ticket Agencies (NAICS 561599)

Appendix: Basic Reference Sources   253
Index   271

Introduction to
the Second Edition

The recreation and entertainment industries continue to evince the most dynamic economic development in the world. Individual and corporate investment, expansion of existing facilities, and consumer participation and expenditure have maintained this record growth.

While the structures of the various recreation and entertainment industries have to this point remained relatively consistent with the pattern outlined in the first edition, major changes have taken place in the last decade in the way information is delivered and in its availability and modes of access. These changes can be summarized in three words: fax, e-mail and internet.

The emphasis in this edition is on these information delivery changes.

In addition, the following changes in the contents of the publication have been instituted.

♦ *Industry Classification* ♦

In 1997 the United States Office of Management and Budget created the *North American Industry Classification System*, an expanded and more detailed replacement for the *Standard Industrial Classification* system used in the first edition the identify industries. This edition has employed in the Table of Contents and in each chapter the new system because it recognizes industries not only in the United States but in Canada and throughout the continent.

♦ *Directories* ♦

Many directories, primarily lists of association members, previously included, have not been listed but can be found by referencing "Associations" entries.

♦ *Management-Industry-Market* ♦

Many references that were included in the first edition have not been continued because they are identified and often more easily accessed via one or more of the "Databases" or "Associations" websites.

♦ *Periodicals* ♦

Periodicals included in this edition have been limited to those which accept advertising since the factor of products and services is considered a vital element in the understanding of the industry. Newsletters and association magazines and periodicals have been referenced in the "Associations" entries.

♦ *Databases* ♦

Databases listed under this heading have been limited to those which offer a wide spectrum of information and references about a particular Industry. References to many other databases can be found listed as part of an entry for an Association and for non-association Periodicals.

♦ *Associations* ♦

In the first edition numerous associations which did not represent business enterprises, e.g., professionals, guilds, advocacy groups, amateur participants, were included since they provided information relevant to business operations. Most of these associations have been eliminated from the current listing but, where appropriate, for their business information and when accessible online, have been included in the "Databases" category.

Between the first and second editions over 50 percent of the publications and Associations changed either their name or their address. Indications are that this movement will continue. In addition, population growth in the United States, Canada, and the UK is causing major area code telephone changes. Thus, the address data found in this publication may, in the future, prove faulty.

It is recommended that persons wishing to contact an association or publisher check one of the following references: *Associations Unlimited*, published by the Gale Group and found in most major libraries online, or the *National Trade and Professional Associations* (NTPA) directory, for current information. Fortunately, three forms of address often remain the same: the last seven digits of a phone or fax number (unless the association or publisher moves), the e-mail address, and the website.

1. *The Fitness Industry*

NAICS 71394.

FITNESS CENTERS. For Fitness Shops and Equipment and Apparel Manufacturing and Servicing SEE Chapter 8.

◆ *Directories* ◆

1. *Gyms Locator*. Birmingham AL. Hot New Products. online. website: http://www.fitnesszone.com/gyms/ Listing of health clubs in the United States. Access is by city and state or by zip code.

2. *Health Clubs*. Marina del Rey CA: Fitscape. online. website: http://www.fit-net.com/gyms/ Listing of clubs worldwide. Access is by map of the US and world. For each state, country clubs are listed by name with address, phone, fax, e-mail, and area map pinpointing location of club.

3. Giordano, Frank S. *World Fitness Guide: European Edition*. San Diego CA: StayFit, c1992. 293p. Listing of fitness centers in Europe.

4. International Health, Racquet and Sports Association. *Passport*. Boston MA: Author. Annual. $50.00. website: http://www.ihrsa.org/passport/ Guide to the more than 3,000 IHRSA member clubs throughout the world who participate in IHRSA's reciprocal guest access program. Also available in database format on the Internet but is accessible only by club name. The Internet site gives information on location, phone, guest fees, and facilities.

◆ *Management* ◆

5. *Physical Fitness Center.* Irvine CA: Entrepreneur Magazine. c1992. 200p. $59.50. Step-by-step guide to the decision, opening, operating, managing, and marketing. Includes bibliographical references and an index.

6. Grantham, William C. *Health Fitness Management.* Champaign IL: Human Kinetics, c1997. 269p. $37.95. A comprehensive resource for managing and operating programs and facilities.

7. International Health, Racquet and Sports Association. *Profiles of Success.* Boston MA: Author. Annual. $400.00. Based upon IHRSA's annual Industry Data Survey. Presents key information on club operations and finances. Report details revenue and expense ratios, equipment inventories, facilities, programs, and membership growth and retention rates.

8. International Health, Racquet and Sports Association. *Ultimate Source.* Boston MA: Author. Series. $10-$25 each. An extensive and frequently updated series of publications relevant to the daily operations of a club. Covers all aspects of management, purchasing, training, marketing, and public relations.

9. International Health, Racquet and Sports Association. *Uniform System of Accounts for the Health, Racquet and Sportsclub Industry.* Boston MA: Author, c1998. $185.00. Comprehensive guide to established accounting procedures for the industry. Establishes an industry standard for revenue and expense recognition, provides a sample chart for accounts, explains how to calculate ratios, suggests methods of budgeting, and more.

10. Patton, Robert W. *Developing and Managing Health/Fitness Facilities.* Champaign IL: Human Kinetics, c1998. 364p. Textbook.

◆ *Industry* ◆

11. Gimmy, Arthur E. and Woodworth, Brian B. *Fitness, Racquet Sports, and Spa Projects.* Chicago IL: American Institute of Real Estate

Appraisers, c1989. 191p. A guide to appraisal, market analysis, development, and financing. Includes bibliography.

12. International Health, Racquet and Sports Association. *Fitness Industry Technology.* Boston MA: Author. Annual. $50.00. Publication designed to simplify the equipment purchasing process. Organized by product category with charts and graphs for equipment comparison.

13. International Health, Racquet and Sports Association. *State of the Health Club Industry.* Boston MA: Author. Annual. $275.00. Presents charts and graphs that chronicle the growth of the exercise industry. Examines internal and external factors that shape the industry and influence the prospects of growth. A directory of major fitness club companies and a compendium of cutting-edge club programs is included.

♦ *Market* ♦

14. Abdilla, Brenda. *Marketing for Results.* Fort Washington PA: CMB Books, c1996. 118p. $15.00. Provides a menu of approaches for successfully recruiting and retaining members.

15. American Sports Data. *American Health Club Experience.* Boston MA: International Health, Racquet and Sports Association, c1996. 24p. $50.00. Presents answers to the most important questions which consumers ask about health clubs. Describes factors which influence successful recruitment and member retention.

16. American Sports Data. *Why and Where People Exercise.* Boston MA: International Health, Racquet and Sports Association. c1995. 20p. $25.00. Study examining the relative value people place on exercise, training, weight control, and other factors in deciding on a fitness program. Examined age, sex, and preferred environment (i.e., club, home, work).

17. Annesi, James J. *Enhancing Exercise Motivation.* Los Angeles CA:

FM Books, c1996. 120p. A guide to increasing fitness center member retention.

18. Brooks, Christine. *How Consumers View Health and Sports Clubs.* Boston MA: International Health, Racquet and Sports Association, c1997. 132p. $150.00. In-depth research into the consumers perceptions of health, fitness, and sports clubs. Identifies attitudes which act a major barriers to club membership.

19. Fitlinxx. *Why People Quit.* Boston MA: International Health, Racquet and Sports Association, c1997. 68p. $150.00. Study of the factors which lead to club attrition and how to deal with them. Attention given to new member retention. Discusses the role of the staff in member retention. Presents case studies of four clubs.

20. Gerson, Richard F. *Fitness Director's Guide to Marketing Strategies & Tactics.* Canton OH: Professional Reports, c1992. 149p. Manual.

♦ *Periodicals* ♦

21. *American Fitness Magazine.* Sherman Oaks CA: Aerobics and Fitness Association of America. 6 issues. $27.00. Edited for fitness professionals. Features information on latest trends and research in health and exercise.

22. *Club Industry.* Atlanta GA: Primedata Intertec. Monthly. $68.00. Edited for owners and operators of fitness and health facilities as well as other membership clubs. Features news, opinions, program design, financial and operational statistics, and industry products and trends.

23. *Fitness Management.* Los Angeles CA: Leisure Publications. Monthly. $24.00. website: http://www.fitnessworld.com Provides non-technical management and other information to owners, managers, and buyers of fitness centers. Topics include motivation, marketing, law, and finance. Includes annual products and services source guide.

24. *Fitness Products News.* Arlington Heights IL: Adams Business Media. Bimonthly. free. Provides information on new products, trends, and solutions. Includes expert advice, success stories, and useful pull-out charts.

25. *IDEA Fitness Manager.* Boston MA: IDEA: The International Association for Fitness Professionals. 5 issues. membership. Provides information on program, staff, motivation, and financial management. Includes articles on start-up, new programs, marketing, and industry issues. Newsletter format.

26. *IDEA Health & Fitness Source.* Boston MA: IDEA: The International Association for Fitness Professionals. 10 issues. membership. Primarily a publication for users but is essential resource for owners and operators because of extensive coverage of new trends and products, motivational guidelines, and fitness research.

27. *National Fitness Trade Journal.* Denver CO: National Health Club Association. 6 issues. free. Provides information on new products, trends, and marketing advice. Includes reports on insurance and finances.

◆ *Databases* ◆

28. *AFFA.* Sherman Oaks CA: Aerobics and Fitness Association of America. online. website: http://www.afaa.com Resource to articles on "your body" and "lifestyle" in relationship to fitness. Provides information on certification of fitness trainers. Connection to other fitness databases.

29. *Fitclubs: Your Guide to the Health & Fitness Club Industry.* New York NY: iZing Interactive. online. website: http://www.fitclubs.com Primarily a directory to fitness associations, clubs, suppliers, and career opportunities. Gives detailed data about each fitness activity. Provides access to specific administration information on club operation via club ID and password.

30. *IDEA: the Health and Fitness Source.* Boston MA: IDEA: The International Association for Fitness Professionals. online. website: http://www.ideafit.com The most extensive source for the latest fitness and health news, information, and research. Provides access to publications, marketing opportunities, and educational products. Lists job opportunities. Gives tips on fitness and answers frequently asked questions. Offers search capabilities and links to other resources.

31. *UKFitlinks.* London ENG: Paul Furness. online. website: http://www.gifford.co.uk/~atoll/ukfitlinks Fitness links.

♦ *Associations* ♦

32. American Spa and Health Resort Association. P.O. Box 585. Lake Forest IL 60045. phone: (847) 234-8851; fax: (847) 295-7790 Association of small and diverse fitness enterprises and resorts. Serves as an information exchange and contact with data and statistical resources. Conducts inspections and certifies qualifying facilities. Sets standards.

33. The Fitness Industry Association. Argent House, 103 Frimley Rd. Camberley, Surrey ENG GU15 2PP. phone: 441276676275; fax: 44127629776 Association of operators and suppliers. Provides training and materials for persons interested in entering the fitness business. Seeks to standardize the industry practices.

34. International Health, Racquet and Sports Association. 263 Summer St. Boston MA 02210. phone: (617) 951-0055; free phone: (800) 228-4772; fax: (617) 951-0056. email: info@ihrsa.org website: http://www.ihrsa.org (annotation, same as #18, 1st edition)

35. International Physical Fitness Association. 415 Court St. Flint MI 48503. phone: (810) 239-2166; fax: (810) 239-9390. (annotation, same as #17, 1st edition)

36. International Spa and Fitness Association. 113 S. West St., Suite 400. Alexandria VA 22314-2851. phone: (703) 838-2930; fax: (703) 898-0484. Association of owners, directors, professionals, manufacturers, and others related to the fitness industry. Conducts marketing and public relations efforts. Publishes newsletter.

37. National Health Club Association. 12596 W. Bayard Ave., 1st Floor. Denver CO 80228. phone: (303) 753-6422; free phone: (800) 765-6422; fax: (303) 986-6813. Association of fitness centers and health clubs. Provides insurance and financial services. Promotes aerobic standardization. Publishes periodical. Formerly: Fitness Trade Association/National Fitness Association.

38. National Swim and Recreation Association. P.O. Box 322. Chalfont PA 18941. phone: (215) 822-0710; fax: (215) 822-5872. Association of operators of swim clubs. Publishes newsletter. Formerly: Swim Facilities Operators of America.

2. *The Skiing Industry*

NAICS 71392.

SKIING FACILITIES. For Ski Shops and Equipment and Apparel Manufacturing and Servicing SEE Chapter 8. For Ski Schools and Pro Shops SEE Chapter 15. For Professional Ski Tournaments SEE Chapter 22.

♦ *Directories* ♦

39. *Blue Book of European Ski Areas.* New York NY: Publishers Group International. Biennial. $18.95. Information on over 150 ski areas organized by country. For each area gives addresses (including e-mail and web), costs, terrain and runs, facilities, services, and travel information.

40. *White Book of Ski Areas US & Canada.* Washington DC: Inter-Ski Services. Biennial. $21.95. Information on over 800 ski areas organized by region. For each area gives address, statistics, hours and rates, facilities, services, and travel information.

41. Cross Country Ski and Nordic Center. *North American Directory Database.* Winchester NH: Cross Country Ski Areas of America. online. website: http://www.xcski.org/ccsaa-directory.htlm. Listing of CCSAA members state by state as well as Canada, Scotland, and France. Each listing contains a description as well as a checklist of on-site services.

42. National Ski Areas Association. *Membership Directory.* Lakewood CO: Author. Annual. $350.00. Listing contains addresses, phone, fax, e-mail, websites, and contacts for each member.

43. World Ski Association. *Regional/Resort Index.* Lakewood CO: Author. online. website: http://www.worldski.com/directory/ Listing of ski resorts as well as sport shops, restaurants, and other activities in resorts located by region in the United States and in Canada and Europe. Serves as a reservation and discount service directory for members of the WSA.

♦ *Management* ♦

44. Cross Country Ski Areas of America. *Cross Country USA: A Ski Area Development Manual.* Winchester NH: Author, c1997. 1v. $100.00. (annotation, same as #25, 1st edition)

45. Laventhol and Horwath. *Ski Area Financial Management Series.* Springfield MA: National Ski Areas Association. c1976-77. out of print. (annotation, same as #26, 1st edition)

♦ *Industry* ♦

46. Cross Country Ski Areas of America. *Cross Country Ski Area Operations Survey.* Winchester NH: Author. Annual. $50.00. (annotation, same as #34, 1st edition)

47. National Ski Areas Association. Economic Analysis of United States Ski Areas. Lakewood CO: Author. Annual. $200.00. Annual review of financial data and ski area characteristics, e.g., size, days of operation, capacity, skiers, and ticket prices. Includes economic ratios, probability, and regional variation factors.

48. _____. *Knottke National End-of-Season Survey.* Lakewood CO: Author. Annual. $100.00. Survey of regional and national skier and snowboarder visit data. Studies relationships between location, length of season, lift capacity, and night skiing.

49. Sierra Nevada College. *NSAA Industry and Salary Survey*. Lakewood CO: National Ski Areas Association. Annual. $400.00. Description and survey of 150 ski area positions. Present data on salaries, paid vacations, discounts and privileges, insurance, disability and retirement plans, and other benefits.

50. SnowSports Industries America. *Facts and Figures On The On-Snow Industry*. Lakewood CO: National Ski Areas Association. Annual. $450.00. Compilation of more than ten ski industry studies. Includes statistics and analysis of demographics, habits, number and type of visits, retention, and other factors.

51. University of Colorado. Business Research Division. *1976-1993 Economic Analysis of North American Ski Areas*. Boulder CO: Author, c1994. $150.00. Seventeen years of financial information. Economic and critical ratios by regions. Includes data on operations, property value, and insurance.

◆ *Market* ◆

52. Canadian Ski Council. *Canadian Skier/Snowboard Survey*. Mississauga ON: Author, c1998. $100.00. Most extensive regional and national study of demographics and consumer patterns ever completed. Based on 12,800 interviews. Complemented by "Market Segmentation Research Report" ($120.00) compiled from 1,154 questionnaires collected at eight Canadian ski areas.

53. Leisure Trends Group. *National Skier/Boarder Opinion Survey*. Boulder CO: Author. Biennial. $450.00. Reflects the results of on-slope interviews with over 20,000 skiers in the US. Identifies important demand differences between age groups, gender, residency, and skiing interests. Complemented by "Historical Perspective" survey ($250/$500) based upon 90,000 interviews.

♦ *Periodicals* ♦

54. *Ski Area Management.* Woodbury CT: Beardsley. Bimonthly. $32.00. website: http://www.saminfo.com. Edited for managers of North American ski resorts. Articles on operations, technology, products, construction, and maintenance. Specials issues: "Product and Suppliers Directory;" "Lift Construction Index."

55. *Ski Tech.* Waitsfield VT: Ski Racing International. 5 issues. $16.00. Provides product information for retail ski shops, professional ski instructors, and servicers of ski equipment.

56. *Skiing Trade News Buyers Guide.* New York NY: Times Mirror. 2 issues. free. website: http://www.skinet.com. Edited for owners and managers of ski shops and sporting goods stores. Regular features include columns on sales training, shop management, and merchandising techniques. Provides data on new ski products and skiwear.

57. *Snowboarding Business.* Oceanside CA: Transworld Media. 6 issues. free. website: http://www.twsnet.com. Edited exclusively for the snowboarding industry. Articles on current news, retailing, surveys, products, and company profiles.

58. *Wintersports Business.* Santa Fe NM: Miller Freeman. 10 issues. free. Edited for manufacturers, retailers, and distributors. Provides news and feature coverage of equipment, apparel, and accessories in the ski, snowboarding, and winter resort industry.

♦ *Databases* ♦

59. *CCSAA's Nordic, Cross Country & Snowshoeing Information Center.* Winchester NH: Cross Country Ski Areas Association. online. website: http://www.xcski.org. North American ski area directory. Information on industry and services, equipment, publications, travel and ski fests, terminology, and other websites.

60. *Great Skiing and Snowboarding in Canada.* Mississauga ON: Canadian Ski Council. online. website: http://www.skicanada.org. Information on nordic, cross country, and snowboarding. Data on ski areas in Canada, deals and events, industry newsletter and statistics, and much more. Also French edition.

61. *NSAA/OITAF National International Trade Show.* Lakewood CO: National Ski Areas Association. online. website: http://www.nsaa.org. Information about the NSSA, member update, its media center, government affairs, regional shows, a catalog of skiing and industry publications, market and marketing strategies, a skiing data and reservation service for the USA, and links to skiing databases worldwide.

62. *World Ski and Public Snowboard Associations.* Lakewood CO: World Ski Association. online. website: http://www.worldski.com. Regional/Resort Index for US, Canada, and Europe. Information on industry services and activities, ski and sports retail shops, lodging, restaurants, travel planning and deals, festivals, and "tips."

◆ *Biblio/Index* ◆

63. Morales, Leslie Anderson. *Ski Resort Design: a Bibliography.* Monticello IL: Vance, c1990. 6p. Annotated list of design and construction books and articles.

◆ *Associations* ◆

64. Canadian Ski Council. 7035 Fir Tree Dr., Unit 36. Mississauga ON L5S 1V6. phone: (905) 677-0020; fax: (905) 677-2055. website: http://www.skicanada.org. Association of lifts, resorts, instructors, and manufacturers. Compiles statistics. Conducts research. Publishes newsletter, directory, surveys, and research.

65. Cross Country Ski Areas of America. 259 Bolton Rd. Winchester

NH 03451. phone: (603) 239-4341; fax: (603) 239-6387. e-mail: ccsaa@xcski.org. website: http://www.xcski.org. Association of owners, operators, and suppliers of cross country skiing areas. Compiles statistics. Conducts research. Publishes newsletter, directory, manuals, handbooks, statistics. Formerly: National Ski Touring Operators' Association.

66. National Ski Areas Association. 133 S. Van Gordon St. Lakewood CO 80228. phone: (303) 987-1111; fax: (303) 986-2345. e-mail: info@nsaa.org. website: http://www.nsaa.org. Association of alpine ski area and resort owners, operators, and suppliers. Compiles statistics. Conducts research. Publishes newsletter, directory, research, and manuals.

67. Ski Area Management. P.O. Box 644. Woodbury CT 06789. phone: (203) 263-0888; fax: (203) 266-0452. Association of firms that sell ski lifts, over-snow vehicles, and snow grooming equipment. Aids suppliers in reaching customers. Seeks standardization of equipment. Formerly: Ski Area Suppliers Association.

3. The Skating Industry

NAICS 71394

ICE AND ROLLER SKATING FACILITIES. For Skating Shops and Ice and Ice and Roller Equipment and Apparel Manufacturing and Servicing SEE Chapter 8. For Skating Schools and Pro Shops SEE Chapter 15. For Professional Skating Leagues SEE Chapter 20. For Professional Skating Tournaments SEE Chapter 22.

♦ *Directories* ♦

68. *Arenas & Rinks*. Louisville KY: SkateAmerica. online. website: http://www.iceskate.com/arenas/arenas.htm Listing of rinks and ice skating clubs in the US organized by states. For each rink and/or club gives city, name, and phone.

69. *Skateparks*. Escondido CA: Transworld Skateboarding. online. website: http://www.skateboarding.com/skateparks/ Listing of parks in the US and Canada. Organized by state and province. Access via map. Under each state or province parks listed alphabetically by name with address, phone, park terrain, and directions for locating.

70. *UK Roller Skate Rink Directory*. Ipswich ENG: Federation of Artistic Roller Skating. online. website: http://www.british-roller-skating.org.uk/rinks/ Listing of rinks and rinks located in sports centers. Arranged alphabetically by rink name under each category. For each rink gives name, address, phone, fax, e-mail, website, and brief description of facilities.

71. Ice Skating Institute of America. *Skating Rinks.* Dallas TX: Author. online. website: http://www.skateisi.com/rinks.htm Listing of member rinks. Organized by districts in the US Separate list of international member rinks. Arranged alphabetical by state under each district. For each rink gives city, name of rink, and phone.

72. Roller Skating Association International. *Rink Locator.* Indianapolis IN: Author. online. website: http://www.rollerskating.org/ Listing of member rinks. Organized by state. Rinks listed alphabetically by city within each state. Listing for Canada and international. No information about each rink but name and city in which located.

♦ *Management* ♦

73. Ice Skating Institute of America. *Operations Manual.* Dallas TX: Author c1997. $25.00. Resource for policy, job descriptions, organization, safety, rink services, and much more.

♦ *Industry* ♦

74. Roller Skating Association International. *Roller Skating Industry Guide.* Indianapolis IN: Author, c1996. 300p. $75.00. Overview of all industry aspects, how to become involved, site selection and construction, marketing, facilities, activities, operations, management, and legal matters. Loose-leaf.

♦ *Market* ♦

75. Sports Marketing Research Group. *Sportrac: US Recreational Ice* *and Figure Skating.* New York NY: Find/SVP, c1995. 82p. $1000.00. Study of the extent to which people are using facilities and purchasing items. Provides detail profile of participant by gender, age, income level, education, and other factors.

◆ *Periodicals* ◆

76. *Inline Retailer & Industry News.* Boulder CO: Sports & Fitness. Monthly. free. Focus on dissemination of business information for the trade. Provides manufacturers with a vehicle to showcase products. Annual "Buyers Guide."

77. ISI Edge. Dallas TX: Ice Skating Institute of America. Bimonthly. membership. Geared to ISI members involved in day-to-day rink operations. Features articles on operations, maintenance, marketing, and successful customer programming. Calendar of ISI events and competitions.

78. *Roller Skating Business.* Indianapolis IN Roller Skating Association International. Bimonthly. $30.00. Edited for rink operators. Features articles on management, operations, maintenance, marketing, and safety.

79. *Skateboarding Business.* Oceanside CA: Transworld Media. 6 issues. free. Edited for manufacturers, wholesalers, and retailers. Features industry news, new product information, profiles, market data, and retailing tips. Calendar of industry events in each issue.

◆ *Databases* ◆

80. *British Artistic Roller Skating.* Ipswich ENG: Federation of Artistic Roller Skating. online. website: http://www.british-roller-skating.org.uk Provides reference to events, competitions, rinks, products and sales, and calendar of skill tests with listing of requirements for each proficiency level.

81. *Roller Skating Resources.* George Robbins. online. website: http://www.netaxs.com/people/grr/roller/ Provides reference to many roller skating websites and documents. Features conventional roller skating, roller skating rink directory, roller skating organist directory, skating book, and other skating resources and links.

82. *SkateWeb: The Figure Skating Page.* Boston MA: Sandra Loosemore. online. website: http://www.frog.simplenet.com/skateweb/ Provides reference to many ice skating websites and documents. Features current news, articles on all aspects of figure skating, an event list, current business information and trends, a directory of clubs and rinks, and a picture page.

83. *Transworld Skateboarding.* Escodido CA: Transworld Skateboarding. online. website: http://www.skateboarding.com Provides reference to events, competitions, skateparks, questions and answers, tips, and shopping information and products. Indexes issues of Transworld Skate Magazine. Contains "Message Board."

◆ *Biblio/Index* ◆

84. Huls, Mary Ellen. *Ice Rink Design and Construction: a Bibliography of Recent Literature.* Monticello IL: Vance, c1988. 5p. Annotated list of design and construction books and articles.

◆ *Associations* ◆

85. Ice Skating Institute of America. 355 W. Dundee Rd. Buffalo Grove IL 60089-3500. phone: (847) 808-7528; fax: (847) 808-8329. e-mail: isi@skateisi.com. website: http://www.skateisi.com Association of rink owners, builders, suppliers, and wholesalers, retail merchants, skating school owners and instructors, and individual skaters. Provides construction assistance and program development. Organizes competitions, trade shows. Publishes directories, periodicals, management handbooks. Computer database, directory.

86. Roller Skating Association International. 731 Georgetown Rd., Suite 123. Indianapolis IN 46268-4157. phone: (317) 875-3390; fax:

(317) 875-3394. e-mail: rsa@oninternet.com. website: http://www. rollerskating.org Association of skating center owners, manufacturers and suppliers to the industry, and coaches. Provides members with business and marketing advice. Publishes directory, business operations manuals, magazines, promotional materials, videos, and teaching tools.

4. *The Bowling Industry*

NAICS 71395

BOWLING CENTERS. For Bowling Shops and Equipment and Apparel Manufacturing and Servicing SEE Chapter 8. For Bowling Schools and Pro Shops SEE Chapter 15. For Professional Bowling Tournaments SEE Chapter 22.

♦ *Directories* ♦

87. *Bowling Alleys Around The World*. Shefield ENG: Bruce Hartlet. online. website: http://www.shef.ac.uk/~sutbc/alleys/ Listing of alleys in the United Kingdom and Ireland, The United States of America, Norway, The Netherlands, and Canada. Alleys are listed by name, address, and phone under each country or state.

88. *Bowling Center Listings*. Irvine CA: Complete Bowling Index. online. website: http://www.bowlingindex.com/centers/ Listing of centers by regions in the US with separate international listing. States are listed alphabetically with their region. Under each state centers are arranged by city in which located. Only information given on each center is its name.

89. *BPAC Member Centres*. Markham ON: Bowling Proprietors Association of Canada. online. website: http://www.mapa.com/canbowl/centres/ Listing of alleys by province. Access is by map. Centers are arranged alphabetically by name under each province. The city in which the center is located follows the name.

90. *Where are Duckpins?* DT Publishing. online. website: http:// www.duckpins.com/ducks/ Listing of alleys by state. Access is by map. Centers are alphabetized under each state. Gives name, phone, address, and number of lanes for each center.

◆ *Management* ◆

91. *Bowling Center.* Irvine CA: Entrepreneur Magazine. c1992. 200p. $59.50. Step-by-step guide to the decision, opening, operating, managing, and marketing. Includes bibliographical references and an index.

92. Lichstein, Larry. *Profitable Pro Shop.* Mechanicsville VA: Bowling Emporium, c1996. $125.00. Complete guide to starting, budgeting, equipping, retailing, operating, and managing the shop as a major activity within a center. Provides mechanical information on ball processing.

93. Picchietti, Remo N. *Liability Management.* Deerfield IL: Tech-Ed, c1992. 132p. $40.00. Do's and don'ts for accident prevention and employee safety training.

94. Picchietti, Remo N. *Science of Bowling Maintenance 2000.* Deerfield IL: Tech-Ed, c1990. 400p. $40.00. Covers all aspects of the mechanics of bowling center operations. Profusely illustrated. Recognized as industry's foremost authoritative work.

◆ *Industry* ◆

95. Bowling, Inc. *Bowlers Encyclopedia.* Greendale WI: Author. c1998. 225p. $7.95. Statistics, records, honors, competition and data on organization involved in the bowling industry in the United States.

◆ *Market* ◆

96. Bowling Proprietors' Association of America. *People Enjoy Bowling.* Greendale WI: Author (based upon US Bureau of the Census 1993 data), c1998. 7p. free. Statistics on bowling participation by geographic, demographic, and census categories.

97. Florence, Rich. *Telemarketing — A Survival Guide for Today's Bowling Proprietor.* Mechanicsville VA: Bowling Emporium, c1996. $29.95. Guide to implementing a successful program.

◆ *Periodicals* ◆

98. *Bowlers Journal.* Chicago IL: Luby. Monthly. $24.00. Edited for center owners and operators, pro shops, and retailers. Features reports on management trends and profiles, tournaments, industry trends, new products, and rules and legislation.

99. *Bowling Center Management.* Chicago IL: Luby. 11 issues. $44.00. Official publication of the Bowling Proprietors' Association of America. Edited primarily for owners and operators. Key management tool. Features new management, technical, and marketing concepts and industry and tournament news.

100. *Bowling Industry, International.* Westlake Village CA: Crown. Monthly. $38.00. Edited for owners, pro shop operators, manufacturers, and distributors. Features articles on management techniques, employee motivation, customer service, financial management, equipment maintenance, and merchandising. Includes industry and market surveys and business and company profiles.

101. *Bowling Proprietor.* Arlington TX: Bowling Proprietors' Association of America. Monthly. $30.00. Edited for center owners. Covers business practices, equipment, marketing and promotions, and general industry news.

◆ *Databases* ◆

102. *Bowling Headquarters.* Greendale WI: Bowling, Inc. online. website: http://www.bowl.org. Information and news on bowling in general and specifically on the ABC, WIBC, USAB, and YABA. Accesses employment opportunities.

103. *Brian Mclean's Canadian Bowling.* Winnipeg MB: Canadian Tenpin Federation. online. website: http://www.tenpin.org Information and link service to Canadian and other websites. Includes news of the Federation, ABC and WIBC, tournaments, Commonwealth Games, bowling addresses, and youth bowling.

104. *Complete Bowlingindex.* Irvine CA: Kina & White Advertising. online. website: http://www.bowlingindex.com Information and link service to all aspects of bowling industry worldwide. "Site navigator" to news, bowling centers, industry tournaments, who's who, instruction, products, pro shops, centers and equipment for-sale, and a chat line. Industry page contains industry news, product information, and links to finance, marketing, insurance, and support services. Bowling organization links are provided for national, regional, youth and collegiate, women's, 5-pin, duckpin, and international associations.

105. *Duckpin Bowling Pages.* DT Publishing. online. website: http://www.duckpins.com News, alerts, comments, history, rules, specs, records, directory, and links to all aspects of duckpin bowling particularly in the Eastern United States.

106. *5-Pin Bowling: A Real Canadian Sport.* Terry Burns. online. website: http://www.cvnet.net/burnstd/ News, results, history, and the game as well as "links and stuff" to Canada's unique bowling activity.

107. *Lawn Bowls.* Tony Hedges. online. website: http://www.lawnbowls.co.uk/ An Internet magazine promoting lawn bowling worldwide. Features news, a directory of sites worldwide (in process), a shop list, and details of the game.

◆ *Associations* ◆

108. Bowling Proprietors' Association of America. 615 Six Flags Dr. Arlington TX 76011. phone: (817) 649-5105; fax: (818) 633-2940. e-mail:

bpaainc@aol.com website: http://www.bpaa.com (annotation, same as #74, 1st edition)

109. Bowling Proprietors' Association of Canada. 250 Shields Circle, Suite 10A. Markham ON L3R 9W7. phone: (905) 479-1560; fax: (905) 479-8613. Association of owners of alleys. Promotes participation and competition. Represents members, business, labor, government, and public interests.

110. Duckpin Bowling Proprietors of America. 164 Turner Ave. Cranston RI 02920-2740. phone: (401) 942-7120; fax: (401) 434-3664. Association of owners of alleys, suppliers, and bowlers. Promotes participation and competition.

111. National Association of Independent Resurfacers. 5806 W. 127th St. Alip IL 60658. phone: (708) 371-8237. Association of firms and individuals in the business of resanding and refinishing bowling lanes. Establish standards. Conducts schools and seminars. Publishes newsletter, directory.

5. *The Racquet Sports Industry*

NAICS 71934.

HANDBALL, RACQUETBALL, SQUASH, OR TENNIS FACILITIES.
For Tennis Shops and Tennis Equipment and Apparel Manufacturing
and Servicing SEE Chapter 8. For Tennis Schools and Pro Shops SEE
Chapter 15. For Professional Tennis Tournaments SEE Chapter 22.

♦ *Directories* ♦

112. *Tennis Clubs.* Irvine CA: Professional Club Marketing Association. online. website: http://www.tennis-clubs.com Listing of US clubs. Access is by map. Select state. Cities listed alphabetically under each state with number of clubs located therein. Cities and clubs will be listed in alphabetical order. Extent of information for each club is in process of development during 1999.

113. *TennisCountry Travel & Camps.* JJ Unlimited. online. website: http://www.tenniscountry.com/travel/ Worldwide listing of tennis resorts and camps. Separate directory for each. Arrangement is by country alphabetically. Arrangement under country is alphabetical by name. For each gives location and phone.

114. *US Tennis Information.* Palo Alto CA: TennisOne. online. website: http://www.rhinodev.com/tennisone/us.htlm Listing of club, resort, school, and tournament tennis facilities in the US Access via map. Each state divided into major regions subdivided by metropolitan areas. Under each area facilities are listed alphabetically by name with phone number. Current tennis news within each metropolitan area is included.

115. International Health, Racquet and Sports Association. *Passport.* Boston MA: Author. Annual. $50.00. website: http://www.ihrsa.org/ passport/ Guide to the more than 3,000 IHRSA member clubs throughout the world who participate in IHRSA's reciprocal guest access program. Also available in database format on the Internet but is accessible only by club name. The Internet site gives information on location, phone, guest fees, and facilities.

◆ *Management* ◆

116. *Racquetball Club.* Irvine CA: Entrepreneur Magazine. c1992. 200p. $59.50. Step-by-step guide to the decision, opening, operating, managing, and marketing. Includes bibliographical references and an index.

117. International Health, Racquet and Sports Association. *Profiles of Success.* Boston MA: Author. Annual. $400.00. Based upon IHRSA's annual Industry Data Survey. Presents key information on club operations and finances. Report details revenue and expense ratios, equipment inventories, facilities, programs, and membership growth and retention rates.

118. International Health, Racquet and Sports Association. *Ultimate Source.* Boston MA: Author. Series. $10-$25 each. An extensive and frequently updated series of publications relevant to the daily operations of a club. Covers all aspects of management, purchasing, training, marketing, and public relations.

119. International Health, Racquet and Sports Association. *Uniform System of Accounts for the Health, Racquet and Sportsclub Industry.*

Boston MA: Author, c1998. $185.00. Comprehensive guide to established accounting procedures for the industry. Establishes an industry standard for revenue and expense recognition, provides a sample chart for accounts, explains how to calculate ratios, suggests methods of budgeting, and more.

120. US Tennis Court and Track Builders Association. *Guidelines for Tennis Court & Running Track Construction*. Ellicott City MD: Author. c1992. $25.00. Available for free printing off USTC&TBA website. Updated frequently.

◆ *Industry* ◆

121. Collins, Bill and Hollander, Zander. *Bill Collins' Tennis Encyclopedia*. Visible, c1997. 700p. $19.95. Considered the "Bible" of the tennis world. Features history, statistics, rules, biographies, rankings, and much more.

122. Gimmy, Arthur E. and Woodworth Brian B. *Fitness, Racquet Sports, and Spa Projects*. Chicago IL: American Institute of Real Estate Appraisers, c1989. 191p. A guide to appraisal, market analysis, development, and financing. Includes bibliography.

◆ *Market* ◆

123. Audits & Surveys Worldwide. *National Survey of American Tennis Players*. North Palm Beach FL: Tennis Industry Association. Periodically. $450.00. Study of players in the United States by age, sex, demographics, level of participation, and frequency. About 1000 persons who participate more then four times each year are interviewed.

◆ *Periodicals* ◆

124. *Platform Tennis News*. Upper Montclair NJ: American Platform Tennis Association. Quarterly. membership. Official publication of

APTA. Features news, schedules, rankings, new product information, and placement opportunities.

125. *Tennis Industry.* New York NY: Tennis Industry. Bimonthly. $18.00. website: http://www.tennisindustry.com Provides information on equipment and retailing with emphasis on merchandising. Special columns on new products and court construction.

♦ *Databases* ♦

126. *ITF — Tennis on Line.* London ENG: International Tennis Federation. online. website: http://www.itftennis.com Provides news and views on tennis worldwide. Features information on competitions, results, rankings, facts and figures, and many links to other tennis organizations and resources. Certain "Terms and Conditions" apply to accessing information in this database.

127. *Tennis Org UK.* North Wales ENG: Worldsystems. online. website: http://www.tennis.org.uk Premier tennis search engine. Features current news, association links, tournament information and results, players and rankings, tennis rules, tips, and techniques, references to other tennis sites, shopping information, health and general fitness news, a chat "club house," and a design service.

128. *TennisCountry.* JJ Limited. online. website: http://www.tenniscountry.com Features an information and news bank, data on tournaments and results, rankings and other tennis statistics, a worldwide directory of tennis facilities, a store of tennis merchandise, and much more.

129. *TennisOne.* Palo Alto CA: Rhino Development. online. website: http://www.rhinodev.com/tennisone/ Provides a bulletin board of current news worldwide plus ratings and rankings, two newsletters, information on tennis products, a pro column and lesson library, a directory of tennis organizations and sites, and a specific term search capacity.

130. *USTA.* White Plains NY: United States Tennis Association. online. website: http://www.usta.com Website is a major source of tennis information in the US Features news, tournament schedules and results, professional tennis information and standings, and news from the USTA regional sections including local bodies and their events.

131. *USTC&TBA.* Ellicott City MD: US Tennis Court and Track Builders Association. online. website: http://www.ustctba.com Centralized resources for information on all aspects of tennis courts. Features construction guidelines, industry resources and addresses, a searching method for locating specific builders by state, information, and product.

◆ *Biblio/Index* ◆

132. Phillips, Dennis J. *Tennis Sourcebook.* Metuchen NJ: Scarecrow, c1995. 530p. $81.00. Emphasis is on the game, not the business prospective, but a major resource nevertheless.

◆ *Associations* ◆

133. American Platform Tennis Association. P.O. Box 43336. Upper Montclair NJ 07043. phone: (973) 744-1190; fax: (973) 783-4407. website: http://www.platformtennis.com Association of court owners and individual players. Provides management counseling, and seminars. Sanctions competitions. Publishes periodicals, and handbooks.

134. International Health, Racquet and Sports Association. 263 Summer St. Boston MA 02210. phone: (617) 951-0055; free phone: (800) 228-4772; fax: (617) 951-0056. e-mail: info@ihrsa.org website: http://www.ihrsa.org (annotation, same as #108, 1st edition)

135. US Tennis Court and Track Builders Association. 3525 Endicott Mills Dr., Suite N. Ellicott City MD 21043-4547. phone: (410) 418-

4875; fax: (410) 418-4805. website: http://www.ustctba.com, Association of contractors who build tennis courts, manufacturers who supply materials for construction, and accessory suppliers, designers, architects, ands consultants. Provides specifications and counsel on construction. Certifies builders. Publishes manuals.

6. The Golf Industry

NAICS 71391, 71399.

GOLF COURSES, COUNTRY CLUBS, MINIATURE GOLF COURSES, OR DRIVING RANGES. For Golf Shops and Equipment and Apparel Manufacturing and Servicing SEE Chapter 8. For Golf Schools and Pro Shops SEE Chapter 15. For Professional Golf Tournaments SEE Chapter 22.

◆ *Directories* ◆

136. *Golf Courses of the World*. Global Image. online. website: http://www.worldgolf.com/golfcourses.html Listing of courses worldwide. Select country. Under each, access to course information is by map. Cities under countries, states, or regions are listed alphabetically. Courses are listed alphabetically by name under each city. For each course gives address, phone, type, number of holes, yardage, par, rating, slope, date opened, designer, and, for many, "course comments."

137. *Golf Index*. Glendale CA: Travel Publications. 2 issues. $40.00. Listing of courses worldwide. Edited for travel agents. Organized by state and country. Arranged alphabetically by city and names of course under each city. For each course gives phone. Special section for golf tours.

138. *Golf UK and Ireland*. GolfEurope. online. website: http://www.golfeurope.com/clubs/ Listing of courses. Access is by map. Select country. For England, Scotland, Wales, and Ireland, an additional map selection by region is required. Clubs are listed alphabetically under region. Each gives name, address, phone, secretary, directions, number of holes, yardage, par, slope, and course reviews.

139. *Private Golf Courses.* Irvine CA: Professional Club Marketing Association. online. website: http://www. privategolfcourses.com Listing of US courses. Access is by map. Select state. Cities listed alphabetically under each state with number of courses located therein. Select city and courses will be listed in alphabetical order. Each course entry gives address of the course, phone and fax, number of holes, yardage, par, slope, rating, designer, year built, season, and dress code. All PCMA course listings can be accessed in combination from any of their three websites.

140. *Public Golf Courses.* Irvine CA: Professional Club Marketing Association. online. website: http://www. publicgolfcourses.com Listing of US courses. Access is by map. Select state. Cities listed alphabetically under each state with number of courses located therein. Select city and courses will be listed in alphabetical order. Each course entry gives address of the course, phone and fax, number of holes, yardage, par, slope, rating, designer, year built, season, and dress code. All PCMA course listings can be accessed in combination from any of their three websites.

141. *Resort Golf Courses.* Irvine CA: Professional Club Marketing Association. online. website: http://www.resortgolfcourses.com Listing of US courses. Access is by map. Select state. Cities listed alphabetically under each state with number of courses located therein. Select city and courses will be listed in alphabetical order. Each course entry gives address of the course, phone and fax, number of holes, yardage, par, slope, rating, designer, year built, season, and dress code. All PCMA course listings can be accessed in combination from any of their three websites.

142. National Golf Foundation. *NGF's Golf Course Directory.* Jupiter FL: Author, c1997. 1000p. $199.00. Listing of over 14,000 US facilities. For each gives address, phone, type of course, number of holes, and more.

◆ *Management* ◆

143. Beard, James B. *Turf Management of Golf Courses.* Chelsea MI: Ann Arbor Press, c1998. 642p. $106.00. Encyclopedia of design and maintenance of fairway, green, rough, bunker, tee, putting green, and range. Features chapters on irrigation, seeding, fertilizing, products, and pests with guidelines and conversion tables. Emphasizes management techniques and efficient equipment usage and maintenance.

144. Gimmy, Arthur E. and Benson, Martin E. *Golf Courses and Country Clubs: Guide to Appraisal, Market Analysis, Development, Finance.* Chicago IL: Appraisal Institute, c1992. 163p. $60.00. Provides instruction on conducting a preliminary appraisal. Highlights such topics as best-use analysis, cost approach, income approach, and sales comparison approach. Includes examples and a section on valuation.

145. Hurdzan, Michael J. *Golf Course Architecture: Design, Construction and Restoration.* Chelsea MI: Sleeping Bear, c1996. 406p. $82.00. Reference book on the art and science of course building. Discusses site feasibility, design process, specifications, bids, layout, turfgrass, hazards, irrigation, economies, computer modeling, and the "recreation ideal."

146. Miniature Golf Development of America. *Putting Around the 21st Century.* Jacksonville FL: Author, c1997. 1v. $295.00. Reference book on all aspects of construction and operation of a miniature course. Extensive diagrams, charts, and tables.

147. National Golf Foundation. *How to Plan, Build and Operate a Successful Golf Range.* Jupiter FL: Author, c1998. 147p. $150.00. Step-by-step manual. Includes chapters on site selection, market analysis, feasibility study, revenue projections, financing, permits and zoning, design and construction, and marketing. Contains site plans and operational/financial profiles.

148. Pannell Kerr Foster PC. *Accounting for Public and Resort Golf Courses.* New York NY: Author, c1998. 86p. $45.00. Complete accounting and financial management manual. Provides examples and charts for accounting specifically designed for privately-owned courses.

149. Williams, Debra L. *Serious Business of Miniature Golf.* State College PA: Author, c1993. 1v. $30.00. Manual on the design, construction, and operation of a facility separate from or part of a larger amusement complex.

♦ *Industry* ♦

150. Muirhead, Desmond and Rando, Guy L. *Golf Course Development and Real Estate.* Washington DC: Urban Land Institute, c1994. 180p. $60.00. Addresses the needs of developers wishing to build a facility as part of a real estate development. Discusses selection, feasibility, design, environment, construction, operation, and marketing. Presents charts on comparative costs of various development options and a forecast of future developments.

151. National Golf Foundation. *Global Dimensions of the Golf Industry.* Jupiter FL: Author, c1998. 240p. $45.00. Collection of 113 articles on facilities, golfers, industry issues, marketing, and services worldwide. Describes development of courses in many countries on all continents. Examines all types of courses and facilities. Articles focus on golf tourism, women, resort development, ownership, and domes.

152. National Golf Foundation. *Operating and Financial Performance Profiles of Golf Facilities in the US.* Jupiter FL: Author. Annual. $150.00 each. Separate reports on "Daily Fee," "Municipal," and "Private" 18- and 9-hole courses. Operating data, revenues, merchandise, food, and beverage sales, expenses, net income, capital investment, rounds played, and much more nation-wide and by region.

153. National Golf Foundation. *Operational Profile of Canadian Golf Facilities.* Jupiter FL: Author, c1992. 36p. $70.00. Research report which profiles nationally and by region facilities by type, number of holes, fees, rounds played, membership, and employees. Data from 1990 but in many instances compares 1986 to 1991.

♦ *Market* ♦

154. National Golf Foundation. *Golf Consumer Spending in the United States.* Jupiter FL: Author, c1997. 105p. $115.00. Research report indicating where golfers are making their purchases. Breakdowns are given for expenditures at courses, pro shops, and a variety of off-course stores. Comparisons by gender, age, and frequency of play. Expenditures are listed in total and under 15 product categories.

155. National Golf Foundation. *Golf Participation in Canada.* Jupiter FL: Author, c1991. 60p. $100.00. Study of core, occasional, and junior golfers. Measurement is by age, gender, income, education, occupation, and geographic region. Comparison with past data included in many instances.

156. National Golf Foundation. *Golf Participation in the United States.* Jupiter FL: Author. Annual. $250.00. Ongoing national survey. Surveys households in the categories of core, occasional, junior, senior, beginning, private, and public. Measurement is by age, gender, income, education, and occupation. Provides statistics on rounds played, frequency of play, national and state participation rate, and total number of players nationally and regionally.

♦ *Periodicals* ♦

157. *Crittenden Golfinc.* San Diego CA: Crittenden Marketing. Monthly. $25.00. website: http://www.crittengolfinc.com Edited for owners, developers, investors, architects, planners, and other course decision makers. Features articles on finance, engineering, design, development, and marketing.

158. *Golf Business.* Charleston SC: Waterfront. Monthly. $59.00. Official publication of the National Golf Course Owners Association. Features articles on new concepts in golf operations. Promote the exchange of ideas. Contains columns on management, marketing, operations, employment, and related activities and services.

159. *Golf Club Management.* Weston-super-Mare, ENG: Association of Golf Club Secretaries. Monthly. membership. Official publication of the Association of Golf Club Secretaries. Features articles on the operation of British courses, trends, and news.

160. *Golf Course Management.* Lawrence KS: Golf Course Superintendents Association of America. Monthly. $48.00. Contains long articles on turf management, course design, construction, maintenance, and products. Special "Show" issue in January.

161. *Golf Course News.* Yarmouth ME: United Publications. Monthly. free. Edited for superintendents, managers, directors, and others involved in course construction and maintenance. Focus is on maintenance and preservation. Includes regular columns on sod, chemistry, accessories, vehicles, and design.

162. *Golf Range & Recreation Report.* New Canaan CT: Golf Range and Recreation Association of America. Bimonthly. $75.00. Edited for owners, operators, managers, and developers of driving ranges, practice centers, teaching facilities, and family entertainment centers with a golf component. Features articles on operations, marketing, equipment, and merchandise. Profiles model ranges and instructional programs.

163. *Golf Range Times.* Richmond VA: Forecast Golf Group. Bimonthly. $40.00. Focus is on news of value to range developers, owners, and suppliers.

♦ *Databases* ♦

164. *Golf Club Secretaries.* Weston-super-Mare, ENG: Association of Golf Club Secretaries. online. website: http://www.agcs.co.uk Focus on activities of the AGSC but includes a broad spectrum of information on the British world of golf, competitions, and links to clubs online. Includes a listing of golf publications, the association's information library, and training courses.

165. *Golf.Com.* New York NY: NBC Sports. online. website: http://www.golf.com Focus on news, tournaments, commentary. Features business, real estate, equipment, pro shop information. Additional data on women, kids, travel, and "your game."

166. *Golfersweb.* Golfersweb. online. website: http://www.golferweb.com Dedicated to golfers. Features course news, bulletin board, chat room, pro tips, weather, course directory, selected courses, products, and links to other sites.

167. *Golfweb.* New York NY: CBS. online. website: http://www.golf web.com Probably the broadest information site. Features news, activities, tournament data, commentary, newsletter, instruction, course guide, people, games, forum, chat, fantasy, travel, equipment, and pro shop data.

168. *NGF.* Jupiter FL: National Golf Foundation. online. website: http://www.wgf.org Foremost resource to business information. Gives access to general and consulting services, construction activities, the National Institute of Golf Management, frequently asked questions, calendar, publications catalog, and an extensive list of other golf websites.

169. *USGA.* Fair Hills NJ: United States Golf Association. online. website: http://usga.org Website of the controlling organization of golf in the US Extensive news coverage of amateur and professional golf, rules and the golfing system, the golf shop, and location of golfing associations.

170. *World Golf.* Global Image. online. website: http://www.world-golf.com Everything you want to know about pro golfing tournaments, names, statistics, rankings, schedules. Worldwide course directory. Also includes rules, tips, hole-in-one information, travel, classified ads, and more.

◆ *Associations* ◆

171. American Society of Golf Course Architects. 221 N. LaSalle St. Chicago IL 60601. phone: (312) 372-7090; fax: (312) 372-6160. e-mail:

asgca@selz.com website: http://www.golfdesign.org Association of architects and designers of golf courses. Publishes newsletter, directory, resource bibliography.

172. Golf Course Builders Association of America. 920 Airport Rd., Suite 210. Chapel Hill NC 27514. phone: (919) 942-8922; fax: (919) 942-6955. e-mail:gcbaa@aol.com website: http://www.gcbaa.org Association of course contractors and suppliers. Provides guidance and services. Conducts research. Conducts seminars. Publishes newsletter, directory, manuals, bibliography, and building cost statistical guide.

173. Golf Range and Recreation Association of America. P.O. Box 1265. New Canaan CT 06840. phone: (203) 972-6201; fax: (203) 972-1667. e-mail:grraa@aol.com Association of owners, operators, managers, and developers of driving ranges, practice centers, teaching facilities, and family entertainment centers with a golf component. Publishes magazine.

174. Miniature Golf Development of America. P.O. Box 32353. Jacksonville FL 32237. phone: (904) 781-4653; fax: (913) 781-4843. e-mail: info@minigolf.com website: http://www.minigolf.com Association of operators of courses, arcades, driving ranges, alternative golf facilities, batting cages, and go-kart tracks. Conducts research. Develops national promotions. Provides operational guidelines. Publishes magazine, manuals, statistics.

175. National Golf Course Owners Association. 1470 Ben Sawyer Blvd., Suite 18. Mt. Pleasant SC 29464-4535. phone: (803) 881-9956; free phone: (800) 933-4262; fax: (803) 881-9958. e-mail: info @ngcoa.com website: http://www.ngcoa.com Association of owners and operators of privately owned courses. Provides information on operations, management, regulations, taxation, marketing, and community relations. Conducts seminars and trade show. Compiles statistics. Publishes magazine, newsletter, manuals, directory.

176. National Golf Foundation. 1150 S. US Hwy. 1, Suite 401. Jupiter FL 33477. phone: (407) 744-6006; free phone: (800) 733-6006; fax: (407) 744-6107. e-mail: info@ngf.org website: http://www.ngf.org

Association of golf-oriented businesses including: facilities, developers, manufacturers, service organizations, teachers, and other golf associations. Serves as the research and planning organization for the industry. Promotes public course development. Provides seminars and consulting services. Publishes newsletter, large variety of operations and marketing manuals, statistical reports.

177. United Golfers' Association. P.O. Box 5746. Evanston IL 60204-5746. Association of clubs with predominately black members. Sponsors tournament and convention.

7. The Membership Club Industry

NAICS 71399.

PRIVATE MEMBERSHIP CLUBS. For Fitness and Health Clubs SEE Chapter 1. For Racquet Clubs SEE Chapter 5. For Golf Clubs SEE Chapter 6. For Yacht Clubs SEE Chapter 10.

◆ *Directories* ◆

179. *City Clubs.* Irvine CA: Professional Club Marketing Association. online. website: http://www.city-clubs.com Listing of US clubs. Access is by map. Select state. Cities listed alphabetically under each state with number of clubs located therein. Select city and clubs will be listed in alphabetical order. Extent of information for each club is in process of development during 1999.

180. International Health, Racquet and Sports Association. *Passport.* Boston MA: Author. Annual. $50.00. website: http://www.ihrsa.org/passport/ Guide to the more than 3,000 IHRSA member clubs throughout the world who participate in IHRSA's reciprocal guest access program. Also available in database format on the Internet but is accessible only by club name. The Internet site gives information on location, phone, guest fees, and facilities.

♦ *Management* ♦

181. Club Managers Association of America. *Club Renovations: How to Have a Successful Outcome.* Alexandria VA: Author, c1997. 222p. $49.50. Handbook of articles and references provided by professionals. Emphasis on "How to Survive." Provides names of clubs recently renovated.

182. Club Managers Association of America. *Uniform System of Financial Reporting for Clubs.* Dubuque IA: Kendall/Hunt, c1996. 87p. $95.00. Presents a total financial reporting system for club managers, controllers, and officers. Includes latest changes in financial reporting. In addition to general operational activities includes sections of food, beverages, apparel, and other activities and facilities. The main sections deal with the financial statement, supporting operating statements, and departmental schedules. A computer disc is included that contains examples for all statements found in the book.

183. International Health, Racquet and Sports Association. *Profiles of Success.* Boston MA: Author. Annual. $400.00. Based upon IHRSA's annual Industry Data Survey. Presents key information on club operations and finances. Report details revenue and expense ratios, equipment inventories, facilities, programs, and membership growth and retention rates.

184. International Health, Racquet and Sports Association. *Ultimate Source.* Boston MA: Author. Series. $10-$25 each. An extensive and frequently updated series of publications relevant to the daily operations of a club. Covers all aspects of management, purchasing, training, marketing, and public relations.

185. National Golf Foundation. *Private Clubs: Management and Operations.* Jupiter FL: Author, c1998. 204p. $45.00. Though emphasis is on private golf clubs, the topics are applicable to any membership club. Articles focus on management, record keeping, legal issues, member activities, fees, theft, food and beverages, banquets, dress codes, and personnel management.

186. Pannell Kerr Foster PC. *Federal Taxes and the Private Club*. New York NY: Author. Annual. $25.00. Newsletter providing current and background information.

187. Perdue, Joe. *Contemporary Club Management*. East Lansing MI: Educational Institute, American Hotel & Motel Association, c1997. 535p. $75.00. In partnership with Club Managers Association of American and hospitality educators. Includes chapters on operations, management, service, leadership, marketing, human resources, food service, and club entertainment.

♦ *Industry* ♦

188. Hilger Flick & Co. *Club Operations Report*. Washington DC: National Club Association, c1997. 1v. $119.00. Statistical analysis of dues, capital assessments, membership, programs, golf courses, restaurant and bar operations, and more.

189. Pannell Kerr Foster PC. *Clubs in Town and Country*. New York NY: Author. Annual. $50.00. Statistical review incorporating operating and financial data on private clubs in the US.

♦ *Market* ♦

190. Club Managers Association of America. *Club Membership Drives and Marketing*. Alexandria VA: Author, c1996. 195p. $43.00. Articles on how to identify the market and strategies for successfully tapping it. Includes sample marketing plans, membership drive programs, membership letters, applications, and agreements, and club promotions and events. Samples of materials included.

191. National Club Association. *Essentials of Marketing: Guide to Building Club Expertise*. Washington DC: Author, c1995. 84p. $75.00.

Manual designed to help identify and evaluate potential and competition, to survey, set market goals, and develop strategies.

♦ *Periodicals* ♦

192. *Club Director.* Washington DC: National Club Association. Bimonthly. membership. Edited for officers, directors, owners, and general managers of private clubs. Focuses on financial operations, strategic planning, personnel management, capital improvements, taxation, policy and procedures, and trends in the industry.

193. *Club Industry.* Atlanta GA: Primedata Intertec. Monthly. $68.00. Edited for owners and operators of fitness and health facilities as well as other membership clubs. Features news, opinions, program design, financial and operational statistics, and industry products and trends.

194. *Club Management.* St. Louis MO: Finan. 6 issues. $21.95. Official publication of the Club Managers Association of America. Edited for club executives. Features news trends, products, and services. Information on management and marketing activities and ideas. Special columns on design and construction and equipment.

195. *Private Clubs.* Dallas TX: Associate Clubs. 6 issues. $15.00. Primarily a publication for members of clubs. Focus is on information about activities and clubs worldwide. Goal is to encourage and assist club member in visits to associated clubs worldwide. Helpful to owners and operators in understanding club operations, promotions, and member motivations.

♦ *Databases* ♦

196. *Canadian Society of Club Managers.* Toronto ON: Canadian Society of Club Managers. online. website: http://www.cscm.org

Information resource for managers and other administrators as well as the general public. Provides industry updates, association news, access to an association library and links to other related associations.

197. *ClubNet.* Alexandria VA: Club Managers Association of America. online. website: http://www.cmaa.org Official website of the Club Managers Association of America. Provides news, an index referencing learning activities, services, "Buyers Guide," internships, international club network, professional development, placement, Bookmart," online publications, "Clubs on the Web," conferences and expositions, and member directory.

198. *NCA Resource Center.* Washington DC: National Club Association. online. website: http://www.natlclub.org/resource_center.htm Comprehensive database referencing key subjects for which information can be found in the NCA Resource Center. Over 30 major headings and several hundred subcategories. Topics range from "Children" to "Tax Issues."

199. *PCMA.* Irvine CA: Professional Club Marketing Association. online. website: http://www.pcma.net Official website of the Professional Marketing Association. Provides international directories of private clubs. News and data for marketing and managers. Informs on latest trends in marketing. Educates through seminars. Provides access to consulting services. Newsletter online.

200. *Virtual Club.* St. Louis MO: Finan. online. website: http://www.club-mgmt.com Resource for club industry professionals. Provides news, top stories, online searching, e-mail, message board, mailing lists, and classifieds. Information sections on dining room, golf courses, sports, and boards.

♦ *Associations* ♦

201. ClubCorp International. 3030 LBJ Freeway, Suite 500. Dallas TX 75234. phone: (972) 243-6191 website: http://www.clubcorp.com Association of private athletic, city, and country clubs. Serves as a link for members and managers between clubs. Publishes periodical, directory.

202. International Health, Racquet and Sports Association. 263 Summer St. Boston MA 02210. phone: (617) 951-0055; free phone: (800) 228-4772; fax: (617) 951-0056. e-mail: info@ihrsa.org website: http://www.ihrsa.org (annotation, same as #18, 1st edition)

203. National Club Association. 1120 20th St., NW, Suite 725. Washington DC 20036. phone: (202) 822-9822; free phone: (800) 625-6221; fax: (202) 822-9808. website: http://www.natlclub.org Provides support and information to assist club leaders in addressing legal, governance, and business concerns. Helps clubs with financial matters. Lobbys in behalf of club issues at the federal level. Conducts research. Compiles statistics. Publishes periodical, directory, manuals.

8. The Sporting Goods Industry

NAICS 33992, 42191, 45111, 45331, 532292.

SPORTING GOODS MANUFACTURERS, WHOLESALERS, STORES. For Recreation Vehicles (land) SEE Chapter 9. For Recreational Vehicles (water) SEE Chapter 10. For Games and Toys SEE Chapter 11.

◆ *Directories* ◆

204. *American Sportfishing Members Locator*. Alexandria VA: American Sportsfishing Association. online. website: http://www.asafishing. org Listing of member companies. Access is by company name, product category, brand name, city, and country. An alphabetical listing by first letter of company name is also available. For each member gives name, product category, brand name(s), address, phone, and website. Also published in print.

205. *NSGA Buying Guide*. Mount Prospect IL: National Sporting Goods Association. Annual. $250.00. Listing of over 10,000 suppliers. Access is by product and name of company. For each company gives address, phone, fax, agents and wholesalers, and products. Members of NSGA have access to "Guide" via Internet website.

206. *Snowlink*. McLean VA: Snow Sports Industries America. online. website: http://www.snowlink.com Separate listings of retailers, products, resorts, and clubs. List of retailers is accessed by zip code and various radii mileages around the zip code. Retailers are listed alphabetically by name with address, phone, and website. Products are accessed by product line and specific type. Companies are listed alphabetically under each with address, phone, and website. Resorts and clubs have separate lists and are accessed similarly by region and state. Listing is under name with address, phone, and website. Websites listed are linked.

207. *Sportlink.* North Palm Beach FL: Sporting Goods Manufacturers Association. online. website: http://www.sportlink.com Separate listings for products and producers. Products list is accessed by major category, then by specific activity or sport, and, finally, by specific product. Producers are listed alphabetically by company name with phone, fax number, city in which located, and websites. Websites are linked.

208. *Where to Shoot.* Newtown CT: National Shooting Sports Foundation. online. website: http://www.nssf.org Listing of ranges. Access is via state, then by type of organization, e.g., club, then by type of facility, e.g., handgun-outdoor. For each gives name, address, and website. Websites are linked. Alternative access is by zip code.

◆ *Management* ◆

209. *Sporting-Goods Store.* Irvine CA: Entrepreneur Magazine. c1992. 200p. $59.50. Step-by-step guide to the decision, opening, operating, managing, and marketing. Includes bibliographical references and an index.

210. Industry Insights, Inc. *Cost of Doing Business.* Mount Prospect IL: National Ski and Snowboard Retailers Association, c1998. 60p. $110.00. Survey of 54 retailers. Inventory of profitability based upon performance, revenue, income statements, and several standard financial ratios. Specifically examine snowboarding, ski shops, and single and multiple establishment.

211. National Shooting Sports Foundation. *So You Want To Build A*

Shooting Range. Newtown CT: Author, c1998. 18p. $25.00. Step-by-step guide to decision making including how to write a business plan, predicting demand, estimating costs, potential revenue, marketing, and financing. Provides examples of how to formulate each step.

♦ *Industry* ♦

212. American Sportfishing Association. *Economic Impact of Sport Fishing in the US.* Alexandria VA: Author, c1996. 55p. $55.00. Overview and statistical study of the impact nationally and regionally of fishing activities and purchases. Number of persons involved and expenditures on equipment, supplies, licenses, and related acquisitions examined.

213. Sporting Goods Manufacturers Association. *Industrial Financial Study.* North Palm Beach FL: Author. Annual. $300.00. Compendium of company sales and financial records. Based upon actual sales. Presents 26 key financial ratios including margins, productivity, and profitability. Organized for ease of comparison.

214. Sporting Goods Manufacturers Association. *Sporting Goods Import Report.* North Palm Beach FL: Author. online. website: http://www.sportlink.com/research/ Some analysis but largely charts. Import valuation and percent of change 1990-1997. List of largest import increases and decreases 1992-1997. Imported by country 1995-1997. Statistics and charts of imports by individual 1992-1997.

215. Sporting Goods Manufacturers Association. *State of the Industry.* North Palm Beach FL: Author. online. website: http://www.sportlink.com/research/ Examine changes in technology, lifestyles, generation trends, new marketing techniques, equipment, apparel, and footwear fashions, and geographical trends. Reports market segmentation and market share by outlet. Presents overview by specific sports.

♦ *Market* ♦

216. Find/SVP. *Market Research Reports: Sporting Goods.* New York NY: Author. Series. $1000-$2500. An annually published market survey of many sporting goods markets. Published individually. Table of contents of latest found on Find?SVP website. Focuses on owners and their reasons for ownership. Numerous statistics and charts comparing activities and ownership by age, gender, type of weapon.

217. National Sporting Goods Association. *Sporting Goods Market.* Mount Prospect IL: Author. Annual. $225.00. Survey of 100,000 households on purchases of equipment and apparel. Provides unit and price point information, sales by channel of distribution, and demographics of purchasers.

218. National Sporting Goods Association. *Sports Participation in 1997.* Mount Prospect IL: Author, c1997. $525.00. Sampling of 15,000 to 20,000 households covering 32 sports in Series 1 and 28 other activities in Series 2. Demographic data includes gender, age, income level, and education. Geographic analysis includes nine US census regions, states, and 47 metropolitan areas. Part of a series of studies conducted on a two-year cycle.

♦ *Periodicals* ♦

219. *American Firearms Industry.* Fort Lauderdale FL: National Association of Federally Licensed Firearms Dealers. Monthly. $15.00. Edited for retailers. Covers all aspects of the outdoors market. Features new products, sales program, legislation and regulations, law enforcement, and security issues. Special "Show" issue" in January.

220. *Archery Business.* Minnetonka MN: Ehlert Publishing Group. 7 issues. free. Edited for the business side of bowhunting and archery. Includes trade news, industry statistics, marketing and product trends, new product R&D, tips for effective retailing.

221. *ASR Trade Expo Show Guide.* Laguna Beach CA: Miller Freeman. 2 issues. free. website: http://www.asrbiz.com Guide to the Action Sports Retailer Trade Expo. Edited for retailers and manufacturers of all types of sports apparel. Provides information on the products of over 800 manufacturers.

222. *Bowlers Journal.* Chicago IL: Luby. Monthly. $24.00. Edited for center owners and operators, pro shops, and retailers. Features reports on management trends and profiles, tournaments, industry trends, new products, and rules and legislation.

223. *Bowling and Billiard Buyers Guide.* Chicago IL: Luby. Annual. free. Edited for bowling and billiard center owners and operators, pro shops, and dealers. Listing of products and their distributors.

224. *Fishing Tackle Retailer.* Montgomery AL: B.A.S.S. 11 issues. free. Edited for retailers. Features news and trends, new products, merchandising and sales techniques, industry statistics, and regional news. Special features in each issue.

225. *Fishing Tackle Trade News.* Camden ME: Down East Enterprise. Monthly. free. Edited for retailers, dealers, wholesalers, and manufacturers. Features news and product information. Articles on demographics, markets, and leaders in the industry.

226. *Golf Pro.* New York NY: Fairchild. 10 issues. $9.95. Edited for the pro shop and golf specialty retailers. Features information on design and trends in equipment and apparel. Articles on demographics, marketing, and successful golf merchants.

227. *Golf Product News.* Fair Lawn NJ: Golf Publishing Enterprises. 8 issues. free. Edited for owners of facilities, professionals, and merchandisers. Features new products, changes, merchandising, and shop operations. Special focus each issue.

228. *Golf Shop Operations.* Trumbull CT: New York Times. 10 issues. $72.00. website: http://www.golf.com/gso Edited for shop owners and managers. Emphasis is on how to operate and manage successfully and profitably.

229. *Golf Source Magazine.* Freehold NJ: Robertson Williams. Quarterly. $45.00. Edited for the retailer. More of a buyers' guide than a magazine. Focus is on products, comparison between brands, and product detail and analysis.

230. *Harpers Sports and Leisure.* Watford ENG: Harpers. 19 issues. $80.00. website: http://www.harpub.co.uk Edited for UK manufacturers, distributors, and retailers. Features product news and updates, statistical data, and trade show information. Various sports industries featured each month, e.g., golf in December issue.

231. *Hockey Business News.* Los Angeles CA: Straight Line Communications. 8 issues. free. Edited for in-line retailers. Features news and events, industry trends and forecasts, new product news, industry surveys, research data, revenues and marketshare, and marketing and promotion tips.

232. *Inline Retailer & Industry News.* Boulder CO: Sports & Fitness. Monthly. free. Focus on dissemination of business information for the trade. Provides manufacturers with a vehicle to showcase products. Annual "Buyers' Guide."

233. *Material Matters.* Fair Lawn NJ: Golf Publishing Enterprises. 4 issues. free. Edited for golf apparel retailers. Focus is on new products, trends, and companies.

234. *Outdoor Press.* Spokane WA: Outdoor Press. Weekly. $30.00. Edited for people involved in all aspects of sports. Focus is on news, events, regulations, products, "where to go," and "what to do."

235. *Outdoor Retailer.* Laguna Beach CA: Miller Freeman. Monthly. free. website: http://www.outdoorbiz.com Edited for specialty retailers and manufacturers dealing in camping, hiking, water sports, winter sports, and fishing. Emphasis is on apparel. Feature articles on new products, market trends, and merchandising. Annual buyers' guide.

236. *Outfitter Magazine.* Phoenix AZ: Virgo. Monthly. $49.00. website: http://www.outfittermag.com Edited for retailers of outdoor apparel. Features new products, trends, fabrics and fibers, mass merchandising, mail order selling, retail profiles, and international marketing. Special features in each issue.

237. *Powersports Business.* Minnetonka MN: Ehlert Publishing

Group. 16 issues. free. Designed as a medium between manufacturers of recreational vehicles and personal watercraft and retailers. Focus is on news, new products, legislative and regulatory issues, market analysis, sales and marketing tips, and dealer-manufacturers coordination.

238. *Retail Focus.* Mount Prospect IL: National Sporting Goods Association. 11 issues. $50.00. Official publication of the NSGA. Focus is on association news, market research, new products, and member profiles.

239. *S.H.O.T. Business.* Los Angeles CA: Peterson. Monthly. $25.00. Edited for sporting firearm and related retailers. Features articles on management, marketing, public relations, finance, and insurance. Special catalog issue published twice each year.

240. *Shooting Industry.* San Diego CA: Publishers' Development Corp. Monthly. $12.50. Edited for licensed gun dealers. Features news, new products, trends, developments in the industry, and marketing techniques. Special emphasis on legislation and regulation.

241. *Shooting Sports Retailer.* New York NY: SSR Communication. 6 issues. $30.00. Edited for retailer. Emphasis is on management and merchandising. Special features include facing sales programs and regulations.

242. *Skateboarding Business.* Oceanside CA: Transworld Media. 6 issues. free. Edited for manufacturers, wholesalers, and retailers. Features industry news, new product information, profiles, market data, and retailing tips. Calendar of industry events in each issue.

243. *Ski Tech.* Waitsfield VT: Ski Racing International. 5 issues. $16.00. Provides product information for retail ski shops, professional ski instructors, and servicers of ski equipment.

244. *Skiing Trade News Buyers Guide.* New York NY: Times Mirror. 2 issues. free. website: http://www.skinet.com Edited for owners and managers of ski shops and sporting goods stores. Regular features include columns on sales training, shop management, and merchandising techniques. Provides data on new ski products and skiware.

245. *Snowboarding Business.* Oceanside CA: Transworld Media. 6 issues. free website: http://www.twsnet.com Edited exclusively for the snowboarding industry. Articles on current news, retailing, surveys, products, and company profiles.

246. *Sporting Goods Business.* New York NY: Miller Freeman. 18 issues. $65.00. website: http://www.sgblink.com Edited for a cross section of the sports industry including manufacturers and distributors. Focus is on trends and their potential effect on retail sales. Articles include industry statistics, market research, and profiles of top producers. Special focus feature in each issue.

247. *Sporting Goods Dealer.* Atlanta GA: Shore-Varrone. 4 issues. $37.00. website: http://www.svi-atl.com Provides news and technical product information, rule changes, merchandising trends, management information for retailers who deal primarily with school, college, and professional teams. Emphasis is on "how-to" operation and marketing. Special focus feature in each issue.

248. *Sports Trends.* Atlanta GA: Shore-Varrone. Monthly. $71.00. website: http://www.sportstrend.com Edited for the full-line sports retailer, department, chain, discount, catalog, etc. Emphasis on new products. Focus feature in each issue.

249. *Sportstyle.* New York NY: Fairchild. Monthly. free. Worldwide news and product information on men's, women's and children's active sportswear and beachwear. Features fashion trends. Covers market and merchandising. Special focus feature in each issue.

250. *Stringer's Assistant.* Del Mar CA: United States Racquet Stringers Association. Monthly. $63.00. Official publication of the USRSA. Edited for members and others interested in learning about new products, techniques and trends.

251. *Tennis Buyers Guide.* Los Angeles CA: Miller. 4 issues. $28.00. Provides current information on equipment, shoes, apparel, and accessories. Reports industry news and trends. Presents merchandising, display, and retailing tips. Includes directory of manufacturers.

252. *Tennis Industry.* New York NY: Tennis Industry. Bimonthly. $18.00. website: http://www.tennisindustry.com Provides information on equipment and retailing with emphasis on merchandising. Special columns on new products and court construction.

253. *Wintersports Business.* Santa Fe NM: Miller Freeman. 10 issues. free. Edited for manufacturers, retailers, and distributors. Provides news and features coverage of equipment, apparel, and accessories in the ski, snowboard, and winter resort industry.

◆ *Databases* ◆

254. *Sporting & Recreational Goods.* Ottawa ON; Industry Canada. online. website: http://www.strategis.ic.gc.ca Industry overview of Canadian sporting goods. Includes directory of manufacturers online, an industry profile, the retail market, statistics, and Canada's international business strategy. One of a major series of Industry Canada business overviews. Internet access to this database is more easily accessed through http://www.csga.com then click on "sporting goods industry."

◆ *Associations* ◆

255. American Sports Fishing Association. 1033 N. Fairfax St., Suite 200. Alexandria VA 22314. phone: (703) 519-9691; fax: (703) 519-1872. e-mail: amsportsfish@delphi.com website: http://www.asafishing.org Association of manufacturers and importers of fishing tackle and allied products. Promotes sport and sponsors "National Fishing Week." Compiles statistics. Conducts research. Sponsors trade show. Publishes newsletter, directory, buyers' guide. Formerly: American Fishing Tackle Manufacturers Association; Associated Fishing Tackle Manufacturers.

256. Archery Manufacturers and Merchants Organization. 4131 NW 28th Ln., Suite 7. Gainesville FL 32606-6681. phone: (904) 377-8262;

fax: (904) 375-3961. Association of manufacturers, distributors, dealers, and suppliers of bows, arrows, and other archery accessories. Promotes and protects sport. Establishes standards. Publishes manuals. Formerly: Archery Manufacturers and Dealers Association; Archery Manufacturers Association; Archery Manufacturers Organization.

257. Archery Range and Retailers Organization. 156 N. Main. Oregon WI 53575. phone: (608) 835-9060; fax: (608) 835-9360. Association of owners of shops and indoor facilities. Functions as a cooperative buying agency. Sanctions indoor leagues. Conducts trade show. Formerly: Archery Lane Operators Association.

258. Association of Golf Merchandisers. 8102 E. Culver St. Mesa AZ 85207. phone: (602) 373-8564; fax: (602) 373-8518. Association of buyers and vendors. Provides networking. Conducts seminars and annual conference. Compiles statistics. Maintains library.

259. Association of Importers-Manufacturers for Muzzleloading. P.O. Box 684. Union City TN 38281. phone: (901) 885-0374; fax: (901) 885-0440. Association of manufacturers and distributors. Lobbys for legislation and regulation. Promotes education and safety. Conducts conference.

260. Billiard and Bowling Institute of America. 200 Castlewood Dr. North Palm Beach FL 33408-5696. phone: (561) 840-1120; fax: (561) 863-8984. website: http://www.sportlink.com Association of distributors and manufacturers. Conducts seminars and trade show. Publishes newsletter, directory, buyers guide, product list, manuals. Affiliated with: Sporting Goods Manufacturers Association.

261. British Sports and Allied Industries Federation. Federation House. Stoneleigh Park ENG CV8 2RF. e-mail: admin@british-sports.co.uk website: http://www.british-sports.co.uk Association of manufacturers. Represents members before government agencies and international bodies. Promotes exports and athletic involvement. Conducts seminars. Sponsors trade show. Compiles statistics. Publishes newsletter.

262. Camping and Outdoor Leisure Association. 58 Station

Approach. South Ruislip ENG HA4 6SA. phone: 441818421111; fax: 441818420090. e-mail: 101703.2503@compuserve.com Association of manufacturers, wholesalers, distributors, importers, and retailers. Promotes outdoor leisure. Publishes periodical.

263. Canadian In-Line and Roller Skating Association. 679 Queens Quay W., Suite 117. Toronto ON M5V 3A9. phone: (416) 260-0018; fax: (416) 260-0798. e-mail: cirsa@ican.net website: http://www.ican.net/~circa Association of manufacturers and retailers. Promotes in-line and roller skating and roller hockey. Sanctions roller hockey leagues, speedskating facilities and training programs. Provides insurance. Sponsors events and competitions. Conducts research. Compiles statistics. Publishes magazine.

264. Canadian Sporting Arms and Ammunition Association. P.O. Box 235. Coburg ON K9A 4K5. phone: (905) 373-1623; fax: (905) 373-1706. e-mail: showgun@eagle.ca website: http://www.eagle.ca/showgun Association of manufacturers, wholesaler, distributors, and retailers. Promotes positive business image. Represents members before government agencies. Maintains library.

265. Canadian Sporting Goods Association. 455 St. Antoine St., W., Suite 510. Montreal PG H2Z 1J1. phone: (514) 393-1132; fax: (514) 393-9512. e-mail: info@csga.ca website: http://www.csga.ca Association of manufacturers, importers, suppliers, and distributors. Represents members' legislative and international trade interests. Conducts surveys. Sponsors trade show. Publishes directory.

266. Diving Equipment and Marketing Association. 2050 S. Santa Cruz St., Suite 1000. Anaheim CA 92805-6816. phone: (714) 939-6399; free phone: (800) 862-3483; fax: (714) 939-6398. e-mail: demo 110@aol.com website: http://www.dema.org International association of organizations promoting sports diving. Promotes industry. Develops standards. Establishes education programs, seminars, conferences, trade shows. Maintains library. Publishes newsletter, manuals. Formerly: Diving Equipment Manufacturers Association.

267. European Fishing Tackle Trade Association. 51 Cloth Fair.

London ENG EC1A 7JQ. phone: 441716060555; fax: 441716060226. e-mail: eftta@martex.co.uk website: http://www.martex.co.uk/eftta Association of manufacturers, wholesalers, and distributors. Promotes and protects interests of members. Develops specifications and establishes standards. Conducts research. Sponsors trade show. Publishes newsletter, directory, handbook. Affiliated with: American Sports Fishing Association.

268. Golf Manufacturers and Distributors Association. P.O. Box 37324 Cincinnati OH 45222. phone: (513) 631-4400. Association of exhibitors at PGA trade shows. Publishes newsletter.

269. International Inline Skating Association. 201 N. Front St., Suite 306. Wilmington NC 28401. phone: (901) 762-7004; fax: (901) 762-9477. e-mail: direction@iisa.com website: http://www.iisa.org Association of manufacturers, retailers, and skaters. Compiles statistics. Certifies instructors.

270. National Association of Federally Licensed Firearms Dealers. 2455 E. Sunrise Blvd., Suite 916. Fort Lauderdale FL 33304-3118. phone: (954) 561-3505; fax: (954) 561-4129. website: http://www.amfire.com Association of persons licensed by the federal government to sell firearms. Provides retailers with low-cost liability insurance, current information on new products, notice of new laws and regulations, and retailing guidance. Compiles statistics. Sponsors trade expo. Publishes periodical, trade show annual, buying directory.

271. National Association of Sporting Goods Wholesalers. 400 E. Randolph St., Suite 700. Chicago IL 60601-7329. phone: (312) 565-0233; fax: (313) 565-2654. Association of wholesalers and manufacturers primarily of fishing and shooting equipment. Conducts research. Sponsors trade show. Publishes directory.

272. National Shooting Sports Foundation. 11 Mile High Rd. Newtown CT 06470-2359. phone: (203) 426-1320; fax: (203) 426-1087. e-mail: info@nssf.org website: http://www.nssf.org Association of retailers, manufacturers, owners and mangers of shooting facilities, and individuals.

273. National Ski and Snowboard Retailers Association. 1699 Wall St. Mount Prospect IL 60056-5780. phone: (847) 439-4293; fax: (847) 439-0111. e-mail: nsgal699@aol.com Association of ski and snowboard stores. Compiles statistics. Provides business services. Publishes newsletter, annual statistical survey.

274. National Snow Industries Association. 245 Victoria St., Suite 810. Westmount QC H3Z 2M6. phone: (514) 939-7370; free phone: (800) 263-6742; fax: (514) 939-7371. e-mail: nsia@netc.net Association of manufacturers, distributors, and suppliers. Works with the Canadian Ski Council to develop marketing programs. Conducts seminars and trade shows.

275. National Sporting Goods Association. 1699 Wall St. Mount Prospect IL 60056-5780. phone: (847) 439-4000; fax: (847) 439-0111. e-mail: nsgal699@aol.com website: http://www.nsgachicagoshow.com Association of retailers, manufacturers, wholesalers, and importers. Provides site location data, business analysis, and marketing services. Conducts research. Compiles statistics. Sponsors Sports Expo. Publishes periodical, directory, research studies, manuals.

276. Professional Clubmakers Society. 70 Persimmon Ridge Dr. Louisville KY 40245. phone: (502) 241-2816; free phone: (800) 548-6094; fax: (241) 2817. e-mail:pcs@ntr.net website: http://www.proclubmakers.org Association of professional builders, fitters, and repairers. Conducts research. Provides seminars and courses. Certifies. Publishes periodical, newsletter, directory.

277. Professional Golf Club Repairman's Association. 2295 Ben Hogan Dr. Dunedin FL 34698. phone: (813) 733-9241; free phone: (800) 746-8493; fax: (813) 787-4361. Association of persons engages in repair and custom manufacturing. Conducts research. Sponsors schools and seminars. Publishes periodical.

278. Scuba Retailers Association. 4 Florence St. Somerville MA 02145. phone: (617) 623-7722; fax: (617) 776-6890. Association of store owners and operators. Compiles statistics. Sponsors trade show. Publishes periodical.

279. Snow Sports Industries America. 8377-B Greensboro Dr. McLean VA 22102-3587. phone: (703) 556-9020; fax: (703) 821-8276. e-mail: siamail@snowsports.com website: http://www.snowlink.com Association of manufacturers, distributors, and suppliers of ski, snowboard, apparel, footwear, and outdoor accessories. Conducts research. Maintains library. Publishes newsletter, research reports, trade and retailer advisories, trade show directory. Formerly: Ski Industries Association.

280. Soccer Industry Council of America. 200 Castlewood Dr. North Palm Beach FL 33408-5696. phone: (561) 840-1171; fax: (561) 863-8984. e-mail: sosgma@aol.com website: http://www.sportsite.com Association of manufacturers, suppliers, and retailers. Promotes growth of game through grassroots programs. Compiles statistics. Publishes newsletter, directory, annual survey. Affiliated with: Sporting Goods Manufacturers Association.

281. Sporting Goods Agents Association. P.O. Box 998. Morton Grove IL 60053. phone: (847) 296-3670; fax: (847) 827-0196. Association of manufacturers' agents. Provides legal counsel. Conducts seminars. Publishes newsletter, directory, yearbook. Formerly: Sporting Goods Representatives Association.

282. Sporting Goods Manufacturers Association. 200 Castlewood Dr. North Palm Beach FL 33408-5696. phone: (561) 842-4100; fax: (561) 863-8984. website: http://www.sportlink.com Umbrella association primarily of manufacturers of goods and apparel. Conducts research. Compiles statistics. Sponsors trade show. Publishes newsletter, directory, research reports. Formerly: Athletic Goods Manufacturers Association.

283. Tackle and Shooting Sports Agents Association. 1033 N. Fairfax St., Suite 200. Alexandria VA 22314-1540. phone: (703) 683-6534; fax: (703) 519-1872. Association of manufacturers' representatives. Publishes newsletter, directory.

284. Tennis Industry Association. 200 Castlewood Dr. North Palm Beach FL 33408-5696. phone: (561) 848-1826; fax: (561) 863-8984.

e-mail: bptia@aol.com website: http://www.sportlink.com Association of manufacturers of equipment and apparel, court builders and architects, suppliers, and distributors. Represents members legislative interests. Conducts research. Compiles statistics. Maintains library. Publishes newsletter, research and statistical studies. Formerly: American Tennis Industry Foundation. Affiliated with: Sporting Goods Manufacturers Association.

285. United States Racquet Stringers Association. P.O. Box 40. Del Mar CA 92014. phone: (619) 481-3545; fax: (619) 481-0624. e-mail: usrsa@aol.com website: http://www.tennisone.com Association of individuals interested in learning and practicing. Provides latest information and consultation. Conducts experiments and seminars. Publishes newsletter, annual digest manual.

286. Water Sports Industry Association, 200 Castlewood Dr. North Palm Beach FL 33408-5696. phone: (561) 840-1185; fax: (561) 863-8984. website: http://www.sportlink.com Association of manufacturers and distributors of equipment and apparel. Compiles statistics. Formerly: Water Ski Industry Association. Affiliated with: Sporting Goods Manufacturers Association.

287. World Federation of the Sporting Goods Industry. Le Hameau, BP 480. Verbier SWI CH-1936. phone: 41277753570; fax: 41277753579. Association of national and commercial organization, companies, and consultants in 98 countries. Promotes free international trade. Represents industry before international bodies. Advocates standardization. Conducts research. Compiles statistics. Publishes directories, research studies, manuals.

9. The Recreational Vehicle Industry

NAICS 336213, 336214, 336991, 336999, 44121, 441221, 441229, 53212, 81149.

RECREATIONAL VEHICLES (LAND). For Recreational Vehicles (water) SEE Chapter 10.

♦ *Directories* ♦

288. *Bike Shops.* Planet C. online. website: http://www.cycling.org/directories/bike–shops.htm Listing of shops in the US Access by state. Within each state the shops are listed alphabetically by name with address, phone, and reference to a map indicating the location of the shop. Additional access to shops is available by zip code and key words. This database is being continually updated.

289. *Cycle Dealers County List.* Royal Tumbridge Wells ENG: Association of Cycle Traders. online. website: http://www.cyclesource.co.uk/directory Listing of British shops. Access by county. Within each county the shops are listed by city, then by name of the shop with address, and phone.

290. *Find an RV Manufacturer.* Reston VA: Recreational Vehicle Industry Association. online. website: http://www.rvia.org/consumers/rvmembersearch.cfm Listing of RVIA member manufacturers. Access via a search form which permits accessing the entire list of members arranged alphabetically, searching by company name, searching by type of manufacturers, and searching by brand name. For each company gives name, address, website, brands, and list of branches/subsidiaries.

291. *RV Dealer Search.* Fairfax VA: Recreational Vehicle Dealers Association. online. website: http://www.rvda.org/dirdirectory/public_search.cfm Listing of dealers. Access via a search form which permits searching by the country as a whole and by all types of dealers, by state and by specific type of dealer, by name, by city, by zip code, and by phone area code. For each gives name, address, phone, e-mail, website, and if member of RVDA.

292. *RV Rental Dealer Locator.* Fairfax VA: Recreational Rental Dealers Association. online. website: http://www.rvra.org/stat_int.htm Listing of dealers in the US, Canada, and Europe. Access via map or list of states. Arrangement under each state is alphabetical by city. Under each city arrangement is alphabetical by dealer name. For each dealer gives name, address, phone, e-mail, website, amenities, fleet, types of vehicles available, and rates.

◆ *Management* ◆

293. *Bicycle/Moped Store.* Irvine CA: Entrepreneur Group, c1992. 190p. $45.00. Guide to establishing and operating a small business. Legal, management, marketing, operations, and financial procedures outlined. Supplies addresses and a brief bibliography. Loose-leaf format.

294. National Bicycle Dealers Association. *Cost of Doing Business Study.* Newport Beach CA: Author. Biennial. $150.00. Study based upon financial records of independent retailers. Includes data on profitability, productivity, margins, and inventory. Statistics on sales and revenue, profits and loss, and turnover.

◆ *Industry* ◆

295. Find/SVP. *Bicycles.* New York NY: Author. c1995. 138p. $895.00. In-depth data on US factory shipments and imports and exports. Profiles over 40 manufacturers. Examines overflooding of the market and factors determining importing and exporting.

296. Motorcycle Industry Council. *Motorcycle Statistics Annual.* Irvine CA: Author. Annual. $25.00. (annotation, same as #343, 1st edition)

◆ *Market* ◆

297. Burke Market Research, Inc. *Survey of Motorcycle Ownership and Usage.* Irvine CA: Motorcycle Industry Council. Every 5 years. membership. (annotation, same as #345, 1st edition)

298. Curtin, Richard T. *RV Consumer.* Reston VA: Recreational Vehicle Industry Association. c1994. 67p. $75.00. Demographic profile based upon almost 3000 interviews. Study examines age, gender, income, and other factors.

299. Recreational Vehicle Industry Association. *Recreation Vehicle & Conversion Vehicle Market Reports.* Reston VA: Author, c1998. 21p. membership. Graphs and charts reflecting, delivery and retail sales of specific types of vehicles in 1997 by month.

◆ *Periodicals* ◆

300. *American Bicyclist.* Northbrook IL: Willow. 10 issues. $34.00. website: http://www.americanbicylist.com CABDA's national bicycle retailing magazine. Edited for store mangers, and key sales personnel. Features product reviews, industry trends, operations, selling, store design, and successful dealers. Special feature each issue.

301. *Bicycle Dealer Strategies.* Beaverton OR: Skies America. 11 issues. free. Edited for managers, buyers, sales personnel, distributors, importers, and manufacturers. Features strategies in sales, marketing, promotion, inventory, merchandising, operations, finance, and personnel. Special feature each issue.

302. *Bicycle Retailer & Industry News.* Santa Fe NM: Miller Freeman. 18 issues. free. Edited for retailers, equipment, bikewear, and accessories manufacturers, and distributors. News and new product periodical.

303. *BMX Business News.* Santa Ana CA: Times Mirror. Quarterly. free. Edited for dealers. Features product development, marketing, industry trends, retailing tips, company and retailer profiles, and a calendar of events.

304. *Dealernews.* Santa Ana CA: Advanstar Communications. Monthly. $25.00. Edited for motorcycle and powersports dealers. Features news, industry trends, marketing, merchandising, and sales techniques, and profiles of successful retailers.

305. *Kart Marketing International.* Wheaton IL: Kart Marketing Group. Monthly. $42.00. Edited for manufacturers, dealers, distributors, and track owners. Features industry news, technology, products, service, marketing techniques, and operation of tracks and concessions. Annual buyers guide ($5.95)

306. *Motorcycle Industry Magazine.* Gardnerville NV: Industry Shopper. Monthly. free. Edited for dealer/retailer. Features news, products, service, events, and people. Primarily emphasis is on operation profitability. Special feature in each issue.

307. *Motorcycle Product News.* Madison WI: Athletic Business. Monthly. free. Edited for motorcycle and personal watercraft dealers. Primarily an industry news magazine. Buyers guide published each December.

308. *Powersports Business.* Minnetonka MN: Ehlert Publishing Group. 16 issues. free. Edited for dealers, distributors, suppliers, and manufacturers of all-terrain vehicles, motorcycles, snowmobiles, and personal watercraft. Designed to facilitate communication between manufacturer and dealer. Features news, product information, product launchings, legislation and regulation, market analysis, and retail trends.

309. *Professional RV Technician.* Tempe AZ: D&S Media. Quarterly. $24.00. Edited for installers, troubleshooters, and servicers. Features news, new products and techniques, information on systems and components.

310. *RV Business.* Ventura CA: TL enterprises. Monthly. free. Edited for manufacturers, distributors, dealers, servicers, lenders, and investors. Features articles on industry developments, new products, tends and concepts, and new technology. Industry directory published annually.

311. *RV News.* Tempe AZ: D&S Media. Monthly. $36.00. website: http://www.rvamerica.com/rvnews/ Reports on developments, new products, trends, events, and the future. Features include monthly shipment figures, production forecasts, trade show data, legislative happenings, and spotlighted events. Regional editions.

312. *RV Trade Digest.* Elkart IN: Continental Communications Co. of Indiana. Monthly. $36.00. Edited for dealers. Focuses on finance, operations, service, new models, products, and personalities. Annual directory issue in June.

♦ *Databases* ♦

313. *Bikelinks.* Dropbears. online. website: http://www.dropbears.com/bikelinks/dir.htm. An A to Z directory of motorcycle subjects. Access to resources via specific subject or, more broadly, by letter, e.g., A, B, or Z.

314. *Cyber Cyclery.* Planet C. online. website: http://www.cycling.org

The Internet bicycling hub. Gives access to e-mail lists, websites, directories, happenings, products, catalogs, magazines, forums, a job board, and classified ads.

315. *CycleSource.* Royal Tumbridge Wells ENG: Association of Cycle Traders. online. website: http://www.cyclesource.co.uk/inform.htm Emphasis on British bicycling but worldwide in scope. Four screens of topics listed under the broad categories of manufacturers, accessories, organizations, magazines, and holiday companies.

316. *RVUSA.* Fairfax VA: RVUSA. online. website: http://www. rvusa.com. This commercial enterprise provides the largest and most diversified access to RV information though access often limited to members of the organization. Topics include all aspects of RV activities, including camps, RV lifestyle, financing, bulletin boards, shows, and awards.

317. *Snowmobiling.* Haslett MI: International Snowmobile Manufacturers Association. online. website: http://www.snowmobile.org This site provides timely and important information. Access to topics such as what is snowmobiling, a calendar of events, feature stories, safety, weather, statistics, clubs and trails nationwide, and associations and manufacturers.

◆ *Associations* ◆

318. Association of Cycle Traders. 31 A High St. Royal Tumbridge Wells ENG TNI 1XN. phone: 441892526081; fax: 441892544278. e-mail: act@cydessource.demon.co.uk website: http://www.cyclesource.co.uk Association of retailers. Establishes safety standards. Negotiates with government agencies. Public relations with media and public. Publishes newsletter. Formerly: National Association of Cycle and Motorcycle Traders.

319. Bicycle Association of Great Britain. Starley House, Eaton Rd. Coventry ENG CV1 2FH. phone: 441203553838; fax: 441203228366.

Association of manufacturers and suppliers of bicycles, accessories, and parts. Purpose is public relations and promotion. Publishes newsletter.

320. Bicycle Manufacturers Association of America. 3050 K St., NW., Suite 400. Washington DC 20007. phone: (202) 342-8485; fax: (202) 342-8451. Association of manufacturers. Lobbys and conducts legislative actions. Compiles statistics.

321. Bicycle Product Suppliers Association. 1900 Arch St. Philadelphia PA 19103-1498. phone: (215) 564-3484; fax: (215) 963-9785. e-mail: assnhqt@netaxs.com Association of wholesalers, suppliers, and manufacturers. Conducts seminars and education programs. Compiles statistics. Publishes newsletter. Formerly: Cycle Jobbers Association; Bicycle Wholesale Distributors Association

322. Bicycle Trade Association of Canada. 455 St. Antoine St., W., Suite 510. Montreal PG H2Z 1J1. phone: (514) 393-1132; fax: (514) 393-9512. e-mail: info@csga.ca website: http://www.csga.ca Association of manufacturers, importers, suppliers, and distributors. Represents members' legislative and international trade interests. Affiliated with: Canadian Sporting Goods Association.

323. Canadian Recreational Vehicle Association. 111 Peter St., Suite 527. Toronto ON M5V 2H1. fax: (416) 971-5411. e-mail: info@crva.ca website: http://www.crva.ca Association of manufacturers and suppliers. Establishes standards. Lobbys.

324. Cycle Parts and Accessories Association. 181 Salem Rd. East Hills NY 11577. phone: (516) 484-7194. Association of producers of bicycle components and accessories. Lobbys and conducts legislative actions. Publishes newsletter and trade reports.

325. International Snowmobile Manufacturers Association. 1640 Haslett Rd., Suite 170. Haslett MI 48840-8607. phone: (517) 332-1760; fax: (517) 332-0856. e-mail: eklin@aol.com website: http://www.snowmobile.org (annotation, same as #388, 1st edition)

326. Light Aircraft Manufacturers Association. 10790 Ivy Bluff Rd.

Bradyville TN 37026. phone: (615) 765-5397; fax: (615) 765-7234. (annotation, same as #389, 1st edition)

327. Lightweight Cycle Manufacturers' Association. 21-25 Tanners Hill. London ENG SE8 4PJ. phone: 441816921734. Association of builders of hand built and frameset cycles and repairers.

328. Motorcycle Industry Council. 2 Jenner St., Suite 150. Irvine CA 92718-3800. phone: (949) 727-4211; fax: (949) 727-4217. Association of manufacturers and distributors. Lobbys and conducts state and federal legislative activities. Compiles statistics. Maintains library. Publishes newsletter, reports. pamphlets. Formerly: Motorcycle and Allied Trades Association; Scooter and Allied Trades Association.

329. National Bicycle Dealers Association. 2240 University Dr., Suite 130. Newport Beach CA 92660. phone. (949) 722-6909; fax: (949) 722-1747. Association of independent retailers. Sponsors workshops. Compiles statistics. Publishes newsletter, manual, pamphlets.

330. National Caravan Council. Catherine House, Victoria Rd. Aldershot ENG GU11 1SS. phone: 441252318251; fax: 441252322596. e-mail: ncc@matex.co.uk website: http://www.martex.co.uk/ncc/ Association of manufacturers, dealers, suppliers, and parks in the UK. Purpose is to represent the members, provide a vehicle for the exchange of information, and set and insure standards. Maintains caravan links locally, nationally, and throughout Europe. Provides counsel. Operates service for insuring, buying, and selling.

331. National Golf Car Manufacturers Association. Two Ravina Dr., Suite 310. Atlanta GA 30346. phone: (770) 394-7200; fax: (770) 395-7698. Association of manufacturers and dealers.

332. Recreation Vehicle Dealers Association of North America. 3930 University Dr., Suite 100. Fairfax VA 22030-2515. phone: (703) 591-7130; free phone: (800) 336-0355; fax: (703) 591-0734. e-mail: rvdanat@aol.com website: http://www.rvda.com Association of dealers and distributors of motor homes, campers, trailers, and other types of recreational vehicles (RVs). Provides legislative and legal information.

Promotes RV safety, clubs, and campgrounds. Sponsors courses, seminars, and trade shows. Compiles statistics. Publishes periodical, newsletters, directory, manuals, brochures. Formerly: Recreational Vehicle Dealers Institute; Recreational Vehicle Dealers of America.

333. Recreation Vehicle Industry Association. 1896 Preston White Dr., P.O. Box 2999. Reston VA 20195-0999. phone: (703) 620-6003; fax: (703) 620-5071. e-mail: info@rvia.org Association of manufacturers, representatives, and suppliers. Lobbys state and federal government and departments. Provides legal and public relations services. Sponsors research, seminars, and trade shows. Compiles statistics. Publishes magazine, newsletters, directories, research reports, manuals, brochures. Formed by merger of: Recreational Vehicle Institute and Recreational Vehicle Division of the Trailer Coach Association.

334. Recreation Vehicle Rental Association. 3930 University Dr., Suite 100. Fairfax VA 22030-2515. phone: (703) 591-7130; free phone: (800) 336-0355; fax: (703) 591-0734. website: http://www.rvra.org Association of dealers. Conducts workshops and seminars. Compiles statistics. Publishes directory. Affiliated with: Recreational Vehicle Dealers Association of North America.

10. *The Boat Industry*

NAICS 336612, 41222, 42191, 71393, 81149.

RECREATIONAL VEHICLES (WATER), MARINAS. For Recreational Vehicles (Land) SEE Chapter 9. For Powerboat Racing SEE Chapter 21. For Water Travel, Cruises SEE Chapter 29.

◆ *Directories* ◆

335. *Boatbuilders.* Denis & Muntener. online. website: http://www. boatbuilding.com/cqbin/links/boatbuilders Listing of canoe, kayak, powerboat, sailboat, and small craft builders in the US. Listed alphabetically by company name under each category. For each company gives access to website.

336. *Marinas.* Gates. online. website: http://www.marinaguide.com/ marinerspage/ Worldwide listing of facilities. Limited to subscribers of the database, but each subscriber has own website giving name, address, photo, lengthy description of facility, amenities, and phone and e-mail address. Access is via world atlas. Listing is by continent and then country and coastline section within each country.

337. *MDi Boating Industry Classified Index: Marina and Moorings Search.* Southampton ENG: MarineData Internet. online. website: http://www.marinedata.co.uk/directory/marina search/ List of sites. Access via sectors of the industry and county location. Each sector can be subdivided by county. Firms are listed alphabetically. For each gives name, address, phone, e-mail address.

338. *MDi Boating Industry Classified Index: Market Search.* Southampton ENG: MarineData Internet. online. website: http://www. marinedata.co.uk/directory/marine market/ List of boatbuilders. Access via county location. Arrangement under county is by city, but the arrangement of cities varies. Facilities are listed alphabetically under each city. For each facility gives name, address, phone, e-mail, number of moorings, capacity, max LOA, max draught, access, location, nearest government station, and facilities.

339. *Paddlesports Industry Resource — Retailers.* Mequon WI: North American Paddlesports Association. online. website: http://www.go paddle.org Listing of stores. Access via name of store or place located. State listings are alphabetical by name of store with city location and phone.

340. *PPA Directory.* Butler KY: Professional Paddlesports Association. online. website: http://www.propaddle.com/directory/ Listing of outfitters in the US, Canada, and Europe. Access is by state with firms listed alphabetically by name. For each outfitter gives name, address, phone, fax, e-mail, and description of facility.

341. *Yacht Clubs ... on the World Wide Web.* Sailing Source/International Sailing Federation. online. website: http://www.sailing.org/ iyru/yachtclub.html Listing of clubs worldwide. ISAF member clubs listed first followed by country by country listing. Clubs are listed alphabetically by name under each country. Click on club name for website.

342. *Yachting Clubs.* Irvine CA: Professional Club Marketing Association. online. website: http://www.yachtingclubs.com Listing of US clubs. Access is by map. Select state. Cities listed alphabetically under each state with number of clubs located therein. Select city and clubs will be listed in alphabetical order. Extent of information for each club is in process of development during 1999.

♦ *Management* ♦

343. American Boat Builders and Repairers Association. *Boatyard & Marina Operator's Manual*. New York NY: Author, c1998. 150p. $150.00. Guide to operations. Covers organization, accounting, personnel, repairs, services, cost and pricing, marketing, regulations, and much more.

344. International Marina Institute. *Financial & Operational Benchmark Study*. Nokomis FL: Author. Annual. $275.00. Provides statistical data and comparative analysis of facilities, employees, capital improvements finances and trends, and ten industrial and financial ratios.

345. International Marina Institute. *Uniform System of Accounts for Marinas and Boatyards*. Nokomis FL: Author, c1997. 40p. $15.00. Provides standard financial organization and accounts structure. Includes mechanism for comparing financial operations with similar organizations.

346. National Marine Representative's Association. *Marine Industry Supplier Information Manual*. Gurnee IL: Author, c1998. 34p. $50.00. Guide to the industry, time frames, pricing, payment, catalogs, packaging, selling, marketing, motivation, and benefits. Includes NMRA survey results and a model rep contract.

♦ *Industry* ♦

347. International Council of Marine Industry Associations. *Boating Industry Statistics*. Egham ENG: Author. Annual. L100.00. (annotation, same as #414, 1st edition)

348. Martec Group. *Study of Trends in the Marine Industry*. Chicago IL: National Marine Manufacturers Association, c1995. 65p. $125.00. Five-year analysis involving over 275 discussions with all segments of the industry. Predicts new directions and trends and prospects for consolidation.

349. National Marine Manufacturers Association. *Import/Export Report on Recreational Boating.* Chicago IL: Author. Annual. $50.00. Statistical summary and commentary on boats and engines.

◆ *Market* ◆

350. National Marine Manufacturers Association. *Boating Registration Statistics.* Chicago IL: Author. Annual. $50.00. A detailed, state-by-state analysis of registrations by hull type, length, materials, and other factors.

◆ *Periodicals* ◆

351. *Boat & Motor Dealer.* Niles IL: Preston. Monthly. free. website: http://www.prestonpub.com Edited for retailers and service providers. Features news, trends, marketing innovations, service and operations discussions. Special feature in each issue.

352. *Boating Industry.* Latham NY: National Trade. Monthly. $38.00. website: http://www.boatbiz.com Edited for manufacturers, distributors, and retailers. Features articles on management, merchandising, selling, marketing, and industry trends. Annual Buyers' Guide issued separately.

353. *Marina/Dock Age.* Niles IL: Preston. Bimonthly. free. website: http://www.prestonpub.com Edited for owners, managers, designers, consultants, builders, and financiers. Features articles on design, success stories, management practices, new developments, government regulations, and trends. Special feature in each issue.

354. *Paddle Dealer.* Springfield VA: Paddlesport. Quarterly. free.

Edited for retailers and service providers. Features articles on merchandising, sales, and marketing, and profiles of successful operations.

355. *Powersports Business.* Minnetonka MN: Ehlert Publishing Group. 16 issues. free. Edited for dealers, distributors, suppliers and manufacturers of all-terrain vehicles, motorcycles, snowmobiles, and personal watercraft. Designed to facilitate communication between manufacturer and dealer. Features news, product information, product launchings, legislation and regulation, market analysis, and retail trends.

356. *Professional Boatbuilder Magazine.* Brooklin ME: Professional Boatbuilder. Bimonthly. free. website: http://www.proboat.com Edited for builders, designers, repairers, and surveyors. Features technical information and articles on management, regulations, and insurance.

♦ *Databases* ♦

357. *Aboard Boats and Yachts Market.* London ENG: Aboard Boats & Yachts. online. website: http://www.aboard.co.uk Market place for information on buying and selling boats. Provides company and product information, sites, statistics, and a register. Also gives nautical news, events, and weather information.

358. *Boatbuilding Community.* Denis & Muntener. online. website: http://www.boatbuilding.com Boatbuilding, design, and repair resource for amateurs and professionals. Provides directories to numerous categories of boatbuilding from builders to building techniques. Features online articles and a project showcase. Has capability of searching topics within the database. Departments include what's new," "what's popular," discussion form, logbook, bookstore, and website construction.

359. *Boating-USA.* Jackson NJ: Caperello. online. website: http://www.boating-usa.com Commercial website for fishing boats and personal watercraft on sale, brokers and dealers, marinas, fishing charters, parts and accessories, and other marine related items. Provides a fishing report and information of shows and exhibitions. Features "interesting ports of call."

360. *MarineData Internet.* Southampton ENG: MarineData Internet. online. website: http://www.marinedata.co.uk Gateway to online resources of the UK leisure marine industry. Provides access to boat dealers, clothing and equipment stores, services, and holiday charters. Contains a "boat industry index," a listing of clubs and associations, an event calendar, a marinas directory, a list of marine magazines, and how to plan a water trip.

♦ *Associations* ♦

361. American Boat and Yacht Council. 3069 Solomon's Island Rd. Edgewater MD 21037-1416. phone: (410) 956-1050; fax: (410) 956-2737. e-mail: info@abycinc.org Association of manufacturers, dealers, repairers, and other professionals. Conducts research. Develops standards. Sponsors seminars. Maintains library. Publishes periodical, directory, standards.

362. American Boat Builders and Repairers Association. 425 E. 79th St., Apt. 11B. New York NY 10012-1006. phone: (212) 396-4246; fax: (212) 396-4243. e-mail: abbra2@aol.com website: http://www.abbra yacht.com Association of boatyards, marinas, and sailmakers. Purpose is to exchange experiences and ideas. Conducts research. Develops standards. Sponsors seminars and training sessions. Publishes newsletter, manual. Formerly: Atlantic Coast Boat Builders and Repairers Association.

363. Association of British Sailmakers. 2 Orchard Rd., Locks Heath. Southampton ENG SO31 6PR. phone: 441489601517; fax: 441489601518. Association of full-time sailmakers and repairers. Purpose is to exchange information and train. Involved with international sail racing. Sponsors seminars and classes. Maintains library. Publishes periodical, technical publication.

364. British Marine Industries Federation. Meadlake Pl., Thorpe Lea Rd. Egham ENG TW2 8HE. phone: 441784473377; fax: 441784439678. Association of companies. Purpose is to promote industry and conduct public relations. Publishes directory, handbooks.

365. Houseboat Association of America. 4940 N. Rhett Ave. Charleston SC 29405. phone: (803) 744-6581. e-mail: bobperkins@ aol.com Association of manufacturers and rental agencies. Purpose is to promote houseboating. Publishes newsletter, directories.

366. International Marina Institute. P.O. Box 1202. Nokomis FL 34274. phone: (941) 480-1212; fax: (941) 480-0081. e-mail: imimarina@aol.com website: http://www.imimarina.com Association of operators and owner/operators of boat storage facilities. Purpose is to gather and disseminate business and technical information. Conducts research. Sponsors seminars and courses. Publishes newsletter, directory, manuals, pamphlets.

367. Marine Retailers Association of America. 150 E. Huron St., Suite 802. Chicago IL 60611-2912. phone: (312) 944-5080; fax: (312) 944-2716. e-mail: info@mraa.com Association of retailers, distributors, servicers, and manufacturers. Purpose is dissemination of information and industry promotion. Lobbys. Compiles statistics. Sponsors seminars. Publishes newsletter, handbook.

368. National Marine Distributors Association. 1810 S. Rittenhouse Sq., Suite 411. Philadelphia PA 19103. phone: (215) 735-3303; fax: (215) 735-3304. Association of wholesalers. Purpose is exchange of information. Maintains library. Publishes periodical, directory, handbooks.

369. National Marine Manufacturers Association. 200 E. Randolph St., Suite 5100. Chicago IL 60601-6436. phone: (312) 946-6200; fax: (312) 946-0388. Umbrella association incorporating Association of Marine Engine Manufacturers; Canadian Marine Manufacturers Association; Marine Accessories Council; Marina Operators Association of America; National Association of Boat Manufacturers; National Association of Marine Products and Services; National Marine Bankers Association; National Sailing Industry Association; PFD Manufacturers

Association; Personal Watercraft Industry Association; Trailer Manufacturers Association. Researcher and publisher.

370. National Marine Representative's Association. P.O. Box 360. Gurnee IL 60031. phone: (847) 662-3167; fax: (847) 336-7126. e-mail: mnra95@aol.com website: http://www.nmra.com Association of independent reps working on commission. Purpose is to exchange information and serve as an employment clearinghouse for manufacturers seeking representatives. Sponsors trade shows. Publishes newsletter, directory.

371. North American Paddlesports Association. 12455 N. Wauwatosa Rd. Mequon WI 53097. phone: (414) 242-5228; free phone: (888) 732-8275; fax: (414) 242-4428. e-mail: info@gopaddle.org website: http://www.gopaddle.org Association of manufacturers, retailers, outfitters, importers, and liveries. Purpose is to promote industry, develop standards, and provide insurance. Conducts research. Compiles statistics. Sponsors education programs. Publishes periodical.

372. Professional Paddlesports Association. P.O. Box 248. Butler KY 41006-0248. phone: (606) 472-2205; fax: (606) 472-2030. e-mail: paddlespt@unidial.com website: http://www.propaddle.com Association of canoeing, kayaking, rafting, and tubing businesses and manufacturers and distributors of equipment in the US and Canada. Purpose is to certify, insure, set standards, promote safety, and service. Lobbys. Sponsors trade show, seminars. Maintains library. Publishes newsletter, directory. Formerly: National Association of Canoe Liveries and Outfitters.

373. Ship and Boat Builders National Federation. Boating Industry House, Vale Rd. Weybridge ENG KT13 9NS. Umbrella organization for the small craft industry. Members are companies. Sponsors seminars, trade show. Compiles statistics. Conducts research. Publishes directory, handbooks.

374. Society of Small Craft Designers. 4294 Fontenoye St., E. Boyne City MI 49712. phone: (616) 582-2924. Association of designers, builders, and manufacturers. Purpose is to foster research, exchange information, and study mutual problems. Lobbys. Publishes newsletter, annual journal.

375. Yacht Architects and Brokers Association. 105 Eastern Ave., Suite 104. Annapolis MD 21403-3300. phone: (410) 349-8614; fax: (410) 349-8616. e-mail: 102146.2421@compuserve.com Association of designers and financial institutions. Purpose is to collect and disseminate information. Provides placement service. Develops standards. Sponsors education programs. Lobbys. Publishes newsletter, directory.

376. Yacht Brokers, Designers and Surveyors Association. Wheel House, Petersfield Rd., Whitehill. Bordon ENG GU35 9BU. phone: 441420473862; fax: 441420488328. Association of professionals in ten countries. Purpose is to develop and maintain standards, establish fees, and provide for exchange of information. Sponsors education programs and workshops. Publishes directory, research papers, brochures.

377. Yacht Harbour Association. Evegate Park Barn, Smeeth. Ashford ENG TN25 6SX. phone: 441303814434; fax: 441303814364. Association of operators of inland and coastal facilities. Purpose is to advance the development of these facilities. Publishes manuals.

11. The Home Amusements Industry

NAICS 33993, 42192, 45112, 45331, 51121.

HOBBIES, TOYS, GAMES, DOLLS, MINIATURES.

◆ Directories ◆

378. *Business Pages: Hobby Industry Directory.* Waukesha WI: Kalmbach. Annual. $25.00. Listing of 1700 manufacturers, distributors, service providers, and allied companies. Arrangement is alphabetical by company name. For each gives address, phone, fax, e-mail, website, and products description. Cross-reference index by product. Issued as part of Model Retailer magazine.

379. *CIMTA Inc., Travel Guide.* Evergreen Park IL: Cottage Industry Miniatures Trade Association. online. website: http://www.cimta. com Worldwide listing of miniature producers and stores. Arrangement is alphabetical by name. For each gives address, phone, e-mail, website.

380. *Hobby Store Search.* Berkley IL: National Retail Hobby Stores Association. online. website: http://www.hobbystores.org/directory/ Listing of US, Canadian, and military stores which sell airplanes, boats, cars, dolls, games, plaster, rocketry, trains, and other toys. Access is via state or type of product sold. For each store gives name, address, and phone.

381. *Official International Toy Center Directory.* Old Greenwich CT: Toy Center. Annual. $12.50. Listing of over 700 manufacturers and representatives who have permanent displays and offices at the Greater Toy Center in New York City. For each description of products.

382. Dyer, Kathleen M. *Needlework FAQ* Author. online. website: http://www.ncal.verio.com/~dyer/documents/nf_ Three separate listings for Designers and Design Companies, Manufacturers and Distributors, and Retailers. Access is by country, worldwide. Arrangement under country is alphabetical by name of company. For each company gives address, phone, fax, e-mail, website, and products.

383. Hobby Industries of America. *Buyers Guide.* Elmwood Park NJ: Author. Annual. $25.00. Listing of over 1000 companies exhibiting and 300+ distributors in attendance at the association's trade show. For each gives address, phone, fax, e-mail, and product information.

◆ *Management* ◆

384. Game Manufacturers Association. *Selling Games to Wholesalers.* Scottsdale AZ: Author, c1997. 56p. $9.99. A basic primer for designing non-electronic games.

385. Model Retailer. *Hobby Shop Handbook.* Waukesha WI: Kalmbach, c1994. $129.00. Essential information for successful hobby retailing. Includes steps on getting started, store design, marketing, selling, management, finance, plans, and technical advice.

386. National Needlework Association. *Starting Out Right.* Zanesville OH: Author, c1991. 42p. $25.00. Kit for initiating a business. Has start-up pointers, market analysis form, industry statistics, and names and phones of distributors.

387. National Retail Hobby Stores Association. *Hobby Shop Owners Guide.* Berkley IL: Author. c1998. $100.00. Outline and some discussion of steps required to open a business. Topics include: reality check, business yardstick, market analysis, advisors, organization, leases, and insurance.

◆ *Industry* ◆

388. Hobby Industry Association. *Annual Size of Industry Report.* Elmwood NJ: Author. Annual. Membership. (annotation, same as #468, 1st edition, add) In each case, these studies stand alone as the only substantive industry data publicly available.

389. Hobby Industry Association. *Size of Craft/Hobby Industry Study.* Elmwood NJ: Author, c1997. 68p. $500.00. Compilation of manufacturers and retailer sales and consumer purchase statistics. Includes comparative data from earlier studies. Executive summary free from association.

390. Ladenson, Sydney and Schoenhaus, Ted. *Toyland: The High-Stakes Game of the Toy Industry.* New York NY: Contemporary Books, c1990. 339p. $25.00. Describes the industry, the competition, the shows, and social issues involved in a multibillion dollar industry where ten companies dominate the industry.

391. Toy Manufacturers of America. *Toy Industry Fact Book.* New York NY: Author. Annual. free. Review of the year. Presents activities of the TMA, a review of major industry events, industry statistics, economics and marketing overview and statistics, and articles on current industry and association emphasis.

◆ *Market* ◆

392. Business Trend Analysis. *US Market for Toys and Games.* Commack NY: Author, c1992. 2v. $1095.00. Examines past performance, current trends, and strategies for the future. Projects markets for the toy, board game, and electronic games industry.

393. Euromonitor. *Toys and Games: The International Market.* London ENG: Author, c1995. 375p. $3,190.00. Report on France, Germany, Italy, Spain, the UK, and US. Video games and competition highlighted. Family income and growth documented for each country. Includes 365 statistical tables. Looseleaf.

394. Hobby Industry Association. *Nationwide Craft/Hobby Consumer Study.* Elmwood Park NJ: Author, c1997. $400.00. Examines attitudes and behavior of consumers towards crafts and hobbies. Presents statistics nationwide, by demographics and region, and by type of interest. Includes comparative data from earlier studies. Executive summary free from association.

395. Massachusetts Port Authority Trade Development Unit. *Toys and Games in the European Union.* Boston MA: Author, c1994. 62p. free. One of a series of reports focusing on trade potentials for American, especially New England firms, in the upcoming European Union market. Special attention given to electronic games.

◆ *Periodicals* ◆

396. *Card Trade.* Iola WI: Krause. Monthly. $25.00. website: http://www.krause.com Edited for dealers. Features industry news and trends, marketing and business tips, and market reports.

397. *Comics Retailer.* Iola WI: Krause. Monthly. $25.00. website: http://www.krause.com Edited for retailers. Features news from publishers, sales figures, and finance, marketing, and inventory tips. Special feature in each issue.

398. *Craft & Needlework Age.* Manatapan NJ: Hobby Publications. Monthly. $20.00. website: http://www.cnamag.com Edited for chain and independent retailers. Features news, new product information, trends, industry surveys, and dealer profiles. Special feature in each issue.

399. *Craftrends.* Peoria IL: Primedia. Monthly. free. Edited for retailers, distributors, and manufacturers. Features articles on merchandising, consumer trends, new products, and management. Special feature in each issue.

400. *Edplay*. Geneva NY: Fahy-Williams. Quarterly. free. Edited for retailers of toys, games, and puzzles. Features merchandising tips, billing, management, personnel, store design, and specialty toys. Special feature each issue.

401. *Games Retailer*. Geneva NY: Fahy-Williams. Quarterly. free. Edited for retailers of games, hobby materials, and gifts. Features articles on new products, merchandising, and store management. Special feature each issue.

402. *Hobby Merchandiser*. Manatapan NJ: Hobby Publications. Monthly. $20.00. website: http://www.hobbymerchandiser.com Edited for retailers and chain store buyers. Emphasis on selling. Features articles on products of all types from airplanes to sports memorabilia. Each issue contains "New Product" report and description. Annual directory issue in December.

403. *Makin' Stamps*. Elmhurst IL: Marking Devices. Bimonthly. $24.00. Edited for art stamp manufacturers. Features articles on production, engraving, customers, management, and industry trends. Special feature each issue.

404. *Model Retailer*. Waukesha WI: Kalmbach. Monthly. $85.00. website: http://www2.modelretailer.com. Edited for retailers and suppliers of models and miniatures. Features articles on new products, merchandising, trade shows, market trends, and profiles of retail stores and manufacturers. Chicago Show Guide in August, Report in October issues.

405. *Needlework Retailer*. Ames IA: Yarn Tree Designs. Bimonthly. $12.00. website: http://www.yarntree.com/nr.htm Edited for independent retailer. Focus is on new products. Features news, trends, events, and shows.

406. *Playthings*. New York NY: Cahners. Monthly. $29.00. Principal industry magazine for merchandisers of toys, hobbies, and crafts. Features articles on sales and promotional techniques, "what's selling," profitable operations, and analysis of industry trends. Special feature each issues. Special issues: "New Products Showcase" in February, April, August, and November; "Licensing Scope" in February and June. Separate "Buyers' Guide" issued annually.

407. *Rubber Stampin' Retailer.* Elmhurst IL: Marking Devices. Bimonthly. $24.00. Edited for retailers. Features articles on products, trends, sales techniques, trade shows, and instructions on new methods of stamping. Special feature each issue.

408. *Specialty Retailer.* New York NY: Adventure Publishing Group. Bimonthly. free. Edited for toy and gift retailers. Features product and manufacturer news, successful merchandising techniques, and new specialty products. Special feature each issue.

409. *Stamp Wholesaler.* Iola WI: Krause. Monthly. $21.00. website: http://www.krause.com Edited for dealers. Functions as the guide and information provider for the philatelic trade.

410. *Toy Book.* New York NY: Adventure Publishing Group. Monthly. $36.00. Principal communication vehicle for toy manufacturers. Primary source for new products and merchandising for retailers.

◆ *Databases* ◆

411. *4 Hobbies.* 4 Anything Network. online. website: http://www.4hobbies.com A broadly-based home amusement industry database. For hobbies gives information and resources, shows and games, clubs, and associations. Provides links to crafts, games, kites, models, puzzles, stamps, toys, and trains. A to Z listing search also available. And much more.

412. *Gamers Central.* Zaandam NET: Games Central. online. website: http://www.gamescentral.net Provides access to the growing world of electronic games off and online. Included is current news, reviews of new and old electronic games, access to the games themselves, a listing of developers and publishers, and links to gaming websites.

413. *Needlecraft Showcase.* Needlecraft Showcase. online. website: http://www.stitching.com Access to a variety of needlecraft and other hobby information via a keyword search mechanism. Includes listings of designers, manufacturers, wholesalers, shopping malls, and services. News, a newsletter, bulletin board. Links to organizations and AOL users.

414. *Toy Directory.* Los Angeles CA: Toy Directory. online. website: http://www.toydirectory.com A commercial service in which wholesalers and retailers advertise. Membership required for access to news, events, publications, and other current industry information. Public access is available for businesses, product information, stock quotes, trade associations and shows, and links to other toy databases.

415. *ToyLinks.* ToyLinks. online. website: http://www.toylinks.com Most recent industry website. Provides access to specific subject via basic and advanced specific subject searches. Contains information on people, stores, collectibles and hobbies, clubs, and events. Product advertising and classifieds. Industry books reviewed.

♦ *Associations* ♦

416. American Specialty Toy Retailing Association. 206 6th Ave., Suite 900. DesMoines IA 50309-4018. phone: (515) 282-8192; fax: (515) 282-9117. e-mail: astra@astratoy.org website: http://www.astratoy.org Association of manufacturers, retailers, sales representatives, and suppliers. Purpose is to provide resources and information exchange. Compiles statistics. Conducts research. Sponsors workshops and seminars. Publishes newsletter, directory, surveys, reports.

417. American Stamp Dealers Association. 3 School St., Suite 205. Glen Cove NY 11542. phone: (516) 759-7000; fax: (516) 759-7014.

Association of dealers and wholesalers. Purpose is exchange of information. Sponsors National Stamp Collecting Week in November. Publishes newsletter, directory.

418. Association of Crafts and Creative Industries. P.O. Box 3388, 1100-H Brandywine Blvd. Zanesville OH 43701. phone: (740) 452-4541; fax: (740) 452-2552. e-mail: acci.info@offinger.com website: http://www.creative-industries.com Association of manufacturers, wholesalers, importers, retailers, and suppliers. Purpose is to promote craft market and assist industry firms. Compiles statistics. Conducts research. Sponsors education programs and trade show. Publishes newsletter, directories.

419. British Association of Toy Retailers. 24 Baldwyn Gardens. London ENG W3 6HL. phone: 441819932894; fax: 441812482701. Association of independent retailers. Publishes periodical, newsletter.

420. British Numismatic Trade Association. P.O. Box 474A. Thames Ditton ENG phone: 441813984290; fax: 441813984291. e-mail: bnta@coins-on-line.com website: http://www.coins-on-line.com.uk/societies/bnta/ Association of coin dealers. Purpose is to promote and safeguard standards for dealing with the public. Publishes directory.

421. British Toy and Hobby Manufacturers Association. 80 Camberwell Rd. London ENG SE5 0EG. phone: 441717017271; fax: 441717082437. Association of manufacturers. Purpose is promotion of industry and representation of member's interests.

422. British Toy Importers and Distributors Association. Somers Mounts Hill. Benenden ENG TN17 4ET. phone: 441580240819; fax: 441580241109. Association of firms in the UK and Ireland. Purpose is promotion and advise. Develops and promotes safety standards. Publishes newsletter, manuals.

423. Canadian Toy Association. P.O. Box 294. Kleinburg ON L0J 1C0. phone: (905) 893-1689; fax: (905) 893-2392. Association of manufacturers and importers. Purpose is industry growth and representation of member's interests before government agencies. Conducts educational programs. Sponsors trade show. Maintains library. Publishes newsletter, directory.

424. Cottage Industry Miniatures Trade Association. P.O. Box 42849. Evergreen Park IL 60805. phone: (773) 233-5522; fax: (773) 233-5506. e-mail: info@cimta.com website: http://www.cimta.com Association of producers and entrepreneurs. Purpose is intercommunications, public relations, product development, and management. Sponsors seminars, trade shows. Publishes newsletter.

425. Game Manufacturers Association. P.O. Box 1210. Scottsdale AZ 85252. phone: (480) 675-0205; fax: (480) 994-1170. e-mail: info@gama.org website: http://www.gama.org Association of companies that produce, license, and sell adventure games, such as boardgames, role playing games, collectable card games, and wargames. Publishes newsletter, directory, manual.

426. Hobby Industries of America. 319 E. 54th St., P.O. Box 348. Elmwood Park NJ 07407. phone: (201) 794-1133; fax: (201) 797-0657. e-mail: hia@ix.netcom.com website: http://www.hobby.org; http://www.i-craft.com Association of manufacturers, wholesalers, retailers, and allied companies in the craft and hobby fields. Purpose is promotion and industry development. Conducts seminars and workshops. Sponsors National Craft Month and trade shows in the US and Europe. Compiles statistics. Publishes newsletter, directory, research studies, brochures. Absorbed: Ceramic Arts Federation International.

427. Home Sewing Association. 1350 Broadway, Suite 1601. New York NY 10018. phone: (212) 714-1633; fax: (212) 714-1655. e-mail: ahsca@aol.com website: http://www.sewing.org Association of manufacturers and retailers of machines, fabrics, patterns, notions, needlework, and crafts. Purpose is the advancement of the industry and employee and consumer education. Sponsors training sessions and trade show. Maintains library. Publishes newsletter, pamphlets. Formerly: American Home Sewing and Crafts Association.

428. International Council of Toy Industries. 1115 Broadway, Suite 400. New York NY 10010. phone: (212) 675-1141; fax: (212) 633-1429.

e-mail: info@toy-icti.org website: http://www.icti.org Worldwide association of manufacturers and retailers. Purpose is to exchange information, enhance toy development, promote safety, and reduce trade barriers. Collects statistics.

429. International Federation of Stamp Dealers' Association. 868/870 Chausee de Waterloo. Brussels BEL B-1180. Association of dealers in 26 countries. Purpose to reduce international barriers to stamp trading. Establishes standards. Publishes newsletter, handbook.

430. Kite Trade Association International. 74 New Montgomery, Suite 230. San Francisco CA 94105. phone: (415) 764-4908; fax: (415) 777-5298. e-mail: kitetrade@aol.com Association of manufacturers, wholesalers, and retailers. Purpose is industry promotion. Sponsors trade show. Compiles statistics. Publishes newsletter, directory.

431. Miniatures Industry Association of America. 1100-H Brandywine Blvd., P.O. Box 2188 Zanesville OH 43702-2188. phone: (614) 452-4541; fax: (614) 452-2552. e-mail: miaa.info@offinger.com website: http://www.miaa.com Association of manufacturers, wholesalers, representatives, and retailers of dollhouses, dolls, and other collectibles. Purpose is industry growth and development. Sponsors National Dollhouse and Miniatures Month and trade show. Publishes directory, long range industry plan.

432. Model Railroad Industry Association. 303 Freeport Rd. Pittsburgh PA 15215. phone: (412) 781-2709; fax: (412) 781-2871. website: http://www.mria.org Association of manufacturers, importers, distributors, and retailers. Purpose is to publicize industry, provide information interchange mechanism, and promote the development of model railroad clubs. Sponsors trade shows. Publishes newsletter, directory, reports, pamphlets.

433. National Association of Doll and Stuffed Toy Manufacturers. 55 John St., 7th Floor. New York NY 10038-3712. phone: (212) 704-0300; fax: (914) 761-0747. Association of companies. Purpose is primarily to represent manufacturers in collective bargaining.

434. National Needlework Association. 1100-H Brandywine Blvd.,

P.O. Box 3388. Zanesville OH 43702-3388. phone: (740) 452-4541; free phone: (800) 889-8662; fax: (740) 452-2552. e-mail: tnna.info@creative-industries.com website: http://www.creative-industries.com/tnna Association of manufacturers, retailers, wholesalers, and representatives. Purpose is to provide a forum and interaction. Develop a strong, growing, and profitable industry. Promote needlearts. Sponsors trade shows, seminars. Publishes manuals.

435. National Plastercraft Association. 1458 S. Seventh St. Louisville KY 40208. phone: (502) 636-2195. Association of manufacturers, distributors, and retailers for the hobby industry. Purpose is to publicize and disseminate information. Sponsors seminars, competitions. Certifies painters, teachers. Publishes newsletter, directory, handbook. Affiliated with: Hobby Industry Association of America. Formerly: Plastercraft Association.

436. National Retail Hobby Stores Association. 5440 W. St. Charles Rd., Suite 103. Berkley IL 60163. phone: (708) 544-3240; fax: (708) 544-3253. e-mail: info@hobbystores.org website: http://www.hobby-stores.org Association of independent businesses. Purpose is to enhance industry, develop interest in hobbies and collecting, communicate news and trends with members, and provide materials on successful retailing. Sponsors trade show and seminars. Publishes newsletter, directory, manual.

437. Non-Powder Gun Products Association. 200 Castlewood Dr. North Palm Beach FL 33408-5696. phone: (561) 842-4100; fax: (561) 863-8984. e-mail: slsgma@aol.com Association of manufacturers and distributors of air guns and ammunition. Purpose is to publicize industry and product use, to promote proper use and safety, and to establish industry standards. Publishes pamphlets.

438. Professional Numismatics Guild. 3950 Concordia Ln. Fallbrook CA 92028. phone: (760) 728-1300; fax: (760) 728-8507. e-mail: info@pngdealers.com website: http://www.pngdealers.com Association of dealers. Purpose is to establish dealer standards, facilitate information exchange, provide authentication programs, prevent theft, and educate collectors. Sponsors an arbitration system. Publishes directory, pamphlets.

439. Radio Control Hobby Trade Association. 560 E. Bonner Rd. Wauconda IL 60084-1104. phone: (847) 526-1222; fax: (847)526-9987. e-mail: rchta@Ind.com Association of manufacturers, distributors, and retailers. Purpose is industry and product promotion. Compiles statistics. Sponsors trade show. Maintains library. Publishes newsletter.

440. Toy Manufacturers of America. 200 Fifth Ave. New York NY 10010. phone: (212) 675-1141; fax: (212) 633-1429. website: http://www. toy-tma.org Association of manufacturers and importers. Purpose is to facilitate communication among members and to represent industry before federal, state, and local government agencies. Lobbys. Sponsors education programs and trade show. Compiles statistics. Publishes directory, industry fact book, pamphlets.

12. The Gift Industry

NAICS 327212, 339914, 45322, 511191.

GIFTS, NOVELTIES, SOUVENIRS, GREETING CARDS, AWARDS.

♦ *Directories* ♦

441. *European Tableware Buyers Guide.* Redhill ENG: dmg Business Media. Annual. $109.45. Listing of manufacturers of qualified table and giftware. Arrangement is alphabetical by company. For each listing gives address, phone, fax, e-mail, website, and senior executives. Cross references by type of product. Publication also contains calendar of major industry events.

442. *Party & Paper Retailer Source Book.* Norwalk CT: Ward. Annual. $25.00. Listing of manufacturers and importers of paper, tableware, stationary, gift wrap, greeting cards, decorations, invitations, balloons, novelties, and favors. Arrangement is alphabetical with product index. For company each gives address, phone, fax, e-mail, website.

443. Awards and Recognition Association. *Membership Directory and Buyer's Guide.* Chicago IL: Author. Annual. also online. membership. website: http://www.ara.org/index_3.htm Listing of manufacturers, wholesalers, distributors, and servicers. Arranged both alphabetically by company and by product. Each listing gives name, address, phone, fax, contact, products, e-mail, and website. Also listed are retailer members of the association. Website is searchable by state and product.

444. Greeting Card Association. *Greeting Card Industry Directory*. Washington DC: Author. Annual. $95.00. Listing of publishers and suppliers. Arrangement is alphabetical by company name. List is cross-referenced by geographical location, type of product, and brand name. For each company gives address, phone, key personnel, list of products and brands, and types and areas of distribution. Available on CD-ROM.

♦ *Management* ♦

445. *Annual Guide to Full Line Retailing*. New York NY: Miller Freeman. Annual. $35.00. Presents the latest techniques, researches the use of trade shows, catalogs, and the Internet, and provides access to suppliers and allied sources.

446. *Party Goods/Gift Store*. Irvine CA: Entrepreneur Magazine. c1992. 200p. $59.50. Step-by-step guide to the decision, opening, operating, managing, and marketing. Includes bibliographical references and an index.

447. Awards and Recognition Association. *Business Operations Manual*. Chicago IL: Author, c1997. 169p. $149.00. Comprehensive guide for achieving understanding and control over day-to-day operations. Includes information on business structure, order flow, supplier relationships, and extending credit.

♦ *Market* ♦

448. Find/SVP. *US Giftware Market*. New York NY: Author, c1997. 139p. $2250.00. Report divides the $16 billion giftware market into four segments — novelties, decorative accessories, seasonal decoratives, and collectibles. Examines new developments in giftware marketing including electronic home shopping. Profiles major players in the industry.

449. Market Tracking International. *Tableware International File*

1996-2000. Redhill ENG: dmg Business Media. c1995. 1014p. $1400.00. Study of the production, trade and consumption of tableware worldwide. Provides in-depth analysis of the current and future retail market in major countries plus selected secondary and developing markets. Extensive tables and graphs.

♦ *Periodicals* ♦

450. *A & E.* Broomfield CO: National Business Media. Monthly. $39.00. website: http://www.nbm.com/aemag Edited for persons and firms in the award engraving and recognition market. Special features in each issue.

451. *Crafts Report.* Wilmington DE: Crafts Report. Monthly. $29.00. website: http://www.craftsreport.com Edited for retailers and professionals in the business. Features articles on time management, finance, marketing, and law and legislation.

452. *Gift & Stationery Business.* New York NY: Miller Freeman. Monthly. free. website: http://www.giftline.com Edited for retailers. Contains original market research reports. Profiles major retailers.

453. *Gifts & Decorative Accessories.* New York NY: Cahners. Monthly. $42.00. Edited for retailers worldwide. Features articles on marketing, merchandising, promotions, and display. Includes news, people, events, and catalog offerings. Profiles successful store operations. Buyers Directory published separately each September.

454. *Giftware News.* New York NY: Talcott Communications. Monthly. $150.00. website: http://www.giftwarenews.net Edited for gift, stationary, and department stores. In addition to giftware, features articles on stationary, party and paper, tabletop, and decorative accessories. Special feature each issue.

455. *Giftware News UK* Chicago IL: Talcott Communications. Quarterly. $195.00. website: http://www.giftwarenews.net Edited for the

English market. Features news, trends, new products, and events worldwide.

456. *Greetings Today.* Lawrence KS: Alliance Communications Group. Quarterly. $20.00. Edited for retailers. Features articles on merchandising. Contains news, new products, statistical updates, trends, interviews, and profiles.

457. *Party & Paper Retailer.* Norwalk CT: Ward. Monthly. $39.00. website: http://www.partypaper.com Edited for manufacturers and importers of paper, tableware, stationary, gift wrap, greeting cards, decorations, invitations, balloons, novelties, and favors. Emphasis on planning, promotion, and merchandising for holidays. Special feature each issue.

458. *Recognition Review.* Chicago IL: Awards and Recognition Association. Monthly. $42.00. Official Voice of the Awards and Recognition Association. Features articles on management, marketing, and timely promotions. Includes news, new products, and events. Special feature each issue.

459. *Selling Christmas Decorations.* Randolph NJ: Edgell. 2 issues. free. Edited for buyers and retailers. Emphasis on Christmas products. Directory of manufacturers, importers, and manufacturers' representatives in January edition.

460. *Souvenirs, Gifts & Novelties.* Upper Darby PA: Kane. 7 issues. $30.00. Edited for retailers. Reports on new item, trade shows, news, purchasing tips, selling techniques, and trends.

461. *Tableware International.* Redhill ENG: dmg Business Media. 11 Issues. $181.79. website: http://www.dmg.co.uk/tableware/ Provides updates of the latest news and views in the international tabletop, gifts, and home market. Coverage emphasis is Europe, the US, and Japan. Separate European Tableware Buyers Guide issued annually.

◆ *Databases* ◆

462. *GiftBusiness.* Capistrano Beach CA: J. Ford. online. website: http://www.giftbusiness.com Commercial website for assisting industry professionals to gain and communicates information. Provides classified ads, a bulletin board, and a support center.

463. *Giftline.* New York NY: Miller Freeman. online. website: http://www.giftline.com Provides an overview of the gift market from new products in collectibles, gifts, gourmet, accessories, and stationary to reviews of new books on these subjects, and an "industry insider" look at marts, shows, and links.

464. *Party & Paper Retailer.* Norwalk CT: Ward. online. website: http://www.partypaper.com Broad spectrum view of many aspects of the party supply industry. Covers current news, bulletin board, directories of US and global suppliers, a worldwide calendar of trade shows, articles on store operations, results of industry surveys, contents of periodical, and a long list of frequently asked questions.

♦ *Associations* ♦

465. Awards & Recognition Association. 35 E. Wacker Dr., Suite 500. Chicago IL 60601-2105. phone: (312) 782-5252; free phone: (800) 344-2148; fax: (312) 236-1140. website: http://www.ara.org Association of suppliers and retailers. Purpose is to publicize the growth and development of awards and recognition items. Sponsors trade shows. Publishes periodical, newsletter, directory and buyers guide. Formerly: Trophy Dealers and Manufacturers Association.

466. Canadian Gift and Tableware Association. 265 Yorkland Blvd., Suite 301. North York ON M2J 1S5. phone: (416) 497-5771; fax: (416) 497-3448. e-mail: info@gift.org Association of manufacturers. Purpose is to promote, enhance communication among members, and represent members' commercial and regulatory interests. Lobbys.

467. Gift Association of America. 608 W. Broad St. Bethlehem PA 18018-5221. phone: (610) 861-9445; fax: (610) 861-0948. Association of retailers, wholesalers, and industry affiliates of gifts, china, glass, and decorative accessories. Sponsors trade shows. Publishes newsletter, directory. Formerly: Gift and Decorative Accessories Association of America.

468. Gift Packaging and Greeting Card Association of Canada. 1407

Military Tr. Scarborough ON M1C 1A7. phone: (416) 281-8147; fax: (416) 286-4868. Association of manufacturers and distributors. Purpose is to sport and foster communication among members. Compiles statistics. Conducts research.

469. Giftware Association. 10 Vyse St. Birmingham ENG B18 6LT. phone: 441212362657; fax: 441212371106. website: http://www.giftware.org.uk Association of manufacturers, importers, distributors, and wholesalers. Purpose is to assist members in achieving profitable operations through a variety of support services. Establishes standards. Sponsors trade show and seminars. Publishes newsletter.

470. Greeting Card Association. 1200 G St., NW., Suite 760. Washington DC 20005. phone: (202) 393-1778; fax: (202) 393-0336. website: http://www.greetingcard.org Association of publishers and suppliers. Purpose is public and government relations. Lobbys. Publishes newsletter, directory, manuals, pamphlets. Formerly: National association of Greeting Card Publishers.

471. National Tabletop and Giftware Association. 355 Lexington Ave., 17th Floor. New York NY 10017-6603. phone: (212) 661-4261; fax: (212) 370-9047. Association of manufacturers and distributors. Purpose is to interchange information and serve as unified voice for industry. Conducts education programs. Publishes directory. Formerly: National Tabletop Association.

472. Souvenir and Novelty Trade Association. 7000 Terminal Sq., Suite 210 Upper Darby PA 19082. phone: (610) 734-2420; fax: (610) 734-2423. souvenirmag@aol.com Association of manufacturers, distributors, and retailers. Purpose is trade promotion. Collects statistics. Sponsors seminars and competitions. Publishes periodical, reports, manuals.

473. Tableware Distributors Association. Etruria. Stoke-on-Trent ENG ST4 7AF. phone: 441728212473; fax: 441728278308. Association of manufacturers and distributors in the UK. Purpose is to represent membership with various constituencies and foster interchange of information. Publishes newsletter.

13. The Amateur Photography Industry

NAICS 325992, 333315, 334419, 42141, 42162, 44313, 812922.

AMATEUR PHOTOGRAPHIC EQUIPMENT AND SUPPLIES, PHOTOFINISHING.

♦ Directories ♦

474. *The Source.* Jackson MI: Photo Marketing Association International. online. website: http://www.pmai.org/01links.htm Listing of photo/imaging manufacturers and stores with websites worldwide. Arrangement of directory is alphabetical. Click on name to access website.

♦ Management ♦

475. McCurry, William. *Guerrilla Managing for the Imaging Industry.* Jackson MI: Photo Marketing Association International, c1996. 300p. $23.00. Written specifically for the small and medium-sized photo/imaging firm. Focuses on techniques to assist owners in hiring and training personnel. Includes forms, worksheets, and checklists. Author also has book on marketing management available in combination with this publication.

♦ *Industry* ♦

476. Photo Marketing Association International. *Cost of Doing Business Survey*. Jackson MI: Author, c1998. 215p. $243.00. Examines income statements and balance sheets of a variety of types and sizes of companies. Presents findings in narrative, composite, and financial ratio formats.

477. Photo Marketing Association International. *Industry Trends*. Jackson MI: Author. Biennial. $125.00 each. A two work set, US and international, covering 25 countries worldwide. Analyzes and presents extensive statistics on the consumer and professional markets and channels of distribution.

♦ *Market* ♦

478. Frost & Sullivan. *US Consumer Photography Equipment and Accessory Market*. New York NY: Author, c1997. 535p. $1995.00. Details the impact potential of new technologies, e.g., digital, on marketing, positioning, and business strategies in this swift changing market. Profiles the campaigns of the top producers plus examples of successful end-users. Provides data on revenue and sales on new and current products.

479. Photo Marketing Association International. *Consumer Photographic Survey*. Jackson MI: Author. Biennial. $125.00 each. Surveys are currently conducted for the US, Canada, the UK, and France. Surveys camera ownership and usage, types of cameras owned, photo activities, and expenditures on equipment, supplies, and services. Charts delineate demographic and regional characteristics.

◆ *Periodicals* ◆

480. *Photo Imaging Entrepreneur.* Greensboro NC: Entrepreneurial Publications. Bimonthly. free. Edited for owners and operators of independent photo outlets. Articles focus on operations of minilabs. Emphasis on management and marketing.

481. *Photo Industry Reporter.* Woodbury NY: IRM Publications. 21 issues. free. Edited for dealers, minilabs, mass merchandisers, and chains. Focus on news, new products, trends, and promotions. Special feature each issue. Convention "Extra" published separately each year.

482. *Photo Lab Management.* Santa Monica CA: PLM Publishing. Monthly. $15.00. Edited for managers and production supervisors. Features articles on digital equipment, processing, lab management, and marketing. Includes columns on industry news and new products.

483. *Photo Marketing.* Jackson MI: Photo Marketing Association International. Monthly. $30.00. Official publication of the Photo Marketing Association International. Edited for the photographic industry. Features news, profiles of industry leaders, products and production techniques. Special feature each issue.

484. *Photo Trade News.* Melville NY: Cygnus. Monthly. $20.00. Edited for photo finishing retailers. Features news, new product and processing information, and industry trends. Includes long articles on management and marketing.

485. *Photographic Processing.* Melville NY: Cygnus. Monthly. $35.00. Edited for firms engaged in photofinishing and electronic processing. Features articles on new equipment and processing. Includes tips on management, personnel, and marketing.

◆ *Databases* ◆

486. Photo Marketing Association International. *PMA.* Jackson MI: Author. online. website: http://www.pmai.org Extensive coverage of all aspects of the amateur photography field worldwide. Information includes news, information request system, calendar of events, business directory and links, and a search engine for accessing specific topics.

◆ *Associations* ◆

487. British Photographic Importers' Association. Ambassador House, Brigstock Rd. Thornton Heath ENG CR7 7JG. phone: 441816656181; fax: 441816656447; e-mail: bpia@admin.co.uk Association of companies. Purpose is promotion of photographic and digital photography industry through campaigns, competitions, and consumer research.

488. International Minilab Association. 8 S. Michigan Ave., Suite 1000. Chicago IL 60603. phone: (312) 782-4951; free phone: (800) 262-4419; fax: (312) 580-0165. Association of owners and operators, manufacturers, distributors, and suppliers. Provides technical, marketing, merchandising, management, and financial guidance. Compiles statistics. Conducts research. Sponsors trade show and seminars. Publishes periodical, newsletter, directory, research reports.

489. National Association of Photographic Manufacturers. 550 Mamaroneck St. Harrison NY 10528. phone (914) 698-7603; fax: (914) 698-7609. e-mail: napminc@aol.com Association of manufacturers of equipment, supplies, film, and chemicals. Purpose is to develop interindustry cooperation and public relations with government agencies and educational institutions. Develops standards. Compiles statistics. Conducts research. Maintains library. Publishes newsletter, directory, annual statistical report.

490. National Association of Quick Printers. 401 N. Michigan Ave. Chicago IL 60611-4390. phone: (312) 321-6886; free phone: (800) 234-0040; fax: (312) 527-6789. Association of companies and suppliers. Purpose is to develop recognition, improve quality, and provide management and financial guidance. Compiles statistics. Sponsors research. Maintains library. Publishes newsletter, directory.

491. Photographic and Imaging Manufacturers Association. 550 Mamaroneck Ave., Suite 307. Harrison NY 10528-1612. phone: (914) 698-7603; FAX: (914) 698-7609. e-mail: pima@pima.net website: http://pima.net Association of manufactures of equipment, supplies, film, and chemicals. Purpose is to develop interindustry cooperation and public relations with government agencies and educational institutions. Develops standards. Compiles statistics. Conducts research. Maintains library. Publishes newsletter, directory, annual statistical report.

492. Photo Marketing Association International. 3000 Picture Pl. Jackson MI 49201. phone: (517) 788-8100; fax: (517) 788-8371. e-mail: pma_information_central@pmai.org website: http://www.pmai.org (annotation, same as #580, 1st edition)

493. Photographic Manufacturers and Distributors Association. 1120 Avenue of the Americas, 4th Floor. New York NY 10036. phone: (908) 679-3460; fax: (908) 679-2294. e-mail: pmda@aol.com Association of companies and importers of photographic equipment. Purpose is cooperation among companies, education, international relations, and standardization. Formerly: Photographic Merchandising and Distributing Association.

14. The Musical Instrument Industry

NAICS 339992, 42199, 45114, 53229, 81149.

MUSICAL INSTRUMENTS.

♦ Directories ♦

494. *Music Yellow Pages Business Directory*. New York NY: National Music and Entertainment. online. website: http://www.musicyellow-pages.com/bizdir.htm Listing of manufacturers, suppliers, wholesalers, and retailers. Access is alphabetical by first letter of company name. For each gives phone, fax, toll-free number and web address. Referencing by product is accessed via a separate "Category Index."

495. *Purchaser's Guide to the Music Industries*. Englewood NJ: Music Trades. Annual. $15.00. Listing of piano, organ, chime, band, and concert instrument manufacturers, electronic equipment and accessories producers, sheet music publishers, and trade associations. Arrangement is alphabetical by name with referencing from type of product. For each firm gives name, address, phone, fax, and products.

♦ Management ♦

496. Music Industries Association — England. *So You Want to Open a Music Shop*. West Horsley ENG: Author, c1997. 58p. L15.00. Guide to establishment of an instrument, accessories, and print music shop. Chapters on planning, design, management, finance, operations, and merchandising, each written by a "working expert."

◆ *Industry* ◆

497. NAMM International Music Products Association. *Music USA.* Carlsbad CA: Author. Annual. $45.00. Statistical review of the music products industry. Contains data on over 20 instrument and accessory categories, shipped from manufacturers to retailers. Includes economic and social indicators affecting the industry.

◆ *Market* ◆

498. American Music Conference. *Music USA.* Chicago IL: Author. Annual. $45.00. Survey of amateur music participation.

◆ *Periodicals* ◆

499. *Drum Business.* Cedar Grove NJ: Modern Drummer. Bimonthly. free. website: http://www.moderndrummer.com Edited for stores selling acoustic, electronic, and related equipment. Features articles on effective management and marketing. Includes profiles news, tips, and coverage of new products. Special feature each issue.

500. *Music & Sound Retailer.* Port Washington NY: Retailer Publishing. Monthly. $18.00. Edited for store owners offering full line of instruments. Features articles spotlighting manufacturers, dealers, and industry and market trends. Includes news, new products, dealer events, and personnel changes.

501. *Music Trades Magazine.* Englewood NJ: Music Trades. Monthly.

$16.00. Edited for retailers and wholesalers of musical instruments and accessories. Features articles on management, success stories, merchandising, and selling. Includes news, new products, personnel changes, stock quotations, and forecasts.

502. *Musical Merchandise Review.* Newton MA: Larkin. Monthly. $24.00. website: http://www.mmrmagazine.com Edited for retailers of instruments, sound equipment, and sheet music. Features articles on merchandising, promotion, and selling. Includes news, new products from a non-technical prospective, personnel, and store openings. Special feature each issue.

♦ *Databases* ♦

503. *4 Musicians.* 4 Anything Network. online. website: http://www.4anything.com/business/ A broadly-based musical instrument industry database. Gives access to instruments, software for musicians, music publishers, information and resources, coda, sheet music and recordings, music lessons, services and organizations, and composers and musicians. Links to many other sources. A to Z listing search also available.

504. *Music Yellow Pages.* New York NY: National Music and Entertainment. online. website: http://www.musicyellowpages.com More than just a phone-book type directory. A comprehensive directory to information on the music industry. Directories to companies, alphabetically and by category, to trade shows. Industry news and online links. Information and site searching tools. Classifieds and advertising.

♦ *Associations* ♦

505. Guitar and Accessories Marketing Association. 38 W. 21st St., 5th Floor. New York NY 10010-6906. phone: (212) 924-9175; fax: (212) 675-3577. e-mail: assnhdqs@aol.com Association of stringed instrument manufacturers. Purpose is promotion of guitar playing. Sponsors education programs. Publishes newsletter. Formerly: National Association of Musical Merchandise Manufacturers; Guitar and Accessories Manufacturers Association; Guitar and Accessories Music Marketing Association.

506. International Association of Electronic Keyboard Manufacturers. 38 W. 21st St., Room 1106. New York NY 10010-6906. phone: (212) 924-9175; fax: (212) 675-3577. e-mail: assnhdqs@aol.com Association of manufacturers. Purpose is promotion of playing of electronic instruments. Sponsors seminars. Compiles market data for members.

507. Music Industries Association — England. Wix Hill House, Epsom Rd. West Horsley ENG KT24 6D2. phone: 441483223326; fax: 441483222748. e-mail: office@mia.org.uk website: http://www.mia.org.uk Association of manufacturers, distributors, and retailers. Purpose is the promotion of musical playing as leisure activity and advising members of marketing and promotion actions. Publishes newsletter.

508. Music Industries Association of Canada. 1210 Sheppard Ave., E., Suite 109. North York ON M2K 1E3. phone: (416) 490-1871; free phone: (877) 490-6422; fax: (416) 490-9739. website: http://www.miac.net Association of manufacturers, distributors, and retailers of instruments, accessories, sound reinforcement products, and sheet music. Purpose is promotion and interchange of information. Sponsors trade show. Compiles statistics. Publishes newsletter.

509. NAMM International Music Products Association. 5790 Armada Dr. Carlsbad CA 92008. phone: (619) 438-8001; free phone: (800) 767-6266; fax: (619) 438-7327. website: http://www.namm.com Association of retailers, manufacturers, distributors, jobbers, wholesalers, and publishers of music and instruments. Purpose is to enhance professional development of members and general public. Sponsors education seminars and trade show. Compiles statistics. Maintains library. Publishes newsletter, annual statistical report. Formerly: National Association of Music Merchants.

510. National Association of Band Instrument Manufacturers. 38

W. 21st St., 5th Floor. New York NY 10010-6906. phone: (212) 924-9175; fax: (212) 675-3577. e-mail: assnhdqs@aol.com Association of manufacturers and importers. Purpose is interchange of information.

511. National Council of Music Importers and Exporters. 38 W. 21st St., 5th Floor. New York NY 10010-6906. phone: (212) 924-9175; fax: (212) 675-3577. e-mail: assnhdqs@aol.com Association of companies. Purpose is to provide information on federal, state, and local regulations, work with government agencies, serve as a contact for foreign manufacturers. Lobbys. Publishes newsletter. Formerly: National Association of Music Importers; National Council of Music Importers.

512. Piano Manufacturers Association International. 4020 McEwen St., Suite 105. Dallas TX 75244-5109. phone: (214) 233-9107; fax: (214) 490-4219. website: http://www.pianonet.com Association of manufacturers and suppliers. Purpose is to promote piano playing and provide interchange of information among members. Sponsors National Piano Foundation and trade show. Compiles statistics. Formerly: National Piano Manufacturers Association of America.

513. Piano Trade Suppliers Association. 78-80 Borough High St. London ENG SEi 1XG. phone: 441714032300; fax: 441714038140. Association of suppliers of parts especially piano. Small association. Limited activities.

15. *The Recreation/ Entertainment School Industry*

NAICS 61161, 61162.

SCHOOLS PREPARING FOR CAREERS OR PARTICIPATION IN RECREATION OR ENTERTAINMENT.

♦ *Directories* ♦

514. *British Riding Schools.* Penzance ENG: Association of British Riding Schools. online. website: http://www.equiworld.net/abrs/ Listing of schools. Access is alphabetical by county. For each school gives address, phone, and website.

515. *Drama Schools UK.* London ENG: Conference of Drama Schools. online. website: http://www.drama.ac.uk/schools.html Listing of schools subscribing to this website. Access to each school's website.

516. *Sailing Schools.* Southampton ENG: International Sailing Federation. online. website: http://www.sailing.org/iyru/sailschools.html Listing of schools worldwide. Access to each school's website.

517. *ShawGuides.* New York NY: ShawGuides. online. website: http://www.shawguides.com Series of directories designed for learning

vacations and activity development. Directories for Cooking Schools —
Recreational, Golf Schools and Camps, Photography Workshops, Tennis Schools and Camps, and Water Sports. Access is by countries,
regions, states in the US, types of activities, levels of proficiency and
months open. For each gives name, address, phone, fax, e-mail, website, and description. Access directly via website available.

♦ *Management* ♦

518. International Sailing Federation. *ISAF National Training Scheme
Manual.* Southampton ENG: Author. online. website: http://www.sailing.org/iyru/manual.html Collection of articles written by experts on
all major aspects of organizing and operating a sailing school.

519. National Golf Foundation. *Golf Schools: An Expanding Enterprise.* Jupiter FL: Author, c1997. 130p. $45.00. Collection of articles
about types of schools, programs and teaching methods, unique training centers, and special programs by gender and age.

♦ *Periodicals* ♦

520. *Dance Teachers Now.* Raleigh NC: SMW Communications. 10
issues. $29.95. website: http://www.dance-teacher.com Edited for
teachers in business. Features articles on sustaining business, success
stories, and management resources. Special features in February,
July/August, and November issues.

521. *NAKMAS Journal.* Ashford ENG: National Association of
Karate and Martial Arts Schools. Monthly. free. Official publication.
Features articles on events, legal, legislative, and medical concerns, and
technical subjects. Includes profiles of schools.

♦ *Databases* ♦

522. *BASI.* Aviemore SCO: British Association of Ski Instructors.
online. website: http://www.basi.org.uk Overview of skiing courses

and instruction available by type and level. Information on dates and accommodations. Extensive links and a directory.

523. *PADI.* Rancho Santa Margarita CA: Professional Association of Diving Instructors. online. website: http://www.padi.com Worldwide diving education in 174 countries worldwide. Information on centers, courses, certification, and products. Contains a bulletin board, directory of offices, and details of a "Travel Network."

524. *Sailors Choice.* Dana Point CA: Makai Promotions. online. website: http://www.sailerschoice.com/schools.html Sailing and boating instruction, schools, seminars, and schooling primarily in the US, Canada, and Caribbean. Includes home study courses, boat building, and cruse charter school information.

525. *SNOW PRO.* Quebec PQ: Canadian Ski Instructors Alliance. online. website: http://www.snowpro.com Overview of skiing instruction available in Canada. Includes information on certification, course description, training facilities, and schedule.

526. *World's Best Golf Schools.* Miami FL: Golf-Travel. online. website: http://www.golf-travel.com/f_dest.schools.html Designed for the learning-traveler. Information on golf schools, instructional programs, and related facilities. Institutions selected on the basis of reputation. For each school gives location, address, phone, fax, e-mail, website, instructional approach, student ratio, accommodations, description of facilities, and cost. Includes guides to golf resorts and golf links.

◆ *Associations* ◆

527. American Sail Training Association. P.O. Box 1459, 47 Bowen's Wharf. Newport RI 02840. phone: (401) 846-1775. Association of schools involved in training for the ocean-going tall ships. Publishes newsletter, directory, manuals.

528. Association of British Riding Schools. Queens Chamber, 38/40 Queen St. Penzance ENG TR18 4BH. phone: 441736369440; fax: 441736351390. website: http://www.equiworld.net/abrs/ Association of schools, proprietors, and trainers. Purpose is standardization and certification. Publishes handbook.

529. Association of Ski Schools in Great Britain. Abernethy Outdoor Centre. Nethybridge SCO PH25 2ED. phone: 441479821279; fax: 441479821279. Association of schools. Dedicated to high standards and uniform methods of teaching. Administers tests for certification. Promotes safety standards.

530. Conference of Drama Schools. 24 Dovercourt Rd. London ENG SE22 8ST. phone: 441812994516. website: http://www.drama.ac.uk Association of schools. Purpose is to support the training of actors, stage managers, and theater related professionals. Develops standards.

531. International Sailing Schools Associations. 5. rue Jean Bart. Paris FRA F-75006. phone: 33145484370; fax: 33142226052. Association of clubs and associations maintaining schools. Purpose is promotion and standardization. Publishes newsletter, directory. Affiliated with International Sailing Federation.

532. National Association of Karate and Martial Arts Schools. 21 Queen St. Ashford ENG TN23 1RF. phone: 441233647003; fax: 441233647002. e-mail: nakmas@aol.com website: http://www.nakmas. co.uk Association of staff members of accredited schools. Develops standards. Certifies schools. Provides consultant services. Sponsors tournaments. Publishes periodical.

533. National Association of Sailing Instructors and Sailing Schools. 15 Renier Ct. Middletown NJ 07748. phone: (908) 671-6190. e-mail: nasiss@aol.com Association of schools and instructors. Purpose is to set standards and develop training programs and secure recognition for these programs from the Coast Guard, insurance agencies, and the general public. Accredits schools. Certifies instructors. Publishes newsletter, directories, manuals.

534. National Bowling Pro Shop and Instructors Association. P.O. Box 5634 Fresno CA 93755-5634. phone: (209) 225-0256; free phone: (800) 659-9444; fax: (209) 226-6213. Association of instructors who operate as part of centers or own separate retail outlets and equipment manufacturers. Sponsors education programs. Compiles statistics. Publishes periodical.

535. National Federation of Sea Schools. Fletchwood Lane, Totton. Southampton ENG SO40 7DZ. phone: 441703869956; fax: 441703869956. e-mail: info@nfss.co.uk website: http://www.nfss.co.uk Association of sailing and motor cruising schools. Purpose is representation, joint advertising and marketing, exhibitions, and public relations. Publishes newsletter.

536. National School Sailing Association. 17 Ickwell Rd., Northill. Biggleswade ENG SG18 9AB. phone: 441767627370; fax: 441767627370. website: http://www.nssa.co.uk Association of schools, centers, and organizations providing sailing courses for young people. Publishes periodical.

537. National Swim School Association. 776 21st Ave., N. St. Petersburg FL 33704-3348. phone: (727) 896-7946; fax: (727) 896-3933. e-mail: nssa@shamrockgroup.com website: http://www.shamrockgroup.com Association of schools, owners, managers, and instructors. Purpose is to promote professionalism, disseminate information on trends and techniques, and promote effective teaching. Sponsors seminars. Compiles statistics. Conducts research. Maintains library. Publishes newsletter.

538. Organization of Professional Acting Coaches and Teachers. 3968 Eureka Dr. Studio City CA 91604. phone: (323) 877-4988; fax: (323) 877-4988. In the US, Drama Schools are rare and not associated. This is the closest to an instructional body. Purpose is to provide guidelines for professional conduct, to prepare instructional materials, and to assist students in selection of coaches. Conducts research. Maintains library. Publishes books and tapes.

539. Professional Ski Instructors of America. 133 S. Van Gordon St., Suite 101. Lakewood CO 80228-1700. phone: (303) 987-9390; fax: (303) 988-3005. website: http://www.psia.org/http://www.aasi.org Association of ski schools and professional alpine and nordic ski teachers. Certifies teachers. Compiles statistics. Conducts research. Develops clinics and seminars. Publishes periodical, newsletter, manuals. Affiliated with National Ski Areas Association.

16. *The Entertainment Agency Industry*

NAICS 512199, 56131, 7114.

BOOKING AND CASTING AGENCIES, AGENTS AND MANAGERS FOR ATHLETES OR ENTERTAINERS.

◆ *Directories* ◆

540. *Agents.* Los Angeles CA: Screaming in the Celluloid Jungle. online. website: http://www.celluloidjungle.com/agents.html Writers Guild of America guild-signatory listing of agents and agencies. Access is by state. For each agent or agency gives name, address, phone, and fax.

541. *Directory of British Entertainment Agents.* London ENG: Agents' Association (Great Britain). online. website: http://www.agents-uk.com Listing of agencies and entertainment acts including agency news. Agents accessed by name, type, and location. Name of agency must be known for name access. Websites for type and area are listed alphabetically under group and geographical region. Area agents are located by a map. All listings are websites.

542. *Model Search Magazine Worldwide Model & Talent Agency Guide.* Burbank CA: Model Search Magazine. Annual. $69.00. Contains over 2,000 model/talent agencies, casting directors, and TV/film studios worldwide. Arrangement is alphabetical by agency with subject index. For each agency gives contact name, address, phone, fax, e-mail, and website.

543. *Sports Agents Directory.* Brighton MA: American Netsite Builders. online. website: http://www.sports-agents.com Commercial website under development. Listing of agent websites. Among purposes is to provide agents with opportunity to list qualifications and services. Designed to assist athletes in choosing an agent. Site is envisioned to include bulletin board.

544. *TV Talent Agents.* New York NY: TVWeather. online. website: http://www.tvweather.com/tv_talen.htm Listing of agencies involved with broadcast TV actors and other employees. Arrangement is alphabetical by name of agency. For each entry gives name, address, phone, fee charged, and brief description of services.

◆ *Management* ◆

545. *Personal Managers.* Hollywood CA: Silver Screen, c1996. 89p. $16.00. Explains what a manager does and the relationship between agents, actors, and managers. Includes articles by a leading manager and a casting director. Personal managers in Los Angeles area listed with address and phone.

546. Frascogna, Xavier M. and Hetherington, H. Lee. *This Business of Artist Management.* New York NY: Watson-Guptill, c1997. 304p. $21.95. Reference to artist management in the music field. Guidance to such topics as career planning, image formation, business and legal advice, and money management.

547. Litwak, Mark. *Dealmaking in the Film & Television Industry...* Los Angeles CA: Silman-James, c1994. 346p. $26.95. Addressed to the non-legal audience. Step-by-step process. Includes examples of various forms and documents.

548. Ruxin, Robert H. *An Athlete's Guide to Agents.* Boston MA:

Jones and Bartlett, c1993. 192p. $30.00. Primer for would-be agents, sports attorneys, and athletes in search of an agent. Written primarily from the prospective of the athlete. Outlines the activities and actions of the agent. Contains sample contracts, explanation of the draft, and salary tables.

♦ *Industry* ♦

549. Press, Skip. *Writer's Guide to Hollywood Producers, Directors, and Screenwriter's Agents.* Rocklin CA: Prima, c1998. 454p. $23.00. Compendium of agent listings. Way to proceed in choice of successful road to Hollywood career. Overview of the role of agents in this quest.

550. Rose, Frank. *The Agency: William Morris and the Hidden History of Show Business.* New York NY: HarperBusiness, c1995. 532p. $45.00. A look at the history of talent agencies from the prospective of the largest and most influential organizations in the business.

551. Singular, Stephen. *Power to Burn: Michael Ovitz and the New Business of Show Business.* Secaucus NY: Carol Publishing Group, c1996. 224p. $40.00. The new world of theatrical talent as seen through the eyes of a major power broker in the new world of show business.

♦ *Market* ♦

552. Dell, Donald L. *Minding Other People's Business: Winning Big for Your Clients and Yourself.* New York NY: Villard, c1989. 237p. $42.00. Somewhat dated, but still one of the best overviews of the controversial world of the sports agent. Case studies.

553. Simon, Ron. *The Game Behind the Game: Negotiating in the Big Leagues.* Stillwater MN: Voyageur, c1993. 271p. $40.00. Case studies of a major sports agent in negotiating contracts for professional athletes. Overview of the role and workings of the agent.

♦ *Associations* ♦

554. Agents' Association (Great Britain). 54 Keyes House, Dolphin Sq. London ENG SW1V 3NA. phone: 441718340515; fax: 441718210261. e-mail: gensec@agents-uk.com website: http://www.agents-uk.com Association of entertainment agencies. Purpose is to represent and protect member's interests. Collective voice for negotiations and legislation. Maintains library. Publishes newsletter, directory.

555. Association of Talent Agents. 9255 Sunset Blvd., Suite 930. Los Angeles CA 90069-3381. phone: (310) 274-0628; fax: (310) 274-5063. e-mail: atajetton@aol.com Association of agency companies in the motion picture, stage, television, radio, and literary industries. Purpose is contract guidance, interpretation, and rulings, negotiation and arbitration, and establishing contract standards. Lobbys at state labor level. Conducts seminars. Compiles statistics. Maintains library. Publishes newsletter. Formerly: Artists Managers Guild.

556. International Group of Agents and Bureaus. 6845 Parkdale Pl., Suite A. Indianapolis IN 46254-5605. phone: (317) 297-0872; fax: (317) 387-3387. e-mail: info@igab.org website: http://www.igab.org Association of speakers in over 100 countries bureaus which have been in business for two or more years. Purpose is to educate the public about the service, promote image, enhance professionalism, and provide services for members. Publishes newsletter.

557. National Association of Performing Arts Managers and Agents. 137 E. 30th St., Suite 3B. New York NY 10016-7337. phone: (212) 683-0801; fax: (212) 683-0801. website: http://www.napama.org Association of professionals who serve artists in the development of their careers. Purpose is to promote standards, exchange information, and seek to develop the influence of members within the arts community. Publishes newsletter.

558. National Conference of Personal Managers. 964 Second Ave. New York NY 10022. phone: (212) 421-2670; fax: (212) 838-5105. Association of managers in the entertainment industry. Publishes newsletter.

Formed by merger of: Conference of Personal Managers, West/Conference of Personal Managers, East.

559. Personal Managers' Association. 1 Summer Rd. East Morlesey ENG KT8 9LX. phone: 441813989796; fax: 441813989796. Association of agents for artists, technicians, and writers in the entertainment industry.

560. Sports Lawyers Association. 11250-8 Roger Bacon Dr., Suite 8. Reston VA: 20190-5202. phone: (703) 437-4377; fax: (703) 435-4390. website: http://www.sportslaw.org Association of lawyers and firms representing athletes, teams, leagues, conferences, and other sports organizations. Purpose is to foster discussion of legal problems affecting sports law and promoting the interchange of perspectives and positions. Establishes rules of ethics. Sponsors seminars and educational programs. Publishes newsletter.

17. Show Business

NAICS 71111, 71112, 71119.

THEATRE COMPANIES, DINNER THEATERS, DANCE COMPANIES, OTHER PERFORMING ARTS COMPANIES.

♦ Directories ♦

561. *AmericanTheatre Web Listings.* New York NY: AmericanTheatre Web. website: http://www.americantheatreweb.com/directory/ Listing of theaters throughout the US in which artistic performances are produced and staged. Access is provided in three ways: alphabetically by name, alphabetically by city under each state, and alphabetically by production. Access to each is by website.

562. *Billboard International Talent & Touring Directory.* New York NY: BPI Communications. Annual. $104.00. Business-to-business listing of show business artists, support companies, agents, and other services. Arrangement is by categories with alphabetical name index. For each entry gives name, address, phone, fax, key personnel, and services.

563. *Cavalcade of Acts and Attractions.* Nashville TN: BPI Communications. Annual. $75.00. Listing of shows, touring shows, carnivals, circuses, fair attractions plus amusement parks, arenas, rodeos, and other public amusements along with agents servicing these organizations and facilities. Arrangement is by categories with name index. For each entry gives name, address, phone, fax, key personnel, and activities.

564. *Official British Theatre Directory*. London ENG: Richmond House. Annual. $34.50. Listing of venues with administrative and technical details. Includes current productions, agents and promoters, organizations, training and educational facilities, and suppliers and services. For each gives address, phone, fax, e-mail, websites, and brief description.

565. *Theatre List*. Toronto ON: Professional Association of Canadian Theatres. Annual. $27.50. Listing of professional theatre companies and facilities in Canada. For each address, phone, fax, e-mail, website, and information on staff, repertoire, festivals, and services. Includes guide to governmental departments, service organizations, and funding agencies.

◆ *Management* ◆

566. Celentano, Suzanne Carmack, and Kevin Marshall. *Theatre Management: A Guide to Producing Plays…* New York NY: Players Press, c1998. 320p. $29.00. Guide to producers, directors, actors, playwrights, designers, technicians, and front-of-house staffs on the production process. In addition to production, covers fund raising, financial, legal, and personnel management, and marketing. Appendices focus on house and box office management, telemarketing, and limited partnership agreements. Numerous production photos incorporated.

567. Farber, Donald C. *Producing Theatre: A Comprehensive Legal and Business Guide*. New York NY: Limelight Editions, c1997. 472p. $25.00. Focus on the paperwork involved in production. Extensive examples of contact, accounting, and other legal documents.

568. Langley, Stephen. *Theatre Management and Production in America*. New York NY: Drama Publishers, c1990. 702p. $37.50. The most comprehensive guide to the industry. Covers commercial, stock, resident, college, community, and other presenting organizations. All aspects of theatre, large and small, presented in textbook format. Extensive bibliography.

569. Shagan, Rena Road Show. *Booking & Tour Management for the Performing Arts.* New York NY: Allworth, c1996. 270p. $19.95. Guide to taking a show on the road. Includes discussion of scheduling, transportation, lodging, and accommodations.

◆ *Industry* ◆

570. Duboff, Leonard D. *The Performing Arts Business Encyclopedia.* New York NY: Allworth, c1996. 256p. $19.95. Listing of business and legal terms and definitions of other practical issues relating to theatre, dance, opera, music, screen, and television. Written for the layman but essential for all performance arts executives.

571. Zietz, Karyl Lynn. *Opera Companies and Houses in the United States.* Jefferson NC: McFarland, c1994. 225p. $49.95. Overview of the industry. The work is arranged by state, city, and company name. Includes history, inaugural performance, staff, and local situation. Companion study on companies and houses in western Europe, Canada, Australia, and New Zealand also published by the same author.

◆ *Market* ◆

572. Andreasen, Alan R. *Expanding the Audience for the Performing Arts.* Washington DC: Seven Locks, c1990. 186p. $10.95. This study offers a six-stage model for the use by both managers and researchers in seeking to achieve and study the potential for new patronage in the attendance at events.

573. Dance/USA. *Invitation to the Dance: Audience Development for the Next Century.* Washington DC: Author, c1999. 120p. $15.00. Final report of the National Task Force on Dance Audiences. Five key areas were focused on in the study: mission, education, audience segmentation, collaborations, merchandising. Documents and statistics gathered by the Task Force included.

574. Kotler, Philip and Scheff, Joan. *Standing Room Only: Strategies for Marketing the Performing Arts.* Cambridge MA: Harvard Business School, c1997. 576p. $60.00. Written primarily for non-profit organizations seeking to maintain their income level in light of decreased governmental funding. Techniques and suggestions applicable to commercial market. Focus is on audience and product definition, pricing, and market positioning. Treats non-profit enterprises as much of a business venture as commercial firms.

♦ *Periodicals* ♦

575. *Back Stage.* New York NY: BPI Communications. Weekly. $75.00. website: http://www.backstage.com Theatre trade newspaper edited for all types of involved professionals. Focuses on auditions, notices, industry news, and service features. Includes regional news.

576. *TCI Magazine.* New York NY: Primedia. 11 issues. $30.00. website: http://www.etecnyc.net Reports on the fields of design, technology, and administration in the performing arts. Features articles on theatre, film, video, dance, opera, concerts, theme parks, and touring shows. Special issues: Buyers Guide, Industry Resources, Architecture, Sound Products, Lighting Products.

577. *Theatre Journal.* Baltimore MD: Johns Hopkins University Press. Quarterly. $28.00. Edited for researchers. Focuses on history and criticism but valuable for its overview of theatre development and practice.

♦ *Databases* ♦

578. *ISPA.* Rye NY: International Society for the Performing Arts Foundation. website: http://www.ispa-online.org Information on features and events. A forum for ideas. Job posting. A site map giving access to topics in the performing arts. But most importantly, an

"Internet gateway" giving access to a variety of resources, research and reference tools, directories, networks, associations, and funding opportunities.

579. *ITI-Worldwide.* Paris FRE: International Theatre Institute. website: http://www.iti-worldwide.org Site of an international non-governmental organization which maintains formal relations with national performing arts centers in 90 countries. Focus is on major international theatre events, ITI publications, and activities of associated organizations.

580. *Playbill-on-Line.* New York NY: American Express. website: http://www.playbill.com Basically, a consumer ticketing service, but includes extensive information and access designed to entice. Presents news, a message board, a chat section, connections to "wired" professionals, feature stories, and sites: the largest compendium of theatre links on the Internet." All this plus performance listings in New York, London, off Broadway, regional, and on tour.

581. *UK Theatre Web.* London ENG: UK Theatre Web. website: http://www.uktw.co.uk Similar to "Playbill-on-Line" in providing news, information on productions, a directory of theatre, dance, opera, mime, and musical productions, listings and tickets, and a variety of theatre weblinks.

◆ *Associations* ◆

582. American Association of Community Theatres. 4712 Enchanted Oaks. College Station TX 77845-7649. phone: (409) 774-0611; fax: (409) 774-8718. e-mail: angloaact@aol.com website: http://www.aact. org Association of theatres, individuals involved, and suppliers. Purpose is to promote excellence through networking, workshops, and publications. Sponsors festival. Publishes periodical, newsletter, directory, handbooks. Formerly: American Community Theatre Association.

583. American Dinner Theatre Institute. P.O. Box 7075. Akron OH

44306. phone: (216) 724-9855. Association of owner/operators. Purpose is to assist in the development of professional, year-around theatres. Provides construction, maintenance, management, and operations advice. Fosters exchange of information on successful productions and profitable food service. Maintains library. Publishes newsletter, directory.

584. Canadian Association of Professional Dance Organizations. P.O. Box 4130, 99 Fourth Ave., Suite E. Ottawa ON K1S 2L0. phone: (613) 234-0970; fax: (613) 234-6952. e-mail: capdo@magi.com website: http://www.culturenet.ca/capdo/ Association of companies, training and retraining institutions, and agencies servicing the dance community. Purpose is to expand the organization and performance of professional dance in Canada.

585. Canadian Popular Theatre Alliance. 11039 Saskatchewan Dr. Edmonton AB T6G 2B4. phone: (403) 439-3905; fax: (403) 433-4782. Association of companies and interested individuals. Purpose is to promote theatre as a source of entertainment and instrument for social change. Seeks audience usually ignored by traditional theatre. Publishes newsletter.

586. Entertainment Services and Technology Association. 875 Sixth Ave., Suite 2302. New York NY 10001. phone: (212) 244-1505; fax: (212) 244-1502. e-mail: info@esta.org website: http://www.esta.org Association of production service companies and designers, manufacturers, and suppliers of entertainment equipment and technology. Purpose is to provide a forum for the exchange of information. Provides credit reporting and insurance for members. Sponsors trade shows. Conducts research. Compiles statistics. Publishes periodical, directory, handbooks. Formerly: Theatrical Dealers Association.

587. Independent Theatre Council. 12 Weston St. London ENG SE1 3ER. phone: 441714031727; fax: 441714031745. e-mail: itc@diocan.co.uk Association of small and middlescale touring and resident companies and facilities. Purpose is to publicize and promote development. Publishes handbooks.

588. International Brotherhood of Magicians. 11137 Southtowne Sq.,

Suite C. St. Louis MO 63123-7819. phone: (314) 845-9200; fax: (314) 845-9220. e-mail: nolinmagic@aol.com website: http://www.magician.org Association of professionals, suppliers, agents, and others interested in magic. Purpose is to promote the industry, discourage fraud, and support creditable merchandise. Encourages humane care and treatment of live animals. Publishes newsletter.

589. International Society for the Performing Arts. 2920 Fuller Ave., NE., Suite 205. Grand Rapids MI 49505-3458. phone: (616) 364-300; fax: (616) 364-9010. e-mail: info@ispa-online.org website: http://www.ispa-online.org

590. International Theatre Equipment Association. 244 W. 49th St., Suite 200. New York NY 10019. phone: (212) 246-6460; fax: (212) 265-6428. Association of companies and individuals involved in providing equipment to theaters and theatrical companies.

591. League of American Theatres and Producers. 226 W. 47th St., Suite 1710. New York NY 10036. phone: (212) 764-1122; fax: (212) 719-4389. e-mail: info@broadway.org website: http://www.broadway.org Association of owners, operators and producers of legitimate theatre. Primary Purpose is labor negotiation and government relations. Sponsors Tony awards. Compiles statistics. Conducts research. Publishes newsletter, statistics, research. Formerly: League of New York Theatres.

592. League of Historic American Theatres. 34 Market Pl., Suite 320. Baltimore MD 21202-4034. phone: (410) 659-9533; fax: (410) 837-9664. e-mail: info@lhat.org website: http://www.lhat.org Association of restored theaters and individuals and organizations involved in the restoration. Purpose is to provide information and networking on preservation, protection, and programming. Sponsors tours, seminars, workshops. Publishes newsletter, directories, brochures.

593. League of Resident Theatres. 1501 Broadway, Suite 2401. New York NY 10036. phone: (212) 944-1501; fax: (212) 768-0785. Association of professional regional theatre companies. Purpose is regional promotion, labor relations, and exchange of information and ideas.

594. National Alliance for Musical Theatre. 330 W. 45th St., Lobby

B. New York NY 10036. phone: (212) 265-5376; fax: (212) 582-8730. Association of professional companies and theaters. Purpose is development and production assistance. Provides grants. Publishes directory, handbook.

595. National Dinner Theatre Association. 8204 Highway 100. Nashville TN 37221. phone: (615) 646-9977; free phone: (800) 282-2276; fax: (615) 622-5439. e-mail: info@dinnertheatre.com website: http://www.webcom.com/ndta/ Association of 40 dinner theatres nationwide. Purpose is to enhance and market their service. Access to each is available via the Internet.

596. National Movement Theatre Association. P.O. Box 1437. Portsmouth NH 03802-1437. phone: (603) 436-6660; fax: (603) 436-1577. e-mail: pontine@nh.altranet.com Association for the promotion of mime theatre. Formerly: National Mime Association.

597. Opera America. 1156 15th St., NW. Washington DC 20005-1704. phone: (202) 293-4466; fax: (212) 393-0735. e-mail: frontdesk@operaam.org website: http://www.operaam.org Association of professional companies and affiliated organizations. Purpose is promotion of industry, assistance in the development of companies, and education and training. Provides consulting services. Sponsors grants, workshops, educational programs. Maintains library. Publishes periodical, newsletter, directories, manuals. Absorbed: Central Opera Service.

598. Professional Association of Canadian Theatres. 30 St. Patrick St., 2nd Fl. Toronto ON M5T 3A3. phone: (416) 595-6455; free phone: (800) 263-7228; fax: (416) 595-6450. website: http://webhome.idirect.com/~pact/ Association of companies. Purpose is labor relations, communications, advocacy, and professional development. Establishes standards. Publishes newsletter, directory, manuals.

599. Society of British Theatre Designers. 46 Bermondsey St. London ENG SE1 3XT. phone: 441714033778; fax: 441713786170. e-mail: office@abtt.org.uk website: http://www.abtt.org.uk Association of set, costume, and lighting designers. Purpose to enhance the standing of members at home and abroad. Sponsors national exhibition, tours, seminars. Publishes manuals, brochures.

600. USITT: The American Association of Design and Production Professionals. 6443 Riding Rd. Syracuse NY 13206-1111. phone: (315) 463-6463; free phone: (800) 938-7488; fax: (315) 463-6525. e-mail: usittno@pppmail.appliedtheory.com website: http://www.usitt.org Association of organizations, manufacturers, suppliers, and individuals specializing in design, production, and technology. Purpose is exchange of information and development of standards. Maintains library. Publishes periodical, newsletter, directories, manuals, standards.

18. The Motion Picture Industry

NAICS 51211, 51212, 512131, 512132, 512191, 512199, 53223.

MOTION PICTURE, TELEVISION, OR VIDEO PRODUCTION AND DISTRIBUTION.

♦ Directories ♦

601. *AV Market Place: The Complete Business Directory...* New York NY: Bowker. Annual. $195.00. Listing of over 5,000 producers, distributors, and servicers of audio, motion picture, and video industries in the US. Arrangement is by state and alphabetical by company under each. Referencing by product, service, and company name.

602. *Cinemedia.* Los Angeles CA: American Film Institute. online. website: http://www.afi.cinemedia.org Internet's largest film and media directory. Listing of all types of media producers, stations, networks, studios, theaters, organizations, schools, actors, films, shows, and festivals. Has research, search, and mail functions. Access to all entities listed is via website.

603. *Film Producers, Studios, Agents & Casting Directors.* Los Angeles CA: Lone Eagle. Annual. $65.00. Listing of studios and companies as well as individuals referred to in the title. Arrangement is by category and alphabetically under each. Each entry gives address, phone, and fax. Producers and casting directors are cross referenced by film title.

604. *Production Companies.* Los Angeles CA: Screaming in the Celluloid Jungle. online. website: http://www.celluloidjungle.com/prodcos.html Listing accessed by letter of the alphabet. Companies listed alphabetically. For each company gives name, address, city, state, and zip code, phone, fax, production type, and major ongoing or recent productions.

605. *Regional Film Theatres.* London ENG: British Film Institute. online. website: http://www.bfi.org.uk Listing of websites of BFI supported theatres. Access is via city with theatres listed alphabetically under each.

◆ *Management* ◆

606. Cleve, Bastian. *Film Production Management.* Boston MA: Focal, c1994. 217p. $29.95. Discusses the process for transforming a screenplay into a movie. Explains script processing, shooting schedules, budgeting, location selection, hiring, and communicating with unions. Provides sample forms and contracts and addresses.

607. Harmon, Renee and Lawrence, Jim. *The Beginning Filmmaker's Guide to A Successful First Film.* New York NY: Walker, c1997. 182p. $14.95. Emphasis on "pitching the product." Discusses the elements of financial acquisition, legal decisions and problems, and marketing and distribution basics. Examples of financial and contractual tools. Lists of festivals, labor organizations, and associations. Includes bibliography.

608. Reid, Roger A. and Wolf, Jill F. *How to Build a Financially Successful Wedding Photography and Video Business ...* Tempe AZ: Perfect Image, c1993. 158p. $19.95. Basic organization for establishing a business out of your home. Marketing secrets and strategies for success.

609. Resnik, Gail and Trost, Scott. *All You Need to Know About the Movie and TV Business.* New York NY: Simon & Schuster, c1996. 335p. $12.00. Written by two entertainment attorneys. Outlines the legal aspects of production and studio operations. Spells out the nature of the job definition from a legal prospective. Especially concerned about protection of creative work and movie "deals."

610. Wiese, Michael. *The Independent Film & Videomaker's Guide.* Studio City CA: Author, c1998. 500p. $29.95. Outlines the activities of the author during 25 years of filmmaking. Gives tips and examples of processes involved in completing a successful production.

♦ *Industry* ♦

611. *BFI Film & Television Handbook.* London ENG British Film Institute. Annual. L17.99. Guide to thousands of cinema and TV contacts. Contains information on production companies, distributors, cinemas, and training courses. Includes extensive facts and figures and listings of award winners.

612. *Producer's Masterguide.* New York NY: Producer's Masterguide. Annual. $125.00. Reference guide to the industry. Includes information on contracts, finance, licensing, regulations, work guidelines, festivals, markets, and a listing by categories of over 30,000 production companies, services, and professionals.

613. Blumenthal, Howard J. and Goodenaugh, Oliver R. *This Business of Television.* New York NY: Watson-Guptill, c1998. 688p. $35.00. Describes how television programming is financed, produced, and distributed. Includes information on audience measurement, advertising, and markets. Discusses regulations and law, networks, cable, and local programming.

614. Sanders, Don and Sanders, Susan. *The American Drive-In Theatre.*

Osceola WI: Motorbooks International, c1997. 160p. $29.95. Traces the history, geography, and ideology of the movement. Includes sections on refreshments and amusement attractions. Insightful analysis of the role of this passing form of entertainment in relationship to the film and television world of today.

615. Squite, James E., ed. *The Movie Business Book.* New York NY: Simon & Schuster, c1992. 479p. $14.00. Collection of articles by movie insiders on the developing, financing, making, and exhibiting movies.

◆ *Market* ◆

616. *Television Industry Tracking Study.* London ENG: British Film Institute, c1995-1997. 2v. £25.00. Qualitative, longitudinal study of 500 viewers over five years. Detailed account of television viewing habits. Charts, statistics, and analysis.

617. *Video Marketing Surveys and Forecasts.* Hollywood CA: VidmaR. Monthly. $4500.00. Tracking service for products, markets, and technologies. Latest statistics and developments. Detailed data on product, sales, and usage. Loose-leaf format.

618. Find/SVP. *Children's Video Market.* New York NY: Author. Annual. $1500.00. Annually updated survey. Covers products, consumers, marketers, and trends, and company profiles. Table of contents of latest found on Find/SVP website (http://www.find/svp.com). comparing activities and ownership by age, gender, type of weapon.

619. Lukk, Tiiu. *Movie Marketing: Opening the Picture and Giving It Legs.* Los Angeles CA: Silman-James, c1997. 240p. $19.95. Focuses on audience. Demystifies marketing issues. Profiles strategies. Defines distribution responsibilities. Includes chapters on merchandising, promotions, and trailers.

620. Sherman, Eric. *Selling Your Film: A Guide to the Contemporary Marketplace.* Acrobat, c1998. 196p. $19.95. Examines how the producer accesses the market. Focus is on marketing avenues and agencies. Includes data on movie goers.

621. *Billboard*. New York NY: BPI Communications. Weekly. $279.00. website: http://www.billboard.com Edited for the music and video industries worldwide. Reports on news, events, people and companies that impact on sales and marketing. Features statistics, charts, and analysis. Emphasis is on the music and recording industries.

♦ *Periodicals* ♦

622. *Box-office*. Chicago IL: RLD Communications. Monthly. $30.00. website: http://www.boxoffice.com Edited for the motion picture theatre industry. Focus on management, operations, trends, production events, and distribution of films. Reviews and charts new releases. Film exposition or topic featured each issue.

623. *Daily Variety*. Los Angeles CA: Cashners Business Information. Daily. $187.00. website: http://www.cashners.com/mainmag/dvar.htm Major source for breaking news in the industry worldwide. Tracks the entire scope of Hollywood and world film activities. Contains reviews and statistics.

624. *Film & Video*. White Plains NY: Knowledge Industry. Monthly. free. Features news articles on motion picture, television, music video, and related production topics. Extensive product and services advertising.

625. *Film & Video News*. Chicago IL: Real Estate News. Monthly. $7.50. Reports on the industry in the Midwest. Focuses on corporate activities, trends, new technology, and services. Features industry leaders and projects.

626. *Film Journal International*. New York NY: Sunshine Group International. Monthly. $45.00. Features production, distribution, exhibition, and allied activities. Includes information on construction, equipment, concessions, censorship, ratings, and other trade-related news. Buying and booking data found in each issue.

627. *Filmmaker Magazine.* Los Angeles CA: Filmmaker Magazine. Quarterly. $16.00. website: http://www.filmmaker.com Magazine of independent filmmaking. Contains articles from working filmmakers on their productions, techniques, problems, and solutions. Seeks to provide an insider's look and the business and creative aspects of the production of indies. Includes information and reports on festivals and competitions. Provides interviews and case studies.

628. *Hollywood Reporter.* Los Angeles CA: Hollywood Reporter. Daily. $149.00. website: http://www.hollywoodreporter.com Edited for professionals in the industry. Features news on film, video, theatre, television, cable, and music. Extensive statistics, charts, and financial data. International news featured on Tuesday and Friday. Over 80 special topic issues published annually. Somewhat abbreviated edition can be accessed via website.

629. *Location Update.* Van Nuys CA: Location Update. Monthly. $49.95. http://www.cineweb.com/reelnews/update/ Covers film and video production in the US and Canada. Each issue sports a state, province, or city as potential locations. For each gives data on facilities, equipment, services, and previous productions.

630. *Locations.* Los Angeles CA: Association of Film Commissioners International. Annually. $5.00. Official publication of the Association of Film Commissioners International, an organization of governmental agents involved in attracting film production. Addresses such production issues as facilities, finance, laws and regulations, and local involvement. Each issue contains directory of member commissioners and a description of their services.

631. *Markee.* Orange City FL: HJK Publications. Monthly. $34.00. Focuses on film and video production in Southern and Southwestern states. Features production data, management, and related crafts and skills. Special feature or state each issue.

632. *Point of View.* Beverly Hills CA: Empire. Quarterly. free. website:

http://www.producersguild.com Edited for producers. Features articles from the business, technical, artistic, and philosophical point of view. Regular columns focus on production teams, women, couples, and similar subjects.

633. *Post.* Port Washington NY: Post Pro. Monthly. $40.00. Edited for the animated, audio, film, and video post production industry. Focus is on news, products, and innovations.

634. *Screen.* Chicago IL: Screen. Weekly. $75.00. Covers news of the Chicago film, video, and television production market. Focuses on production, duplication, distribution, and marketing. Special emphasis each issue.

635. *Screen International.* London ENG: EMAP Business. Weekly. $195.00. Edited for the film, TV, and video industry. Features news, information, statistics, and analysis. Includes articles on production, distribution, and marketing.

636. *Variety.* Los Angeles CA: Cahners Business Information. Weekly. $167.00. website: http://www.cashners.com/mainmag/var.htm Edited for the global entertainment industry. Features news, reviews, and box office statistics. Focus on companies, performance, finance, and marketing.

637. *Video Age International.* New York NY: TV Trade Media. 9 issues. $30.00. Business journal for the film, home video, television, teleproduction industry.

638. *Video Business.* New York NY: Cahners Business Information. Weekly. free. Edited for retailers and distributors of cassettes, discs, DVD, games, and related products. Features news, products, and analysis. Includes reviews, statistics, and charts. Special articles on improving business operations.

639. *Video Store.* Santa Ana CA: Advanstar. Weekly. $48.00. Edited for the retailer. Primary resource for new product information. Includes articles on the industry trends, product development, and market analysis. Special issues survey retailers and consumers.

640. *Video Systems.* Overland Park KS: Primedia Intertec. Monthly. free. website: http://www.intertec.com Edited primarily for operating personnel at independent production facilities. Features articles on technology, equipment, and how-to processes. Focus is worldwide.

641. *Videography.* New York NY: Miller Freeman. Monthly. $30.00. website: http://www.vidy.com Edited for professional in teleproduction facilities and production companies. Features in-depth analysis of trends and techniques employed in production. Special features each issue.

◆ *Databases* ◆

642. *ActorSource.* Los Angeles CA: Christopher Brian Barrett. online. website: http://www.actorsource.com. Personally developed and maintained site. Created for persons interested in starting a career in movies and television. Features resources, links, agents, services, newsgroups, a bulletin board, and a survey page.

643. *British Film Institute.* London ENG: British Film Institute. online. website: http://www.bfi.org.uk Primarily a resource for film funding in the UK. However, contains extensive information on films previously funded, films, television programs, computer games, and other film archives, exhibitions, and training facilities. Press releases and research being conducted by the Institute also included. Online Funding Guide."

644. *Screaming in the Celluloid Jungle.* Los Angeles CA: Screaming in the Celluloid Jungle. online. website: http://www.celluloidjungle. com Primarily a resource for screen writers, but much more broadly oriented. Contains information on script sales. Includes directories of agents and producers with extensive phone listings for related organizations and individuals. Newlines articles and statistics in the industry, production, directing, acting, films in production, box-office receipts, a calendar, glossary, resources, and software. Resources for the writer contain website access to several hundred topics under 24 categories, e.g., reference.

645. *Telefilm Canada.* Montreal CA: Telefilm Canada. online. website: http://www.telefilm.gc.ca The Canadian federal cultural agency dedicated to developing and promoting the Canadian film, television, video, and multimedia industry. Provides access to information on the organization, its financing of Canadian media production, media products, festivals, international relations, and current news.

646. *VideoRetailer.* Keane NH: Video Headquarters. online. website: http://www.videoretailer.com Work of one retailer to enhance the communication of recent news and trends to other retailers worldwide. Emphasizes news and views, new products, marketing opportunities, and purchases and rentals. Provides classified ads, trade show data, and links to the industry and the IVRG.

◆ *Associations* ◆

647. Adult Video Association. 270 N. Canon Dr., Suite 1370. Beverly Hills CA 90210. phone: (213) 650-7121; fax: (213) 654-6850. Association of producers. Purpose is to insure the right of individuals to view what they choose in the privacy of their home. Lobbys for constitutionality of laws affecting adult video. Sponsors publicity campaigns. Supports other anti-censorship organizations. Publishes newsletter.

648. Alliance of Motion Picture and Television Producers. 15503 Ventura Blvd. Encino CA 91436-3140. phone: (818) 995-3600; fax: (818) 382-1793. Association of major producing companies. Purpose is exchange of information.

649. American Film Marketing Association. 10850 Wilshire Blvd., 9th Fl. Los Angeles CA 90024-4321. phone: (310) 446-1000; fax: (310) 446-1600. e-mail: info@afma.com website: http://www.afma.com Association of independent producers and distributors of full length films involved in selling rights in the domestic and foreign markets. Negotiates with foreign producers. Develops standardized contracts. Maintains international arbitration tribunal. Sponsors trade show. Publishes newsletter, fact book.

650. Association for the International Collective Management of Audiovisual Works. 26 rue de St.-Jean. Geneva SWI CH-1203. phone: 41223403200; fax: 41223403432. Association of producers in 13 countries. Purpose to monitor copyright internationally and arrange for proper transfer of royalties.

651. Association of Cinema and Video Laboratories. 959 N. Seward. Hollywood CA 90038. phone: (213) 960-7210; fax: (213) 460-4807. e-mail: info@cfi-hollywood.com website: http://www.acvi.org Association of transfer laboratories. Purpose is exchange of technical and management ideas and solutions. Lobbys and conducts public relations activities. Establishes standards and practice. Publishes handbook.

652. Association of Independent Video and Filmmakers. 304 Hudson St., 6th Fl. New York NY 10013. phone: (212) 807-1400; fax: (212) 436-8519. e-mail: info@aivf.org website: http://www.aivf.org Association of companies, producers, directors, writers, and individuals. Purpose is to publicize and advance the role of the independent film. Provides counsel. Sponsors trade show, seminars. Maintains library. Publishes periodical, directory, exhibitor's guide.

653. Black Filmmaker Foundation. 670 Broadway, Suite 304. New York NY 10012. phone: (212) 253-1690; fax: (212) 253-1689. Association of producers and individuals. Serves as media arts center. Purpose is to develop audience for black filmmakers. Sponsors festivals and educational programs. Maintains library. Publishes newsletter.

654. British Video Association. 167-169 Great Portland St. London ENG W1N 5FD. Association of producers, box manufacturers, printers, duplicators, and wholesalers. Purpose is to protect the copyright and collective market interests of members and industry. Publishes yearbooks, brochures.

655. Canadian Association of Film Distributors and Exporters. 30 Des Trilles. Laval PQ H7Y 1K2. phone: (514) 689-9950; fax: (514) 689-9822. Association of companies. Purpose is to promote development of Canadian producers and the domestic and world market for Canadian products.

656. Canadian Independent Film Caucus. 181 Carlaw Ave., Suite 211. Toronto ON M4M 2S1. phone: (416) 469-2596. Association of producers. Purpose is to promote excellence, advance economic interests, and represent its members before government, labor, and the public. Sponsors promotional programs.

657. Council of Film Organizations. 334 W. 54th St. Los Angeles CA 90037. phone: (213) 752-5811. Association of trade and professional organizations. Purpose is to provide a forum for exchange of ideas. Sponsors competitions. Publishes newsletter.

658. Independent Feature Project. 104 W. 29th St., 12th Fl. New York NY 10001-5310. phone: (212) 465-8200; fax: (212) 465-8525. e-mail: info@ifp.org website: http://www.ifp.org Association of producers and directors. Purpose is to promote the production and distribution of independent films. Provides counsel. Conducts seminars. Sponsors trade shows. Maintains library. Publishes periodical, newsletter, brochures.

659. Independent Film and Video Alliance. 4550 Garnier. Montreal PQ H2J 3S5. phone: (514) 277-0328; fax: (514) 277-0419. website: http://www.culturenet.ca Association of Canadian producers. Purpose is development and promotion. Provides counsel and technical assistance. Sponsors publicity campaigns. Maintains library. Publishes annual report.

660. Independent Film Distributors' Association. 10A Stephen Mews. London ENG W1A 0AX. phone: 441719578957; fax: 441719578968. Association of companies in the UK. Purpose is development of the quality and acceptance of cinema not covered by the major circuits.

661. International Documentary Association. 1551 S. Robertson Blvd., Suite 201. Los Angeles CA 90035. phone: (310) 284-8422; fax: (310) 785-9334. e-mail: ida@artnet.net website: http://www.documentary.org Association of organizations engaged in nonfiction filmmaking. Purpose is to promote the art and science, support the development, and provide a forum for discussion of nonfiction film and video. Provides financial, production, and distribution consultation. Holds screenings of award winning productions. Compiles statistics. Conducts research. Publishes periodical.

662. International Federation of Associations of Film Distributors. 43 Blvd. Maleshebes. Paris FRE F-75008. phone: 33142660532; fax: 33142669692. e-mail: film.paris@wanadoo.fr Umbrella body of 10 national distribution associations. Purpose is to enhance communication between associations and defend the international interests of the group with world organizations and countries.

663. International Motion Picture and Lecturers Association. 1455 Royal Blvd. Glendale CA 91207. phone: (818) 243-7043. e-mail: trwood @worldnet.att.net Association of travelogue film producers and lecturers. Purpose is to foster intercommunication among members. Produces annual festival. Publishes periodical, newsletter, directory.

664. Motion Picture Association. 15503 Ventura Blvd. Encino CA 91436. phone: (818) 995-6600; fax: (818) 382-1784. Association of producers. Purpose is to represent the export interests of the industry. Maintains offices in major countries throughout the world. Limited distribution of information to prospective producers and the general public. Formerly: Motion Picture Export Association of America.

665. Motion Picture Association of America. 1600 I St., NW. Washington DC 20006. phone: (202) 293-1966; fax: (202) 293-7674. website: http://www.mpaa.org Association of major producer/distributors in the US. Purpose is advocacy of the members, protecting producer's rights, fighting censorship, and directing anti-piracy programs. Limited distribution of information. Formerly: Motion Picture Producers and Distributors of America.

666. Music Film and Video Producers' Association. 26 Noel St. London ENG W1V 3RD. phone: 441714342651; fax: 441714349002. Association of production companies.

667. National Association of Television Program Executives. 2425 Olympic Blvd., Suite 550E. Santa Monica CA 90404. phone: (310) 453-4440; fax: (310) 453-5258. e-mail: info@natpe.org website: http://www.

natpe.org Association of representatives of networks, station groups, individual stations, cable systems, and buyers, producers, and distributors. Purpose is to promote and assist in marketing programs. Sponsors major trade conference to accomplish this purpose. Provides counsel and career development assistance.

668. National Association of Theater Owners. 4605 Lankershim Blvd., Suite 340. North Hollywood CA 91602-1891. phone: (818) 506-1778; fax: (818) 506-0269. Association of owners, operators, and executives of motion picture theaters. Purpose is to assist members in the successful operation of their facilities. Compiles statistics. Publishes newsletter, annual, directory, reports. Formerly: Theater Owners of America.

669. National Association of Video Distributors. 700 Frederica St., Suite 205. Owensboro KY 42301. phone: (502) 926-6002; fax: (502) 685-6080. Association of wholesalers of home video products. Promotes industry. Conducts public and governmental relations programs. Publishes directory.

670. Producers Alliance for Cinema and Television. Gordon House, Greencoat Pl. London ENG SW1P 1PH. phone: 441713316000; fax: 441713316700. e-mail: enquiries@pact.co.uk website: http://www.pact.co.uk Association of independent producers in the UK. Purpose is the protection of the rights of its members. Provides financial, production, and facilities counsel. Publishes newsletter, directory.

671. Professional Travelogue Sponsors. 337 S. Madison. Adrian MI 49221. phone: (517) 263-2867. e-mail: awilson@pc3net.com Association of independent entrepreneurs. Purpose to exchange information and works to improve the quality of documentary travel films. Publishes newsletter, directory. Formerly: Professional Travel Film Directors Association.

672. Society of Film Distributors. 22 Golden Sq. London ENG W1R 3PA. phone: 441714374383; fax: 441717340912. Association of companies. Purpose is to protect members distribution rights and to work with other film and governmental organizations on distribution interests.

673. Theater Equipment Association. 244 W. 49th St., Suite 200. New York NY 10019. phone: (212) 246-6460; fax: (212) 265-6428. Association of manufacturers and sellers. Publishes newsletter.

674. Video Software Dealers Association. 16530 Ventura Blvd., Suite 400. Encino CA 91436. phone: (818) 385-1500; fax: (818) 385-0567. website: http://www.vsda.org Association of retailers, distributors, and major producers of video cassettes, games, and software. Purpose is to publicize the industry. Lobbys. Provides counsel. Compiles statistics. Publishes newsletter.

675. Wedding and Event Videographers Association International. 8499 S. Tamiami Trail, Suite 208. Sarasota FL 34238. phone: (941) 923-5334; fax: (941) 921-3836. e-mail: info@weva.com website: http://www. weva.com Association of professionals worldwide. Purpose is to publicize industry, provide information on new technology, and assist in updating skills. Sponsors workshops. Publishes periodical.

19. *The Music Industry*

NAICS 334612, 45122, 51211, 5122, 51223, 71113.

MUSICAL GROUPS, MUSIC PUBLISHING, RECORDING, RE-RECORDING, MUSIC AND RECORD STORES.

♦ *Directories* ♦

676. *AV Market Place: The Complete Business Directory...* New York NY: Bowker. Annual. $195.00. Listing of over 5000 producers, distributors, and servicers of audio, motion picture, and video industries in the US. Arrangement is by state and alphabetical by company under each. Referencing by product, service, and company name.

677. *Billboard International Buyer's Guide.* New York NY: BPI Communications. Annual. $125.00. (annotation, same as #972, 1st edition)

678. *Music Yellow Pages.* West Hempstead NY: National Music & Entertainment. online. website: http://www.musicyellowpages.com Also in print format ($4.95). Probably the most comprehensive listing of US and Canadian companies involved in all aspects of music and related fields. Service is divided into three main sections: "Yellow Pages" an alphabetical listing of categories with names and phone numbers listed for each business under that category; "Business" an alphabetical listing of all businesses referred to in the "Yellow Pages" with phone, fax, e-mail, and website for each; and "Trade Shows" arranged alphabetically. Also "Industry News."

679. *Musical America International Directory of the Performing Arts.* Hightstown NJ: Primedia. Annual. $105.00. Primary emphasis on musical and music-related arts. Listing of companies and related musical organizations. North American and international listings are organized by activity or services. For each organization listed gives name, address, phone, fax, e-mail, website, key personnel, and activities.

680. *Official Country Music Directory.* Rancho Mirage CA: Entertainment Media. Annual. $125.00. Listing of artists, their representatives, products and services, public facilities, and related groups. Divided into 50 categories. Arrangement is alphabetical by name under each. For each entry gives address, phone, fax, key names and profile.

◆ *Management* ◆

681. Everest, Frederick Alton. *How to Build a Small Budget Recording Studio from Scratch...* New York NY: Tab, c1998. 295p. $21.95. Basic introduction to the studio. Not written for a major operation, but is good on theory. Twelve designs included. Concepts and procedures for construction and operation. Not a step-by-step manual.

682. Muller, Peter. *The Music Business-A Legal Perspective.* Westport CT: Greenwood, c1993. 376p. $65.00. Introduction to the major agreements and documents prevalent in the music and recording industry. Examines the relationship of personnel management to these agreements. Presents types of contracts from agency to rights to tours. Bibliography and index.

683. Passman, Donald S. *All You Need to Know About the Music Business.* New York NY: Simon & Schuster, c1997. 416p. $27.50. Comprehensive look at all aspects of the music industry with emphasis on the business and working elements. Detailed examination of organization, finance, contracts, recording companies, and much more.

684. Stim, Richard. *Music Law: How to Run Your Band's Business.* Rochester NY: Layers' Cooperative, c1998. 400p. $65.00. Examines the management and legal aspects of a small operation. A guide to effectively surviving the many legal facets involved in a small operation. Among many major topics are included such seemingly insignificant problems as band name, need for lawyer, members outside activities, ownership of equipment, etc. Forms and agreements appendixed.

685. Sweeney, Tim and Geller, Mark. *Tim Sweeney's Guide to Releasing Independent Records.* Torrance CA: T.S.A. Books, c1996. 149p. $24.95. Guide to establishing an independent record label for yourself or for others. Covers incorporation, finance, contracts, studio operations, personnel, recording and re-recording, distribution, and how to succeed. Many tips and strategies.

♦ *Industry* ♦

686. Brabec, Jeffrey and Brabec, Todd. *Music, Money, and Success: The Insider's Guide to the Music Industry.* New York NY: MacMillan, c1994. 412p. $30.00. Much more than just a tell-it-all work. Explores the complex nature and pitfalls involved in writing, publishing, and recording music. Details the realistic aspects of dollars and cents which it takes to "create" music. Focuses on the role of lawyers, managers, and executives to success.

687. Burnett, Robert. *The Global Jukebox: The International Music Industry.* London ENG: Routledge, c1996. 171p. $22.99. Focus is on the recording industry from the viewpoint of the domination of the worldwide industry recently by five major labels. Examines the role of the oligopolist" firms in relationship to the "independents." Probably the best and most realistic examination of the musical recording industry.

688. Kashif and Greenberg, Gary. *Everything You'd Better Know About the Recording Industry.* New York NY: Brooklyn Boys, c1996. 289p. $39.95. An industry overview from a management prospective. Focus on the role of deals, contracts, incorporation, royalties, publishing and recording, and marketing. Over 150 pages of contacts and forms.

689. Krasilovsky, M. William and Shemal, Sidney. *This Business of Music*. New York NY: Billboard, c1995. 214p. $30.00. Updated version of work first published in 1964. Overview of the production and performance of music and types of people and organizations involved. Examines the "business" of music from viewpoint of operations, activities, personnel, and law.

690. National Music Publishers' Association. *International Survey of Music Publishing Revenues*. New York NY: Author. Annual. $450.00. Data from over 50 countries on music publishing revenues. Income results for performance, reproduction, and distribution. Includes royalties and exchange rates. Statistics on one featured country in each issue.

◆ *Market* ◆

691. Cusic, Don. *Music in the Marketplace*. Bowling Green OH: Bowling Green State University. c1996. 189p. $22.95. Discussion of how popular music is disseminated in the US. Examines product promotion, marketing strategies, and merchandising of popular, classical, jazz, bluegrass, and folk categories. Small independents focused. Accuracy of charts explored.

692. Euromonitor. *Entertainment Software: The International Market*. London ENG: Author, c1995. 375p. $3190.00. Examines the sales potential of all types of software products. Emphasis on recordings but includes video and computer games. Countries covered are France, Germany, Italy, Japan, Spain, the UK and US. Developments in multimedia technology are blurring the divisions between existing product sectors. Includes 365 statistical tables. Loose-leaf.

693. Independent Music Association. *Marketing for the Start-up Record Label*. Saddle River NJ: Author, c1996. 96p. $100.00. Presentation of proven strategies. Topics include publicity, distribution, merchandising, and marketing on radio and the Internet. Case study appendixed.

694. Recording Industry Association of America. *RIAA Statistics.* Washington DC: Author. online. website: http://www.riaa.com/stats. htm Demographic survey and consumer profiles of music buyers. Manufacturer shipment and value statistics. Data on anti-piracy activities and Hispanic music. Updated annually.

695. Smith, Jim. *The Sounds of Commerce: Marketing Popular Film Music.* New York NY: Columbia University. c1998. 256p. $49.50. Detailed historical analysis of the relationship of the film industry and the music industry in the cross-promotion of music generated by mass audience films. Examines how the film and music industries have become intertwined. Studies how film merchandising spells success or failure of its music. Focuses on specific films with highly successful musical scores.

◆ *Periodicals* ◆

696. *Billboard.* New York NY: BPI Communications. Weekly. $279.00. website: http://www.billboard.com Edited for the music and video industries worldwide. Reports on news, events, people and companies that impact sales and marketing. Features statistics, charts, and analysis. Emphasis is on the music and recording industries. Guides issued separately for "International Buyers," "Latin Music Buyers," "International Talent & Touring."

697. *Mix.* Emeryville CA: Primedia Intertec. Monthly. $46.00. website: http://www.mixonline.com Edited for the world of professional recording, sound, and music production. Features articles on all aspects of recording production. Includes information on new products and technology. Profiles successful people and operations. Special feature in each issue.

698. *Music Connection.* North Hollywood CA: Music Connection. Biweekly. $40.00. website: http://www.musicconnection.com Covers the broad spectrum of the music industry from musicians to music to instruments to records. Emphasis is on news, industry developments, and new products. Interviews with musicians and executives is regular feature.

699. *Music Inc.* Elmhurst IL: Maher. 11 issues. $16.50. Edited for retailers. Emphasis on news, trends, and new products. Includes articles on management, personnel, and merchandising. Contains corporate profiles.

700. *Pollstar Magazine.* Fresno CA: Promoters On Line. Weekly. $295.00. website: http://www/pollstar.com Edited for persons in the concert business. Emphasis on activities and statistics. Includes contact information on concerts, fairs, festivals, theme parks, records and their producers, agents, and other music service groups.

701. *Symphony.* Washington DC: American Symphony Orchestra League. Bimonthly. $35.00. Official publication of the American Symphony Orchestra League. Emphasis on issues facing orchestras today. Directed towards management personnel.

♦ *Databases* ♦

702. *American Music Conference.* New York NY: American Music Conference. online. website: http://www.amc-music.com News, online newsletter, standards for music and records, research websites, online resources, and surveys. Provides access to a variety of music topics via a keyword search. Extensive links.

703. *ASCAP Resource Guide.* New York NY: American Society of Composers, Authors, and Publishers. online. website: http://www. ascap.com Information on ASCAP, copyright and publishing materials, the recording industry, concert music, film and TV, theatre and cabaret, jingles, and extensive websites for reference books, periodicals, newsletters, directories, and professional organizations.

704. *British Country Music.* London ENG: British Country Music Internet. online. website: http://www.countrymusic.org.uk News, notice board, chat room, several directories, e.g., bands, tour dates, and listing of music organizations and personnel websites.

705. *IUMA: Internet Underground Music Archive.* New York NY: IUMA. online. website: http://www.iuma.com Access to information and music of over 3000 independent musicians. Also listing of bands, labels, and "cool extras." News and published resources. IUMA seeks to "reinvent the industry" via this alternative website.

706. *MusicSearch.* New York NY: MusicSearch. online. website: http://www.musicsearch.com Directory of companies, artists, products, events, and reviews. Quick search to over 20,000 topics. Meta search to over 100 websites. News, forum, and advertising.

♦ *Associations* ♦

707. American Symphony Orchestra League. 1156 15th St., NW., Suite 800 Washington DC 20005-1704. phone: (202) 776-0212; fax: (202) 776-0224. e-mail: league@symphony.org Association of orchestras, organizations, businesses, and individuals. Purpose is to assist members. Compiles statistics. Conducts research. Provides counsel, employment services. Sponsors educational programs, seminars. Maintains library. Publishes periodical, directories.

708. Association for Independent Music. P.O. Box 998, 147 E. Main St. Whitesburg KY 41858-0988. phone: (606) 633-0946; free phone: (800) 607-6526; fax: (606) 633-1160. e-mail: info@afim.org website: http://www.afim.org Association of record manufacturers, distributors, and retailers. Purpose is sales promotion. Provides forum for industry information exchange. Publishes newsletter, directories, guides.

709. Association of British Orchestras. Francis St. London ENG SW1P 1DE. phone: 441718286913; fax: 441719319959. e-mail: info@abo.org.uk website: http://www.abo.org.uk Association of symphony, chamber, and specialist ensembles and opera and theatre groups. Purpose is to advance professional music in an environment where music can flourish artificially and financially. Maintains library. Publishes newsletter.

710. Association of Professional Recording Studios. 2 Windsor Sq,

Silver St. Reading ENG RG1 2TH. phone: 441189756218; fax: 441189756216. e-mail: info@apra.co.uk website: http://www.apra.co.uk Association of companies and individuals working in the professional audio industry. Purpose is to serve the commercial interest of the members. Sponsors seminars. Publishes newsletter.

711. British Association of Symphonic Bands and Wind Ensembles. 7 Dingle Close, Tytherington. Macclesfield ENG SK10 2UT. phone: 441625430807; fax: 441625430807. e-mail: basbwe@interbs.demon.co. uk Association of companies, organizations, and individuals. Purpose is to advance industry goals and objectives, foster contact and information exchange among members, and assist in the business and financial success of its member's groups. Provides counsel. Conducts clinics and workshops. Maintains library. Publishes periodical, directory.

712. British Phonographic Industry. 25 Savile Row. London ENG W1X 1AA. phone: 441712874422; fax: 441712872252. e-mail: general@bpi.co.uk website: http://www.bpi.co.uk Association of record companies. Purpose is to promote the industry in the UK and throughout Europe. Maintains library. Publishes handbook.

713. Canadian Country Music Association. 5 Director Ct., Suite 102. Woodbridge ON L4L 4S5. phone: (905) 850-1144; fax: (905) 850-1330. e-mail: county@ccma.org website: http://www.ccma.org Association of companies and individuals. Purpose is the promotion of and clearinghouse for members. Publishes newsletter, directory.

714. Canadian Independent Record Production Association. 214 King St., W., Suite 614. Toronto ON M5H 3S6. phone: (416) 593-1665; fax: (416) 593-7563. Association of recording studios. Purpose is to promote small companies, represent member before government, labor, and the public, and organize promotions.

715. Canadian Recording Industry Association. 1250 Bay St., Suite 400. Toronto ON M5R 2B1. phone: (416) 967-7272; fax: (416) 967-9415. e-mail: cria@interlog.com Association of major studios. Purpose is to establish standards and represent member's interests.

716. Chamber Music America. 305 Seventh Ave., 5th Fl. New York

NY 10001-6008. phone: (212) 242-2022; fax: (212) 242-7953. e-mail: info@chamber-music.org website: http://www.chamber-music.org Association of ensembles and their associates. Purpose is to promote professionalism, act as an advocate with government, corporations, and private funders. Provides organizational and financial counsel. Conducts workshops. Compiles statistics. Conducts research. Maintains library. Publishes periodical, newsletters, directories.

717. Country Music Association. One Music Circle S. Nashville TN 37203. phone: (615) 244-2840; fax: (615) 242-7955. website: http://www.countrymusic.org Association of artists, musicians, mangers, agents, promoters, publishers, record companies, and merchandisers. Purpose is promotion and publicity. Sponsors seminars. Conducts surveys. Compiles statistics. Publishes periodical.

718. Country Music Association. 18 Golden Sq., 3rd Fl. London ENG W1R 3AG. phone: 441717433221; fax: 441714343025. website: http://www.countrymusic.org.uk British affiliate of the US association of the same name. Focus is on the UK and Europe. Otherwise, is engaged in similar activities.

719. Gospel Music Association. 1205 Division St. Nashville TN 37203. phone: (615) 242-0303; fax: (615) 254-9755. e-mail: gmatoday@aol.com website: http://www.gospelmusic.org Association of musicians and fans. Purpose is promotion, education, and research. Compiles statistics. Conducts research. Maintains library. Publishes newsletter, directory.

720. Independent Music Association. 10 Spruce Rd. Saddle River NJ 07458. phone: (201) 818 6789; fax: (201) 818-6996. e-mail: imamusic@nis.net website: http://www.imamusic.com Association of record companies, retailers, musicians, and composers. Purpose in promotion, marketing, and distribution of independently produced recordings, increase the playing, and encourage the development of direct and cooperative marketing programs. Sponsors education programs and trade shows. Conducts research. Maintains library. Publishes periodical, guides.

721. Independent Music Retailers Association. 10 Spruce Rd. Saddle

River NJ 07458. phone: (201) 818 6789; fax: (201) 818-6996. e-mail: imamusic@nis.net website: http://www.imamusic.com Association of stores. Purpose is to provide marketing information, work for better producer-retailer communication and relations, and provide member services. Compiles statistics. Conducts research. Maintains library. Publishes periodical, handbooks.

722. International Bluegrass Music Association. 207 E. Second St. Owensboro KY 42303. phone: (502) 684-9025; free phone: (888) 438-4262; fax: (502) 686-7863. e-mail: ibma@occ.uky.campus.mci.net website: http://www.imba.org Association of performers, agents, composers, and publishers, who support the business growth of the industry. Provides counsel, financial support. Sponsors trade show. Compiles statistics. Publishes newsletters.

723. International Federation of the Phonographic Industry. 54 Regent St. London ENG W1R 4PJ. phone: 441718787900; fax: 441718787950. e-mail: info@ifpi.org Association of producers and distributors in over 70 countries. Purpose is to represent members on national and international copyright issues, to promote international legal standards for recordings, and coordinate antipiracy activities worldwide. Provides counsel. Compiles statistics. Maintains library. Publishes newsletter, annual review.

724. International MIDI Association. 23634 Emelita St. Woodland Hills CA 91367. phone: (818) 598-0088. Association of musical software developers. Purpose is to promote the development and spread of electronically produced music with focus on the Musical Instrument Digital interface (MIDI) system. Provides counsel. Maintains library. Publishes newsletter. Formerly: MIDI User's Group.

725. International Recording Media Association. 182 Nassau St., Suite 204. Princeton NJ 08542. phone: (609) 279-1700; fax: (609) 279-1999. e-mail: info@recordingmedia.org website: http://www.recordingmedia.org Association of manufacturers, duplicators, and suppliers. Purpose is to serve as a forum for exchange of management and technical information worldwide. Compiles statistics. Sponsors research and seminars. Publishes directories, handbooks. Formerly: International Tape/Disc Association.

726. Music Distributors Association. 38 W. 21st St., Room 1106. New York NY 10010-6906. phone: (212) 924-9175; fax: (212) 675-3577. e-mail: assnhdqs@aol.com Association of suppliers of sheet music, instruments, and music accessories. Purpose is information interchange among members. Formerly: National Association of Musical Merchandise Wholesalers.

727. Music Industries Association of Canada. 121`0 Sheppard Ave., E., Suite 109. North York ON M2K 1E3. phone: (416) 490-1871; fax: (416) 490-9739. website: http://www.miac.net Association of manufacturers, distributors, and retailers. Purpose is to promote and represent members. Conducts trade show. Compiles statistics. Publishes newsletter.

728. Music Publishers Association. 18-20 York Buildings, 3rd Fl., Strandgate. London ENG WC2n 6JU. phone: 441718397779; fax: 441718397776. e-mail: mpa@mcps.co.uk Association of sheet music companies in the UK. Purpose is to promote and represent members and industry to the government and general public. Publishes newsletter, directory.

729. Music Publishers Association of the United States. 1353 River Rd. Teaneck NJ 07666. phone: (201) 287-1324. website: http://www.mpa.org Association of sheet music companies selling to the concert and education establishment. Purpose is promotion, securing compliance with copyright laws, and anti-piracy activities.

730. NAMM International Music Products Association. 5790 Armada Dr. Carlsbad CA 92008. phone: (619) 438-8001; free phone: (800) 767-6266; fax: (619) 438-7327. website: http://www.namm.com Association of retailers, manufacturers, distributors, jobbers, wholesalers, and publishers of music and instruments. Purpose is to enhance professional development of members and general public. Sponsors education seminars and trade show. Compiles statistics. Maintains library. Publishes newsletter, annual statistical report. Formerly: National Association of Music Merchants.

731. National Association of Recording Merchandisers. 2 Eves Dr.,

Suite 120. Marlton NJ 08053-3188. phone: (609) 596-2221; fax: (609) 596-3268. website: http://www.narm.com Association of retailers, wholesalers, distributors, entertainment software suppliers, and suppliers of related products worldwide. Purpose is to provide a formal network for the interchange of information among members. Publishes newsletter, directories.

732. National Association of School Music Dealers. 4020 McEwen, Suite 105. Dallas TX 75244-5109. phone: (972) 233-9107; fax: (972) 490-4219. website: http://www.nasmd.com Association of retail stores and companies engaged in sales, service, and repair. Purpose is to interchange information and develop coordination between sales agencies and school administrators. Publishes newsletter, directory.

733. National Music Publishers' Association. 711 Third Ave. New York NY 10017. phone: (212) 370-5330; fax: (212) 953-2384. website: http://www.nmpa.org Association of companies. Purpose is protection of publishers' rights. Advises publishers and songwriters of legislation and court rulings. Publishes newsletter, pamphlets. Formerly: Music Publishers Protective Association.

734. Opera America. 1156 15th St., NW. Washington DC 20005-1704. phone: (202) 293-4466; fax: (212) 393-0735. e-mail: frontdesk@operaam.org website: http://www.operaam.org Association of professional companies and affiliated organizations. Purpose is promotion of industry, assistance in the development of companies, and education and training. Provides consulting services. Sponsors grants, workshops, educational programs. Maintains library. Publishes periodical, newsletter, directories, manuals. Absorbed: Central Opera Service.

735. Orchestras Canada. 56 The Esplanade, Suite 311. Toronto ON M53 1A7. phone: (416) 366-8834; fax: (416) 366-1780. e-mail: info@oc.ca website: http://www.oc.ca Association of professional, semiprofessional, and community companies. Purpose is to promote and provide administrative support. Conducts education programs. Compiles statistics. Maintains library. Publishes newsletter, directory, handbooks. Formerly: Association of Canadian Orchestras.

736. Professional Audiovideo Retailers Association. 10 E. 22nd St.,

Suite 310 Lombard IL 60148. phone: (630) 268-1500; fax: (630) 953-8957. e-mail: parahdq@aol.com website: http://www.paralink.org Association of retailers of specialty high end AV equipment. Purpose is to promote the sale of quality equipment and create a forum for the exchange of industry information and new technologies. Provides counsel. Conducts seminars. Certifies professionals. Publishes newsletter, directory, handbooks.

737. Recording Industry Association of America. 1330 Connecticut Ave., NW., Suite 300. Washington DC 20036. phone: (202) 775-0101; fax: (202) 775-7253. e-mail: webmaster@riaa.com website: http://www.riaa.com Association of record companies and distributors. Purpose is promotion, property protection, and public relations. Lobbys. Conducts seminars. Compiles statistics. Conducts research. Publishes newsletter, brochures.

738. Retail Print Music Dealers Association. 4020 McEwen, Suite 105. Dallas TX 75244-5019. phone: (972) 233-9107; fax: (972) 490-4219. website: http://www.printmusic.org Association of stores and publishers. Purpose to serve as the unified voice of the industry.

739. Small Independent Record Manufacturers Association. 1543 Hwy. 138, SE., Suite S-341. Conyer GA 30013. phone: (770) 388-9731; fax: (770) 388-9732. Association of minority-owned companies. Purpose is to create better opportunities for small producers, exchange technical, administrative, and financial advice, and enhance distribution opportunities. Provides counsel. Conducts workshops. Publishes newsletter.

740. Society of Professional Audio Recording Services. 4300 10th Ave., N. Lake Worth FL 33460-2313. phone: (561) 641-6648; free phone: (800) 771-7727; fax: (561) 642-8263. e-mail: info@spars.com website: http://www.spars.com Association of stores and their suppliers. Purpose is to serve as a forum for the exchange of information and new technologies, through members' impact on trends in the AV industry, and address issues confronting members. Evaluates equipment. Conducts seminars. Publishes newsletter.

20. *The Professional Sports Industry*

NAICS 711211.

SPORTS TEAMS AND CLUBS.

◆ *Management* ◆

741. Klinkowitz, Jerome. *Owning a Piece of the Minors.* Carbondale IL: Southern Illinois University. c1999. 160p. $24.95. Amateur's account of purchasing a franchise, Waterloo IA farm team of the Cleveland Indians. Examines all aspects of the finances and marketing required to keep the team alive. Outlines the experiences with achieving community support. Documents the failure and reasons for the end of the "romantic fantasy" and the demise of Waterloo baseball.

742. Morgan, Jon. *Glory for Sale: Fans, Dollars and the New NFL.* Baltimore MD: Bancroft, c1997. 320p. $19.95. A reporter's look at the inner workings of the deal that sent the Cleveland Browns to Baltimore. Profiles the powerful men in the Brown's organization, in the commissioner's office, and in Baltimore with the help of some ex-stars who pulled off the move. Insightful view of the business of professional sports.

743. Quirk, James P. *Pay Dirt: The Business of Professional Team Sports.* Princeton NJ: Princeton University, c1997. 556p. $24.95. Scrutinizes all four major professional team sports: baseball, football, hockey, and basketball. Covers player-reserve clause, free agency, salary structure, franchises, stadiums, and competition.

744. Rothman, Howard. *All That Once Was Good: Inside the National Pastime.* Denver CO: Pendleton Clay, c1995. 262p. $22.95. At a time of hardball team operations and scandal, Rothman examines and tells the positive and financially successful story of the creation and growth of the Colorado Rockies baseball club.

745. Stein, Gil. *Power Plays: An Inside Look at the Big Business of the National Hockey League.* Birch Lane, c1997. 288p. $21.95. Behind the scenes recollections of the past president of the NHL. Comments on players, salaries, owners, violence, Stanley cup, and the financial costs of operating a franchise.

♦ *Industry* ♦

746. Euchner, Charles C. *Playing the Field: Why Sports Teams Move and Cities Fight to Keep Them.* Baltimore MD: Johns Hopkins, c1993. 213p. $39.95. While focusing on the issue of team movement, this work examines the major issues of the continued development of the professional sports industry. The book is as much for planners and city officials as it is for those intimately involved in the industry. Contains three city case studies.

747. Gorman, Jerry and Calhoun, Kirk. *The Name of the Game: The Business of Sports.* New York NY: Wiley, c1994. 278p. $19.95. Examines growth of the industry. Focuses on the impact of television and salaries on the change in the business approach. Looks at the increasingly important role that state-of-the-art facilities and ancillary sources of income have on franchise operations.

748. Johnson, Arthur T. *Minor League Baseball and Local Economic Development.* Urbana IL: University of Illinois, c1993. 273p. $34.95. Case studies charting the economic development of 15 cities from Maine to California which either attracted or lost minor league clubs. Discuss the role and impact of these smaller clubs on the industry and the community served.

749. Noll, Roger G. and Zimbalist, Andrew, eds. *Sports, Jobs, and Taxes: The Economic Impact of Sports Teams and Stadiums.* Washington DC: Brookings Institute, c1997. 420p. $22.95. Collection of articles examining the economic impact of professional sports and their newly constructed stadiums on local economic development, tax revenues, and job creation. Defines criteria for measuring economic impact, justifying subsidies, and construction decisions. Also contains case studies on the building of major league sports facilities. Conclusions are negative.

750. Quirk, James P. and Fort, Rodney D. *Hard Ball: The Perilous Future of Pro Team Sports.* Princeton NJ: Princeton University, c1999. 256p. $22.95. Attempts to explain and project the fundamental economic problems which currently and will continue to face pro teams and their owners and investors. Focuses on squabbles about salaries and financing, deals with cities, ticket costs, and team debt.

◆ *Market* ◆

751. Brooks, Christine M. *Sports Marketing: Competitive Business Strategies for Sports.* Englewood Cliffs NJ: Prentice Hall, c1994. 333p. $73.75. Instructions on marker research, client identification, analysis, interpretation of data, and market exploitation. Provides step-by-step approach for developing a successful marketing strategy.

752. Carter, David M. *Keeping Score: An Inside Look at Sports Marketing.* Grant Pass OR: PSI-Oasis, c1996. 322p. $18.95. Examines the relationship between corporations and the professional sports industry. Studies the links and advantages, role of the corporation in the sport, sport-product identification, and corporation enhancement.

753. Danielson, Michael N. *Home Team: Professional Sports and the*

American Metropolis. Princeton NJ: Princeton University, c1997. 541p. $35.00. Discusses the connection between professional teams and corporate entities and the community in which they locate. Places emphasis on merchandising of the team and its products. Special emphasis on the political aspects. Looks specifically at the impact of baseball, basketball, football, and hockey on cities with a major league team.

754. Schlossberg, Howard. *Sports Marketing.* London ENG: Blackwell, c1996. 214p. $27.95. Global look at the marketing of professional sports. Examines the worldwide development of privately owned professional teams and leagues. Examines the current future market for teams' support and some of the methods employed in achieving consumer support and involvement.

755. Scully, Gerald W. *The Market Structure of Sports.* Chicago IL: University of Chicago, c1995. 207p. $15.00. Identification of the various segments of society to which sports activities appeal. Examines the marketability of each and develops a structure concept for marketers.

◆ *Databases* ◆

756. *CNN Sports Illustrated.* New York NY: Time Warner. online. website: http://www.cnnsi.com Statistics and news on all major professional and amateur leagues and sports. Contents page provides easy access to teams, profiles, players, scores, standings, and statistics. Reviews events and indexes SI articles.

757. *ESPN.* New York NY: ESPN. online. website: http://www.espn. go.com Focuses on professional leagues. Includes news, events, and ticket sources. Sitemap provides alphabetical access to information and statistics on sports and leagues of all kinds worldwide.

758. *NFL Players.* Washington DC: National Football League Players Association. online. website: http://www.playersinc.com Data and view from the player perspective. News events, statistics, and analysis. Games and a store.

759. *NHL Players.* Toronto ON: National Hockey League Player's Association. online. website: http://www.nhlpa.com Stories and statistics about players and association activities. Sections on contracts, player/management relations, players and fans, community service, and league and player statistics.

760. *Sporting News.* New York NY: Times Mirror Interzines. online. website: http://www.sportingnews.com Emphasis on news, events, and team and player activities. Stories and articles by "sideline experts" featured. Chat room and message board. Photos and links.

761. *TSN.* Toronto ON: The Sports News. online. website: http://www.tsn.ca Canadian in origin. North America and all-sports in scope. Contains scoreboard, playing field (major and minor sports), front office, locker room, couchmaster's chat, broadcast booth, and arcade (for just plain fun).

◆ *Biblio/Index* ◆

762. Krause, Jerry V. and Brennan, Stephen J. *Basketball Resource Guide.* Champaign IL: Leisure. c1990. 238p. $22.00. Covers all aspects of the game including leagues and business. Arranged by type of format with author and general subject index.

763. Smith, Myron J., comp. *Baseball: A Comprehensive Bibliography.* Jefferson NC: McFarland, c1986. 915p. $110.00+. Listing of books and articles in 350 periodicals on all aspects of the game. Two supplements: 1985-1992 ($68.50) and 1992-1997 ($59.50) update the original work.

764. Smith, Myron J., comp. *Professional Football.* Westport CT: Greenwood, c1993. 414p. $85.00. Lists English language sources from the beginnings of pro football until 1991. Sections on reference works, general works, and leagues and teams. Includes foreign leagues and postseason activities.

◆ *Associations* ◆

765. American Hockey League. 425 W. Union St., #D3. West

Springfield MA 01089-4108. phone: (413) 781-2030; fax: (413) 733-4767. e-mail: americanhockeyleague@worldnet.att.net website: http://www.canoe.ca/ahl Association of professional teams associated with the National Hockey League. Compiles statistics. Publishes guides. One of two premier minor leagues. Currently eight minor hockey leagues exist and can be accessed via their websites. The SNAP server lists their names and gives access to their websites. The ESPN website accesses their statistics.

766. American League of Professional Baseball Clubs. 350 Park Ave. New York NY 10022. phone: (212) 339-7600; fax: (212) 593-7138. Association of major league teams. Compiles statistics. Maintains library. Publishes guides.

767. Arena Football League. 75 E. Wacker Dr. Chicago IL 60601. phone: (312) 332-5510; fax: (312) 332-5540. e-mail: info@arenafootball.com website: http://www.arenafootball.com Association of professional indoor teams. Compiles statistics. Publishes guide.

768. British National Ice Hockey League. 17 Rodbourne Rd., Manor Farm. Westbury-on-Trym ENG BS10 5AT. phone: 441179048407. e-mail: bnl@cableinet.co.uk website: http://wkweb1.cableinet.co.uk/stan/nhl Association of professional teams in England and Scotland. Compiles statistics. Maintains information center in connection amateur ice hockey associations.

769. Canadian Football League. 110 Eglinton Ave., W., 5th Fl. Toronto ON M4R 1A3. phone: (416) 322-9650; fax: (416) 322-9651. e-mail: info@cfl.ca website: http://www.cfl.ca Association of professional teams. Compiles statistics. Publishes guides.

770. Continental Basketball Association. 400 N. Fifth St., Suite 1425. Phoenix AZ 85004. phone: (602) 254-6677; (602) 258-9985. e-mail: cbagc@netcom.com website: http://www.cbahoops.com Association of professional teams associated with the National Basketball Association. Compiles statistics. Publishes newsletter, guide.

771. Indoor Professional Football League. 4406 Peachtree Rd., NE.

Atlanta GA 30319. phone: (404) 237-5002; fax: (404) 237-5022. e-mail: info@indoorfootball.com website: http://www.indoorfootball.com Association of teams located primarily in the southern US. Compiles statistics. Publishes guide.

772. International Hockey League. 1395 E. Twelve Mile Rd. Madison Heights MI 48071. e-mail: ihl@mindstring.com website: http://www.theihl.com Association of professional teams associated with the National Hockey League. Compiles statistics. Publishes guides. One of two premier minor leagues. Currently eight minor hockey leagues exist and can be accessed via their websites. The SNAP server lists their names and gives access to their websites. The ESPN website accesses their statistics.

773. International League of Professional Baseball Clubs. 55 S. High St., Suite 202. Dublin OH 43107. phone: (614) 791-9300; fax: (614) 791-9009. Association of professional teams in the US and Canada. Compiles statistics. Publishes guide.

774. Major League Roller Hockey. 228 S. Washington St., Suite 115. Alexandria VA 22314. phone: (703) 684-4504. website: http://www.mirh.com Association of professional teams in the US and Canada. Attempting to form a UK Division. Compiles statistics. Publishes guide.

775. Major League Soccer. 110 E. 42nd St., 10 Fl. New York NY 10017. phone: (212) 450-1200; fax: (212) 450-1300. e-mail: info@misnet.com website: http://www.misnet.com Association of professional teams Compiles statistics. Publishes guide.

776. National Association of Professional Baseball Leagues. 201 Bayshore Dr., SE., Box A. St. Petersburg FL 33731. phone: (813) 822-6937; fax: (813) 821-5819. website: http://www.minorleaguebaseball.com Association of 20 professional minor leagues composed of 240 teams. Compiles statistics. Maintains library. Publishes newsletter, guide.

777. National Basketball Association. 645 Fifth Ave. New York NY 10022. phone: (212) 826-7000; fax: (212) 826-0579. website: http://

www.nba.com Association of professional teams. Compiles statistics. Publishes periodical, guide.

778. National Football League. 280 Park Ave., Suite 12-West. New York NY 10022. phone: (212) 540-2000; fax: (212) 681-7582. website: http://www.nfl.com Association of professional teams in the US. Compiles statistics. Publishes guide. Supporting development of US-type professional football teams in the UK, Europe, and Japan.

779. National Football League Europe. Mellier House, 26 A Albermarle St. London ENG W1X 3FA. phone: 441716292992; fax: 441716294055. website: http://www.nfleurope.com Association of professional teams affiliated with the National Football League. Compiles statistics. Publishes guide. Formerly: World League of American Football.

780. National Hockey League. 1251 Avenue of the Americas, 47th Fl. New York NY 10020-1192. phone: (212) 789-2000; fax: (212) 789-2020. e-mail: info@nhl.com website: http://www.nhl.com Association of professional teams in the US and Canada. Compiles statistics. Publishes magazines, guides.

781. National League of Professional Baseball Clubs. 350 Park Ave., 18th Fl. New York NY 10022. phone: (212) 339-7700; fax: (212) 935-5069. Association of major league teams. Compiles statistics. Maintains library. Publishes guides.

782. National Professional Soccer League. 115 DeWalt Ave., NW., 5th Fl. Canton OH 44702. phone: (330) 455-4625; fax: (330) 455-3885. e-mail: npsl1@aol.com website: http://www.npsl.com Association of professional teams. Provides counsel. Conducts seminars. Compiles statistics. Publishes periodical, guide. Formerly: American Indoor Soccer Association.

783. Women's National Basketball Association. 645 Fifth Ave. New York NY 10022. phone: (212) 688-9622; fax: (212) 750-9622. e-mail: info@wnba.com website: http://www.wnba.com Association of professional teams in the US. Compiles statistics. Publishes guide.

21. The Professional Racing Industry

NAICS 711212.

HORSE, DOG, VEHICLE RACE TRACKS AND RACING, POWER-
BOAT RACING. For Recreational Boats see Chapter 10.

♦ Directories ♦

784. *Boat Racing.* New York NY: Performance Marketing. online. website: http://www.boatracing.com Listing of race sites by type of boat racing. Provides direct access to the website for the race. Topical search capability also available.

785. *Greyhound Tracks in North America.* Birmingham AL: National Greyhound Association. online. website: http://www.nga.jc.net/track.htm Listing of tracks. For each gives name, address, fax, purses, total purse, average purse, and website, if available.

786. *Motor Sports Race Tracks.* Troy NY: Krusty Motorsports. online. website: http://www.na-motorsports.com/tracks/ Listing of websites to auto race courses, oval tracks, drag strips, and kart tracks. A search process is available for extracting specific data from these and other sites. Database provides access to organization, school, rally, and many other auto racing websites.

787. *North American Race Tracks.* Atlanta GA: Equibase. online.

website: http://www.equibase.com Listing of horse racing websites. Access is via three methods: alphabetical by track name, by state or province listing alphabetically under each, by location map.

788. *Racing Links.* London ENG: Racenews Internet Services. online. website: http://www.racenews.co.uk/links/ Listing of horsetrack websites worldwide. Divided into "European" and "Rest of the World." Arrangement is alphabetical by country under each grouping. Course websites listed alphabetically under each country.

♦ *Management* ♦

789. Nafzger, Carl F. *Traits of a Winner: The Formula for Developing Thoroughbred Racehorses.* Neenah WI: Russell Meerdink, c1994. 282p. $29.00. Kentucky Derby winning trainer describes four traits essential to a championship racehorse. Emphasizes the management, personnel, and training techniques which must be followed.

790. Strode, William; Williams, Peter and Reed, William F. *Keeneland: A Half-Century of Racing.* Louisville KY: Harmony House, c1986. 135p. $74.95. Somewhat dated, but for the beginner a pictorial look at the principle track for testing the future of a racehorse. One of the most enduring and successful cooperative ventures between owners, racing officials and the public.

791. Waite, Andrew J. *The Great Money Hunt: … An Insider's Practical Guide to Raising Motor Racing Sponsorship.* Nexzuz Motorsports Marketing, c1998. 155p. $69.95. Step-by-step planning guide to a successful search and conclusion. Identifies categories and approaches.

792. Youngson, Mark C. *Auto Racepages.* Detroit MI: Author, c1991. 225p. $29.95. Guide to racing competition. Examines all aspects of getting the car ready and successfully completing the race.

♦ *Industry* ♦

793. Brandon Associates. *Economic Impact of the Horse Industry in the United States: Racing Component.* Washington DC: American Horse

Council, c1996. v.IV. $50.00. Statistical analysis of investment, income, and expenditures by the industry and fans. National and state data. Comparative examination to other forms of recreational investment and expenditure.

794. Brown, Allen E. *History of America's Speedways: Past & Present.* Comstock Park MI: America's Speedways, c1994. 596p. $75.00. Narrative and pictorial study of the major auto racetracks in the US. Names and events predominate.

795. Hagstrom, Robert G. *The NASCAR Way: The Business That Drives the Sport.* New York NY: Wiley, c1998. 288p. $24.95. Examines the people, the drivers, the teams, the corporate sponsors, and the fans who made the series a success. Discusses the role of television from its limited role in the '50s to its major promotional and financial contribution today.

◆ *Periodicals* ◆

796. *Kart Marketing International.* Wheaton IL: Kart Marketing Group. Monthly. $42.00. Edited for manufacturers, dealers, distributors, and track owners. Features industry news, technology, products, service, marketing techniques, and operation of tracks and concessions. Annual buyers guide ($5.95).

797. *Performance Racing Industry.* South Laguna CA: Laguna Coast. Monthly. $25.00. website: http://www.performanceracing.com Edited for racing participants, manufacturers, and retailers interested in the development of the racing performance market. Features new products and engine concepts, merchandising ideas, development trends, and regulations. Special feature each issue including Annual Buyers Guide and Tradeshow. Directory.

798. *Professional NASCAR Garage.* Akron OH: Babcox. Quarterly. free. website: http://www.babcox.com/pngnav.htm Focus is on NASCAR racing. Features articles on race-to-street comparisons, design, performance, racing technology, and safety.

♦ *Databases* ♦

799. *Greyhound Starting Box.* Vancouver WA: World Access Network. online. website: http://www.racing.net Provides access to tracks, track programs, results, handicapping, adoption, simulcast sites, forums, associations, and world links. Searching by specific subject and individual greyhound also provided.

800. *Horse Racing.* New York NY: Miningco. online. website: http://www.horseracing.miningco.com Access to all types of horse racing links from Arabian to thoroughbred worldwide. Spotlights major racing events. Provides bulletin board, chat forum, statistics and other data, and bookstore.

801. *Powerboat Index.* Detroit MI: Island Design. online. website: http://www.islanddesign.com/powerboat-index/ Two part access to websites for boat design and manufacturing information and racing competition.

802. *Racepages.* Brea CA: Marty Kane. online. website: http://www.racepages.com Provides Internet access to auto, bike, and boat racing sites. Sanctioning bodies, associations, and clubs listed. Access to equipment providers included.

803. *Your Guide to Everything Motorsports in Britain.* London ENG: Craig Antill. online. website: http://www.ten-tenths.com News, racing information, and extensive linkage to sites in the UK, Europe, and the world. Emphasis on Formula 1 racing but includes all other formats. Has subject search capability.

♦ *Associations* ♦

804. AMA Pro Racing. 13515 Yarmouth Dr. Pickerington OH 43147. phone: (614) 856-1900; fax: (614) 856-1920. website: http://www.amacycle.org/proracing/ Association of professional motorcyclers and teams. Primary purpose is sanctioning of national level events of all types. Compiles statistics. Publishes guides. Affiliated with: American Motorcycle Association.

805. American Greyhound Track Operators Association. 2000 Seminola Blvd. Casselberry FL 32707. phone: (407) 699-4286; fax: (407) 696-0695. e-mail: info@agto.com website: http://www.agto.com Association of pari-mutuel betting tracks. Purpose is to further the growth of the industry as a sport and business venture through creation of uniform policies and by the exchange of information. Compiles statistics. Publishes newsletter.

806. American Power Boat Association. P.O. Box 377, 17640 E. Nine Mile Rd. Eastpointe MI 48021. phone: (810) 773-9700; fax: (810) 773-6490. e-mail: apbahq@aol.com website: http://www.apba-boating.com Governing body for sanctioned racing in the US. Establishes rules. Conducts speed trials. Compiles statistics. Publishes periodical, directory, reference books, guide, brochures.

807. Championship Auto Racing Teams. 755 W. Big Beaver Rd., Suite 800 Troy MI 48084. phone: (248) 362-8800; fax: (248) 362-8810. e-mail: info@cart.com website: http://www.cart.com Association of incorporated organizations and members. Purpose is to sanction races, promote investment, and publicize activities. Provides counsel. Compiles statistics. Publishes newsletter, directory, guide.

808. Circuits International. P.O. Box 132. Zandvoort NET NL-2040 AC. Association of automobile and motorcycle tracks in 15 countries. Purpose is to develop and promote international racing and to establish uniformity in the operation of tracks. Publishes newsletter.

809. Harness Tracks of America. 4640 E. Sunrise, Suite 200. Tucson AZ 85718-4576. phone: (520) 529-2525; fax: (520) 259-3235. e-mail: harness@azstarnet.com Association of pari-mutuel betting tracks. Purpose is to promote the growth of racing through research and publicity. Provides legal information and counsel. Compiles statistics. Maintains library. Publishes newsletter, directory, statistics, research.

810. Indy Racing League. 4565 W. 16th St. Indianapolis IN 46222.

phone: (317) 484-6526; fax: (317) 484-6525. e-mail: info@irl.com website: http://www.indyracingleague.com Association of teams and persons involved in racing indy-type race cars. Governing body for sanctioning and supervising races in the US. Compiles statistics. Publishes newsletter, directory, guide.

811. International Hot Rod Association. P.O. Box 708, 9 1/2 E. Main St. Norwalk OH 44857. phone: (419) 663-6666; fax: (419) 668-6601. website: http://www.ihra.com Association of promoters, competitors, and drag strip owners. Sanctions drag strips and races. Promotes safety within a competitive environment. Conducts world championship series. Compiles statistics. Publishes newsletter, guide.

812. International Offshore Team Association. P.O. Box 172, St. Peter Port. Guernsey, Channel Islands ENG GY1 3LF phone: 440148136622; fax: 440148136004. e-mail: iota@worldoffshore.com website: http://www.class1.worldoffshore.com/iota/ Association of teams, team owners, pilots, and crew of oceangoing boats. Purpose is to develop "offshore" powerboat racing, establish safety rules, negotiate between teams and race organizers, builders, and sponsors.

813. National Association for Stock Car Auto Racing. P.O. Box 2875, 1801 W. Intl. Speedway Blvd. Dayton Beach FL 32120-2875. phone: (904) 253-0611; fax: (904) 252-8804. website: http://www.nascar.com Sanctions and supervises races. Compiles statistics. Publishes newsletter, guide.

814. National Thoroughbred Racing Association. 303 Peachtree St., Suite 3210. Atlanta GA 30308. phone: (404) 653-6550. e-mail: ntra@intraracing.com website: http://www.ntracing.com Association of owners and breeders. Purpose is to promote, coordinate, and market the sport. Sanctions races. Publishes newsletter, directories, guides.

815. Racecourse Association. Winfield Rd. Ascot ENG SL5 7HX. phone: 441344873537; fax: 441344627333. Association of licensed horserace courses in UK.

816. Racetracks of Canada. 20 Holly St., Suite 204. Toronto ON M4S

3B1. phone: (416) 440-0221; fax: (416) 440-1704. website: http://
www.racetrackscanada.com Association of standard and thoroughbred
facilities. Purpose is to provide opportunity for Canadian horsemen to
enhance a local industry. Publishes newsletter, directory, guide.

817. Thoroughbred Racing Associations. 420 Fair Hill Dr., Suite 1.
Elkton MD 21921-2573. phone: (410) 392-9200; fax: (410) 398-1366.
e-mail: traoffice@pnet.net website: http://www.traofna.com Association of tracks. Purpose is to promote thoroughbred racing. Compiles
statistics. Maintains library. Publishes Directory and Record Book.

818. Union Internationale Motonautique. 1, Avenue des Castelans.
Monaco MC 98000. phone: 37792052522; fax: 37792052523. e-mail:
umi@powerboating.org website: http://www.powerboating.org World
governing body for powerboat racing. Sets rules, sanctions world and
continental championships, and seeks to improve safety of sport. Compiles statistics. Publishes guides.

819. United States Auto Club. 4910 W. 16th St. Speedway IN 46224.
phone: (317) 247-5151; fax: (317) 248-5584. Association of Indianapo-
lis-type car owners and associates. Sanctions major competitions.
Supervises motorsports in the US. Compiles statistics. Conducts safety research. Certifies drivers and vehicles for racing. Publishes newsletter, directory, statistics, guides.

820. United States Trotting Association. 750 Michigan Ave. Colum-
bus OH 43215-1191. phone: (614) 224-2291; fax: (614) 224-4575. e-mail:
info@ustrotting.com website: http://www.ustrotting.com Association
of standardbred tracks, owners of horses, trainers, drivers, officials, and
sponsors. Purpose is to standardize, regulate, and register. Certifies drivers. Compiles statistics. Publishes periodical, directory, guide.

821. Unlimited Hydroplane Racing Association. 721 Cloyden Sq.
Palos Verdes CA 90274. phone: (541) 663-8222. website: http://www.
uhra.com Sanctioning body along with APRA for UH races. Establishes
rules. Compiles statistics. Publishes guides.

22. The Professional Tournament Industry

NAICS 711219, 7113.

INDIVIDUAL PROFESSIONAL SPORTS COMPETITIONS, PRO-
MOTERS OF SPORTS EVENTS.

◆ Management ◆

822. Byl, John. *Organizing Successful Tournaments*. Champaign IL: Human Kinetics, c1998. 174p. $20.00. Textbook. Focus is on organization and options in five tournament sports. Is more concerned with the internal aspects of organization rather than the financial and marketing. Includes examples of draw sheets, scheduling, entry forms, tie-breaking, and the like.

823. Catherwood, Dwight W.; VanKirk, Richard L. and Ernst, G. Young. *The Complete Guide to Special Event Management...* New York NY: Wiley, c1992. 306p. $29.95. Business insights, financial advice, and successful strategies from persons who were consultants to the PGA, the Olympics, and other tournaments. Practical management and marketing advice. Presented also are a series of interviews with successful event promoters.

824. National Golf Foundation. *Tournaments and Events: Organization and Management*. Juniper FL: Author, c1998. 152p. $45.00. Collection of

51 articles. Provides information on development, site planning, sponsorship, rules, and recruiting players. Includes reference to professional participation, tours, and championships.

◆ *Industry* ◆

825. Fredriksson, Kristine. *American Rodeo: From Buffalo Bill to Big Big Business.* College Station TX: Texas A&M University, c1993. 161p. $16.95. Rodeo has become big enterprise. Book describes the history of its rise from show business to weekend sport to major tournament industry.

826. McCormick, Mark H. *The World of Professional Golf.* New York NY: Contemporary Books. Annual. $30.00. Essentially a pictorial view of the happenings. Primary value is to give a digest of the industry and its developments, trends, and changes.

◆ *Market* ◆

827. Graham, Stedman and Goldblatt, Joe Jeff. *The Ultimate Guide to Sports Event Management and Marketing.* Chicago IL: Irwin Professional, c1995. 383p. $32.50. Covers both management and marketing. Examines the relationship between sponsorship, products, and public interest and attendance. Provides step-by-step procedures. Forms for agreements, contracts, and publicity included. Glossary and bibliography.

828. Mullin, Bernard James; Hardy, Stephen and Sutton, William A. *Sport Marketing.* Champaign IL: Human Kinetics, c1993. 249p. $44.00. Textbook. Proposes plan for marketing. Provides overview of marketing concept to be utilized. Describes methods for developing sustainable attendance. Relates factors such as promotion and pricing to customer attitudes and experienced need.

829. Pitts, Brenda G., ed. *Case Studies in Sport Marketing.* Morgantown

WV: Fitness Info Tech, c1998. 235p. $31.00. Profiles a variety of amateur and professional sporting activities. Includes bibliography and index.

♦ *Periodicals* ♦

830. *PGA Magazine.* Troy MI: Quarton Group. Monthly. $23.95. Official publication of the Professional Golfers Association of America. Focus is on articles for members. Includes data and statistics on the PGA Tour. Features on Tour sites.

♦ *Databases* ♦

831. *Boxing Ring.* New York NY: Geocities. online. website: http://www.geocities.com/~boxingweb/ring.html Listing of over 150 boxing and martial arts websites to people and groups. Includes access to IBF, IWBF, NABF, WBA, WBC, WBO.

832. *Complete Wrestling Page.* New York NY: Angelfire. online. website: http://www.angelfire.com/pa/completewrestling Provides news, ratings, data and statistics, media coverage, opinions, latest wrestling "moves," links, and webrings to CWC, WCW, WWF.

833. *Professional Tennis.* Houston TX: United States Professional Tennis Association. online. website: http://www.uspta.org Valuable for its online "Business Tools." Advises the professional how to start, finance, schedule, manage personnel, and market. Informs on rules and regulations. Also provides links to organizations, tours, and "what's new."

834. *Rollarjam.* Nashville TN: World Skating League. online. website: http://www.rollerjam.com. Latest of a long line of inline roller skating competitions (see History). Of special interest because of tie between the World Skating League and The Nashville Network (television system). Information on teams, standings, schedule, and news.

835. *Volleyball Professionals.* Marina del Rey CA: Association of Volleyball Professionals. online. website: http://www.avptour.com New website coming online Spring 1999. For current players, news, competitions, and organization http://www.volleyball.org/pros/

◆ *Associations* ◆

836. American Horse Shows Association. 4047 Iron Works Pkwy. Lexington KY 40511. phone: (606) 258-2472; fax: (606) 231-6662. website: http://www.ahsa.org Association of shows, promoters, and interested individuals. Sanctions and governs competitions. Establishes rules. Licenses judges and stewards. Administers drug tests. Compiles statistics. Conducts research. Publishes periodical, rule book, pamphlets.

837. Association of Professional Bridge Players. 606 Western Ave. Petaluma CA 94952. phone: (707) 766-5021; fax: (707) 763-2621. e-mail: bizamerila@aol.com Association of tournament organizers and professional members of the American Contract Bridge Association. Obtains tournament sponsors. Determines tournament locations. Establishes rules. Publishes newsletter.

838. Association of Surfing Professionals. P.O. Box 309. Huntington Beach CA 92648. phone: (714) 851-2774; fax: (714) 851-2773. e-mail: aspintl@earthlink.net website: http://www.aspworldtour.com Association of tournament directors, sponsors, judges, competitors, and media. Serves as the governing body of professional surfing worldwide. Sanctions locations for World Surfing Tour. Establishes standards. Compiles statistics. Publishes newsletter, ASP World Tour guide.

839. ATP Tour. 201 ATP Tour Blvd. Ponte Vedra Beach FL 32082. phone: (904) 285-8000; free phone: (800) 527-4811; fax: (904) 285-5966. website: http://www.aptour.com Association of players and tournaments. Governing body for circuit. Establishes rules. Promotes sponsors and the game. Publishes newsletter, guide. Formerly: Association of Tennis Professionals.

840. Canadian Professional Rodeo Association. 2116 27th Ave., NE., Suite 223. Calgary AL T2E 7A6. phone: (403) 250-7440. e-mail: prorodeo@iul-ccs.com website: http://www.rodeocanada.com Governing agency for all provincial rodeos. Sanctions and promotes. Certifies professionals. Publishes newsletter.

841. International Professional Rodeo Association. P.O. Box 83377, 2304 Exchange Ave. Oklahoma City OK 73148. phone: (405) 235-6540; free phone: (800) 458-4772; fax: (405) 235-6577. e-mail: oprainfo@int-prorodeo.com website: http://www.intprorodeo.com Association of performers, stock contractors, and producers. One of two rodeo governing bodies (see Professional Rodeo Cowboys Association). Establishes rules governing rodeos. Sanctions tournaments. Trains and certifies judges. Compiles statistics. Conducts surveys. Publishes periodical, surveys, guide.

842. International Table Tennis Federation. 53 London Rd. St. Leonard-on-Sea ENG TN37 6AY. website: http://www.ittf.com World governing body for amateurs and professionals. Sanctions worldwide professional competition, the ITTF Pro Tour. Publishes newsletter.

843. Ladies Professional Golf Association. 100 International Golf Dr. Dayton Beach FL 32124-1092. phone: (904) 274-6200; fax: (904) 274-1099. e-mail: lpga@america.com website: http://www.lpga.com Organizes and supervises tour. Provides counsel to local tournament groups. Supports education programs. Compiles statistics. Publishes periodical, directory, tournament guide. Formerly: Women's Professional Golf Association.

844. National Association of Golf Tournament Directors. 8175 S. Virginia St., Suite 850-391. Reno NV 89511. phone: (702) 852-4646; free phone: (888) 899-2483; fax: (702) 852-0824. e-mail: nagtd@aol.com website: http://www.nagtd.com Association of managers. Purpose is to provide an information network and forum. Certifies programs.

Manages tournament reservation and referral service. Publishes newsletter, directory-guide.

845. National Tractor Pullers Association. 6969 Worthington-Galena Rd., Suite L-1000. Worthington OH 43085. phone: (614) 436-1761; fax: (614) 436-0964. website: http://www.ntpapull.com Association of players and associates. Promotes competitions. Provides counsel. Establishes rules, categories for events, and promotion guidelines. Publishes periodical, newsletter, directory, rulebook, media guide.

846. PGA Tour Tournaments Association. 4 Sawgrass Village Cir., Suite 36. Ponte Vedra Beach FL 32082. phone: (904) 285-4222; fax: (904) 273-5726. e-mail: pgatourta@aol.com website: http://www.pgatour.com/tourn/pga_assn Association of sponsors in the US and Canada. Purpose is to serve as a business information clearinghouse, establish positive relationship with tour professionals, promote and enhance the tournaments, and contribute to the communities in which the tournaments are played. Provides financial, marketing, and media counsel. Assists in finding tour sponsors. Compiles statistics. Publishes newsletter, directory. Formerly: American Golf Sponsors, Professional Golf Tournaments Association.

847. Professional Archers Association. 26 Lakeview Dr. Stansbury Park UT 84074. phone: (801) 882-3817. Association of sponsors, competitors, and archery instructors. Sanctions and supervises tournaments. Conducts instructional school. Publishes newsletter.

848. Professional Bowlers Association of America. P.O. Box 5118, 1720 Merriman Rd. Akron OH 44334-5118. phone: (330) 836-5568; fax: (330) 836-2107. website: http://www.pbatour.org Association of tour competitors. Sponsors the PBA tour. Establishes rules and assists the American Bowling Congress in enforcing its rules and regulations. Promotes cooperation with other bowling organizations. Compiles statistics. Maintains library. Publishes newsletter, tour guide.

849. Professional Cycling Association. 30 Windermere Rd. Wolverhampton ENG WV6 9DL. phone: 441902751831; fax: 441902756989. Association of players and tournament sponsors. Sanctions and schedules competitions. Publishes guide.

850. Professional Golfers' Association. Apollo House, The Belfry, Sutton Coldfield. Birmingham ENG B76 9PT. phone: 441675470333; fax: 441675470674. Association of players. Sponsors tournaments. Protects personal interests of its members. Provides placement service. Publishes periodical.

851. Professional Golfers' Association of America. P.O. Box 109601, 100 Avenue of Champions. Palm Beach Gardens FL 33410-9601. phone: (407) 624-8400; fax: (407) 624-8452. website: http://www.pga.com Association of certified individuals and apprentices association with clubs, courses, and tournaments. Sponsors major tournaments in the US and Ryder Cup matches. Conducts professional training programs. Provides counseling. Compiles statistics. Maintains library. Publishes periodical, tournament guide.

852. Professional Putters Association. P.O. Box 35237. Fayetteville NC 28303. phone: (910) 485-7131; fax: (910) 485-1122. website: http://www.putt-putt.com/ppa/index.htm Association of players, owners, managers, and suppliers of franchised courses. Sponsors competitions. Produces television shows. Compiles statistics. Maintains library. Publishes periodical, newsletter, guide.

853. Professional Rodeo Cowboys Association. 101 Pro Rodeo Dr. Colorado Springs CO 80919-9989. phone: (719) 593-8840; fax: (719) 548-4876. website: http://www.prorodeo.com Association of performers, stock contractors, and producers. One of two rodeo governing bodies (see International Professional Rodeo Association). Establishes rules governing rodeos. Sanctions tournaments. Trains and certifies judges. Compiles statistics. Conducts surveys. Publishes periodical, surveys, guide.

854. Professional Squash Association. 56 Spooner Rd. Chestnut Hill MA 02167. phone: (617) 731-6874; fax: (617) 277-1457. e-mail: psajn@aol.com Association of players, teachers, and marketers. Functions as governing body for handball and softball tournaments. Establishes rules. Organizes worldwide tour. Certifies professionals. Sponsors instruction programs. Publishes newsletter, guide. Formerly: World Professional Squash Association.

855. Professional Women's Bowling Association. 7171 Cherryvale Blvd. Rockford IL 61112. phone: (815) 332-5756; fax: (815) 332-9636. e-mail: pwbaoffice@pwba.com website: http://www.pwba.com Association of competitors. Conducts Ladies Professional Bowlers Tour and other professional tournaments. Compiles statistics. Publishes bowling rules and regulations, annual tour guide, periodical. Formerly: Ladies Professional Bowlers Tour.

856. U.S. Professional Cycling Federation. 7733 Brobst Hill Rd. North Tripoli PA 18066. Association of competitors. Sponsors National Championships and sanctions other professional cycling events. Chooses US team for world competition. Conducts education clinics. Compiles statistics.

857. United States Professional Racquetball Association. 1685 W. Uintah. Colorado Springs CO 80904-2921. phone: (719) 635-5396; fax: (719) 635-0685. website: http://www.uspra.com Association of competitors. Sponsors International Racquetball Tour and Women's International Racquetball Tour. Establishes rules. Publishes newsletter, guide.

858. Women's Professional Billiard Association. 5676 Summit Ave. Memphis TN 38134. phone: (901) 380-1102; fax: (901) 380-0887. website: http://www.wpba.com Association of competitors. Sponsors Classic Billiards Tour. Establishes rules. Sanctions tournaments. Supervises qualifying for professional status. Certifies. Publishes newsletter, guide.

859. Women's Professional Rodeo Association. 1235 Lake Plaza Rd., Suite 134. Colorado Springs CO 80906. phone: (719) 576-0900; fax: (719) 576-1386. e-mail: wpra@rmi.com website: http://www.wpra.com Association of competitors who compete in rodeos sanctioned by the Professional Rodeo Cowboys Association. Conducts seminars and clinics. Maintains library. Publishes newsletter.

860. WTA Tour. 1266 E. Main St., 4th Fl. Stamford CT 06902-3546. phone: (203) 978-1740; fax: (203) 978-1702. website: http://www.wtatour.com Organizes and supervises tour. Establishes rules. Sanctions sites. Publishes newsletter, rule book, player guide.

23. The Public Amusement Industry

NAICS 7113, 71219, 7131.

PRIVATE TOURIST ATTRACTIONS, AMUSEMENT AND THEME PARKS, FAIRS, EXPOSITIONS, AMUSEMENT ARCADES, PROMOTERS OF PERFORMING ARTS.

♦ Directories ♦

861. *Cavalcade of Acts and Attractions.* Nashville TN: BPI Communications. Annual. $75.00. Listing of shows, touring shows, carnivals, circuses, fair attractions plus amusement parks, arenas, rodeos, and other public amusements along with agents servicing these organizations and facilities. Arrangement is by categories with name index. For each entry gives name, address, phone, fax, key personnel, and activities.

862. *Directory of Funparks & Attractions.* Nashville TN: BPI Communications. Annual. $60.00. Listing of theme, amusement, kiddieland, water, state, and national parks, tourist attractions, zoos, museums, and similar public facilities. For each gives address and brief description. Members of the International Association of Amusement Parks and Attractions are identified.

863. *Directory of North American Fairs Festivals and Expositions.*

Nashville TN: BPI Communications. Annual. $60.00. Listing of fairs, festivals, and expositions in the US and Canada which run three days or more. Contains data on managers, demographics, facilities, and budget. Chronological cross reference.

864. *International Amusement Industry Buyers Guide.* Nashville TN: BPI Communications. Annual. $60.00. Listing of manufacturers, importers, and suppliers of rides, games, merchandise, food, and drink products.

865. *Showman's Directory.* Godalming ENG: Lance. online. website: http://www.showmans-directory.co.uk Listing of principle shows and other events in the UK. Includes support agencies and suppliers. Access to websites. Also published in print format.

◆ *Management* ◆

866. *Video Arcade.* Irvine CA: Entrepreneur Group, c1992. 189p. $45.00. Guide to establishing and operating a small business. Legal, management, marketing, operations, and financial procedures outlined. Supplies addresses and a brief bibliography. Loose-leaf format.

867. Caputo, Kathryn. *How to Produce a Successful Craft Show.* Mechanicsburg PA: Stackpole, c1997. 146p. $14.95. Step-by-step procedure. Illustrated examples. Includes index.

868. Connellan, Thomas K. *Inside the Magic Kingdom: Seven Keys to Disney's Success.* Austin TX: Bard Press, c1997. 194p. $20.00. Portrayal of the Kingdom as a model of customer merchandising. Based upon extensive interviews with Disney management and employees. Represents author's assessment of success. Not a Disney PR product.

869. Goldblatt, Joe Jeff. *Special Events: Best Practices in Modern Event Management.* New York NY: Wiley, c1997. 206p. $59.95. Detailed and thorough review of all aspects of planning, producing, managing, marketing, legal, and risk procedures. Useful examples of pluses and minuses.

870. Swarbrooke, John. *The Development and Management of Visitor Attractions.* Oxford ENG: Butterworth-Heinemann, c1995. 381p. $37.95. Emphasis is on the development of public amusements to attract and retain interest of visitors. Continental differences in approach are evident. Good bibliography and index.

♦ *Industry* ♦

871. Adams, Judith A. *The American Amusement Park Industry: A History of Technology and Thrills.* Boston MA: Twayne, c1991. 225p. op. Traces the development of the industry from its show-oriented 19th century roots through the introduction of "rides" to today's focus on the spectacular. Emphasizes the role of the US in today's thrills, technology, and trends. Examines economic, social, and cultural factors.

872. Albrecht, Ernest. *The New American Circus.* Gainesville FL: University of Florida, c1995. 258p. $29.95. A look at the development, rise, and seeming success of the media-oriented, intimate circus emerging from the "street" performers to the hot, hippie Cirque du Soliel. Examines the role of Ringling Brothers and Barnum and Bailey in the circus world of today.

873. Cameron, David Kerr. *The English Fair.* London ENG: Sutton, c1998. 256p. $35.00. Examines the evolution of the fair from early Saxon times through the great fairs of the Middle Ages to the market fair of the recent past to the fairs of today with their emphasis on entertainment rather than trade.

874. Cerver, Francisco Asensio. *Theme and Amusement Parks.* New York NY: Whitney Library of Design, c1997. 168p. $39.95. Site layouts and color photographs of parks worldwide. Brief biographies of designers. Limited text.

875. Throgmorton, Todd H. *Roller Coasters of America.* Oceola WI: Motorbooks International, c1994. 160p. $17.00. Photo-factbook on the primary feature of today's amusement park. Details of the construction and technology of each coaster presented.

◆ *Periodicals* ◆

876. *Amusement Business.* Nashville TN: BPI Communications. Weekly. $129.00. website: http://www.amusementbusiness.com Edited for owners and managers of public amusement facilities and their suppliers. Covers the spectrum of the international live entertainment amusement enterprises. Provides news, attendance, revenue, financial, and operational data. and box scores on top concerts. Special directory for amusement parks, festivals, expositions, and trade shows.

877. *Event Solutions.* Phoenix AZ: Virgo. Monthly. $45.00. website: http://www.vpico.com Edited for professionals who provide venues, planning, services, and products for the industry. Focus on preparation, product use, and execution. Features profiles, special effects, and legal issues. Special feature each issue.

878. *Events Business News.* Cherry Hill NJ: SEN. Quarterly. free. Edited for individuals and companies producing public events and attractions. Features news and articles on fairs, festivals, shows, and sporting events.

879. *Funworld.* Alexandria VA: International Association of Amusement Parks and Attractions. Monthly. $35.00. Trade magazine for executives.

880. *Pollstar Magazine.* Fresno CA: Promoters On Line. Weekly. $295.00. website: http://www.pollstar.com Edited for persons in the concert business. Emphasis on activities and statistics. Includes contact information on concerts, fairs, festivals, theme parks, records and their producers, agents, and other music service groups.

881. *Special Events.* Malibu CA: Miramar. Monthly. $36.00. Edited for professionals who provide product and food services for parties, meetings, galas, and other public events. Focus is on preparation and execution. Special feature each issue.

882. *Tourist Attractions and Parks.* Upper Darby PA: Kane Communications. 7 issues. $35.00. Features articles on promotions, management of facilities, new products, services, and personnel. Annual " Industry Reference Buyers Guide."

883. *What's New for Family Fun.* Arlington Heights IL: Adams Business Media. 9 issues. free. Edited for owners, managers, and operators of family entertainment centers, arcades, theme parks, miniature golf courses, and other for-profit amusement facilities. Provides information on products and services especially games, rides, and other attractions.

♦ *Databases* ♦

884. *CircusWeb: Circuses Past and Present.* New York NY: Graphics 2000. online. website: http://www.circusweb.com Links with circus and related websites, history and lore including operations, references, and glossary of circus terms, and organizations and publications.

885. *Festivals.* Seattle WA: RSL Interactive. online. website: http://www.festivals.com Links to over 25,000 festival websites worldwide. Access is by keyword or via region. Includes news, events, features, and resources for arts, music, shows, sports, and children.

886. *Roller Coaster Database.* Orlando FL: Roller Coaster. online. website: http://www.roller-coast.net Links and statistics on more than 450 roller coasters.

887. *The Fair.* Puyallup WA: Western Washington Fair. online. website: http://www.thefair.com/links/ Links to websites for state fairs and expositions in the US and Canada. Other fair links and resources including linkage to "FairNet," of the Western (US) Fairs Association a database that offers access to worldwide fairground resources (http://www.fairnet.org).

888. *Tim Melago's Directory of Amusement Parks and Roller Coaster Links.* Turtle Creek PA: Tim Melago. online. website: http://www.users.sgi.net/~rollocst/amuse.html Links to parks, centers, and rides and to companies, organizations, and merchandisers who service these enterprises.

◆ Biblio/Index ◆

889. Rebori, Stephen Joseph. *Theme and Entertainment Park Developments: Planning, Design, Development, Management.* Chicago IL: Council of Planning Librarians, c1995. 97p. $15.95. Annotated bibliography of recent books and articles.

◆ Associations ◆

890. American Amusement Machine Association. 450 E. Higgins Rd., Suite 201. Elk Grove Village IL 60007-1417. phone: (847) 290-9088; fax: (847) 290-9192. e-mail: info@coin-op.org website: http://www. coin-op.org Association of manufacturers, distributors, and parts suppliers. Purpose is to promote industry development and protect member companies from copyright infringement by foreign competitors. Lobbys. Publishes newsletter, manual.

891. American Music Festival Association. 12450 Whittier Blvd. Whittier CA 90602. phone: (562) 945-5610; fax: (562) 945-7520. Association of organizations and artists. Purpose is to support the preservation of American music through festivals. Sponsors Music Festivals Tour. Compiles statistics. Conducts research. Provides counsel. Maintains library. Publishes newsletter, guide.

892. American Pyrotechnics Association. P.O. Box 213. Chestertown MD 21620. phone: (410) 778-6825; fax: (410) 778-5013. Association of manufacturers, importers, and distributors. Purpose is to promote safety and inform members of regulations. Works with agents and agencies involved with fireworks displays. Conducts safety programs. Publishes newsletter, handbooks.

893. American Society of Theater Consultants. 12226 Mentz Hill Rd.

St. Louis MO 63128. phone: (314) 843-9218; fax: (314) 843-4955. Association of professionals. Purpose is to improve the planning and construction of theaters and public assembly facilities. Seeks to improve design, use, and enjoyment. Promotes high standards and exchange of information. Conducts research. Collects and disseminates design, technical, and furnishing data.

894. Amusement and Music Operators Association. 450 E Higgins Rd., Suite 202. Elk Grove Village IL 60007-1417. phone: (847) 290-5320; free phone: (800) 937-2662; fax: (847) 290-0409. e-mail: amuseus@aol.com website: http://www.amoa.com Association of firms engaged in coin-operated amusements, music, and vending. Compiles statistics. Conducts research. Provides counsel and educational programs. Publishes newsletter, directory. Formerly: Music Operators of America.

895. Amusement Industry Manufacturers and Suppliers International. P.O. Box 3349. Sarasota FL 34230-3349. phone: (914) 954-3101; fax: (914) 954-3201. e-mail: aims@america.net website: http://www.aimsintl.org Association of manufacturers and suppliers of devices and equipment used in parks, carnivals, and fair companies. Purpose is to exchange information on safety and maintenance. Establishes standards for equipment and safety. Lobbys. Conducts research. Publishes periodical, directory, manuals. Formed by merger of Manufacturers Division of National Association of Amusement Parks and American Recreational Equipment Association.

896. Association of Scottish Games and Festivals. P.O. Box 884, 359 Carlton Rd. Bethel Park PA 15102. phone: (412) 851-9900; fax: (412) 854-5963. e-mail: ligdir@juno.com Association of groups that organize highland games and competitions and bagpipe performances in the US. Purpose is to exchange information. Establishes rules and standards. Compiles statistics. Publishes newsletter.

897. British Arts Festivals Association. 77 Whitechapel High St., 3rd Fl. London ENG E1 7QX. phone: 441712474667; fax: 441712475010. e-mail: bafa@netcomuk.co.uk website: http://www.artfestivals.co.uk Association of professional agencies in the UK. Purpose is to provide a forum for the exchange of experiences and represent the members before government agencies, the media, and the public. Lobbys. Publishes tourist guide.

898. British Association of Leisure Parks, Piers, and Attractions. 25 King's Ter. London ENG NW1 0JP. phone: 441713837942; fax: 441713837925. Association of private sector firms and suppliers. Purpose is to represent the industry before government departments and provide a forum for the exchange of problems and information. Publishes directory, tourist guide.

899. European Festivals Association. 120 B, rue de Lausanne. Geneva SWI CH-1202. phone: 41227386873; fax: 41227384012. e-mail: aef@vix.ch Association of organizers of music, theatre, and dance festivals in Europe. Purpose is to promote and publicize. Publishes guide.

900. International Association for Sports and Leisure Facilities. Carl-Diem-Weg 3. Cologne GER D-50933. phone: 492214912991; fax: 492214971280. Association of organizations and individuals involved in designing, building, and operating facilities in 120 countries. Purpose is to collect, evaluate, and disseminate information on planning, constructing, equipping, and maintaining. Sponsors seminars. Compiles statistics. Conducts research. Maintains library. Publishes periodical, planning guides, conference proceedings.

901. International Association of Amusement Parks and Attractions. 1448 Duke St. Alexandria VA 27314-3403. phone: (703) 836-4800; fax: (703) 836-4801. e-mail: info@iaapa.org website: http://www.iaapa.org Association of outdoor centers and their suppliers. Purpose is promotion and publicity. Compiles statistics. Conducts research. Provides counsel. Publishes periodicals, newsletters, directories, buyers guide, manuals.

902. International Association of Fairs and Expositions. P.O. Box 985, 3043 E. Cairo. Springfield MO 65801. phone: (417) 862-5771; free phone: (800) 516-0313; fax: (417) 862-0156. e-mail: info@iafenet.org website: http://www.infenet.org Association of private, state and county organizations worldwide and related groups. Purpose is to provide a forum for the exchange of information. Sponsors trade show. Lobbys. Compiles statistics. Maintains library. Publishes periodical.

903. International Association of Family Entertainment Centers. 36 Symonds Rd. Hillsboro NH 03244. phone: (603) 464-6498; fax: (603) 464-6497. e-mail: iafecnh@aol.com website: http://www.iafec.org Association of indoor facilities and their suppliers. Conducts education programs and competitions. Compiles statistics. Conducts research. Sponsors trade show. Publishes periodical, newsletter, directory, surveys, research studies, manuals, handbooks.

904. International Council of Air Shows. 481 N. Frederick Ave., Suite 405. Gaithersburg MD 20877-2417. phone: (301) 519-6800; fax: (301) 519-6869. e-mail: icas@airshows.org website: http://www.airshows.org Association of sponsors, performers, producers, US and Canadian military and government officials, airline executives, and suppliers. Purpose is to assist in planning, developing, financing, publicizing, and operating. Publishes periodical, newsletter, directory, industry guide, operations manual.

905. International Council of Folklore Festival Organizations and Folk Art. Badstugard 4. Hudiksvall SWE S-82452. phone: 4665093227; fax: 4665093227. Association of national organizations. Works for international cooperation and exchange of information. Regulates international festivals. Sponsors exhibitions and education programs. Provides counsel. Publishes newsletter, calendar guide.

906. International Federation of Festival Organizations. 4230 Stansbury Ave., Suite 105. Sherman Oaks CA 91423. phone: (818) 789-7596; fax: (818) 784-9141. e-mail: mm412@aol.com Association of organizations and individuals in 62 countries that organize and work with events. Purpose is to coordinate events and calendar. Provides counsel. Publishes periodical, directory.

907. International Festivals and Events Association. P.O. Box 2950, 115 E. Railroad Ave., Suite 302. Port Angeles WA 98362-0336. phone: (360) 457-3141; fax: (360) 452-4695. e-mail: info@ifea.com website: http://www.ifea.com Association of special event producers and suppliers in 33 countries. Serves as a clearing house for planning, finance, management, programming, and promotional information. Provides counsel. Conducts convention and regional seminars. Maintains library. Publishes periodical, directory, manuals.

908. International Sports Show Producers Association. P.O. Box 480084. Denver CO 80248-0084. phone: (303) 892-6800; fax: (303) 892-6322. website: http://www.exposonline.com/isspa Association of organizers and managers. Purpose is to provide a forum for the exchange of information. Publishes newsletter, directory.

909. National Association of Casino and Theme Party Operators. 147 SE. 102nd. Portland OR 97216. phone: (503) 252-6827; free phone: (800) 505-1027; fax: (503) 253-9172. website: http://www.casinoparties.com Association of companies that plan and operate gaming parties and special events. Purpose is to promote industry development nationwide. Publishes newsletter, directory.

910. National Ballroom and Entertainment Association. 2799 Locust Rd. Decorah IA 52101. phone: (319) 382-3871. website: http://www.nbea.com Association of owners and operators. Purpose is promotion and publicity. Publishes newsletter.

911. National Caves Association. 4138 Dark Hallow Rd. McMinnville TN 37110-8629. phone: (931) 668-3925; fax: (931) 668-3988. website: http://www.cavern.com Association of private and publicly owned show caverns. Purpose is to establish standards for preservation and conservation. Conducts promotion campaigns. Lobbys. Publishes newsletter, directory.

912. National Showmen's Association. P.O. Box 662. East Northport NY 11731. phone: (516) 261-2417. Association of carnival owners, operators, entertainers, amusement manufacturers, and associates. Purpose is to promote and expand the amusement show business. Compiles statistics. Affiliated with: Showmen's League of America.

913. Outdoor Amusement Business Association. 4600 W. 77th St. Minneapolis MN 55435. phone: (612) 831-4643; free phone: (800) 517-6222; fax: (612) 831-4642. e-mail: oaba@aol.com website: http://www. oaba.org Association of owners, executives, and employees of fairs and carnivals and persons associated with manufacturing for and supplying these enterprises. Purpose is promotion of the industry. Lobbys. Establishes ethical standards. Provides information center. Publishes newsletter, directory.

914. Showmen's Guild of Great Britain. 41 Clarence St. Staines ENG TW18 4SY. phone: 441784461805; fax: 441784461732. Association of owners and operators of fairground equipment. Purpose is to organize traveling showmen throughout the UK. Establish standards for operations.

915. Showmen's League of America. 300 W. Randolph St. Chicago IL 60606-1705. phone: (312) 332-6236. Association of owners and executives of fairs, expositions, circuses, carnivals, rodeos, auto races, thrill shows, and other indoor and outdoor amusement enterprises. Purpose is to assist members in their profession. Publishes newsletter.

916. Society of Theatre Consultants. 47 Bermondsey St. London ENG SE1 3XT. phone: 441714033778; fax: 441714033778. Association of designers. Purpose is to assist the performing arts in their design of buildings for performance and leisure.

917. Themed Entertainment Association. P.O. Box 11148. Burbank CA 91510-1148. phone: (818) 843-8497; fax: (818) 843-8477. website: http://www.teaonline.org Association of professional developers and producers of facilities for amusement parks, entertainment centers, casinos, resorts, and related public attractions. Purpose is to promote and provide contact between developers and developments. Publishes newsletter, directory, manuals, guides.

918. World Waterpark Association. P.O. Box 14826. Lenexa KS 66285-4826. phone: (913) 599-0300; fax: (913) 559-0520. e-mail: www@waterparks.com website: http://www.waterparks.com Association of facilities and suppliers. Purpose is to provide a forum for exchange of information. Provides counsel. Conducts safety programs. Compiles statistics. Sponsors trade show. Maintains library. Publishes periodical, newsletter, buyers' and developers' guides.

24. *The Gambling Industry*

NAICS 71321, 71329.

CASINOS AND OTHER GAMBLING ESTABLISHMENTS.

◆ *Directories* ◆

919. *American Casino Guide.* Las Vegas NV: Casino Vacation. Annual. $14.95. Listing of over 600 casinos in 32 states. Arrangement is by state with casinos listed by community under each state. Maps of each state show where casinos are located. Also map of Las Vegas with casino locations. Includes informative article about each casino with listing of type of gambling available.

920. *CasinoLinks.* Thought Group. online. website: http://www.casinolinks.com/hotels.index.shtlm Access websites to specific casino-hotels. Sites are indexed by location: US, Caribbean, Europe, other.

921. *Euro Gambling.* Amsterdam NET: RSAC. online. website: http://www.rebus.demon.nl Listing bookmakers, casinos, lotteries, sweepstakes, sports betting, and other gambling sites by country. Arrangement under country is by type of gambling agency. Access is to agency website.

922. *Indian Casinos.* People's Path. online. website: http://www.yvw iiusdinvnohii.net/news/casino.htm Arrangement is more like spot news reports, but you can find websites and current happenings at all casino locations in the US and Canada. Site also contains regulation news, general news, and opinions on Indian casino gambling.

923. Cantor, George. *Where to Gamble*. Visible Ink, c1997. 274p. $19.95. For the gambling enthusiast who wishes to locate all types of gambling establishments plus information about each. Probably not the most complete listing but easily the most interesting.

◆ *Management* ◆

924. Eade, Vincent H. *Introduction to the Casino Entertainment Industry*. Upper Saddle River NJ: Prentice Hall, c1996. 304p. $60.50. Overview of the casino. Examines all aspects of the organization with emphasis on management, operations, personnel, and marketing.

925. Kilby, Jim and Fox, Jim. *Casino Operations Management*. New York NY: Wiley, c1998. 384p. $59.95. Begins with a history of gambling. Following a basic discussion of business aspects of the casino goes into specifics on regulations, the games, cage operations, surveillance, and accounting.

926. Martinez, Ruben. *Managing Casinos: A Guide for Entrepreneurs* ... Detroit MI: Barricade Books, c1995. 431p. $75.00. Primer on inside operations. Overviews the use of management companies. Discusses table management, odds making, and credit. Glossary of terms. Gambling statistics. Lacks index and bibliography.

◆ *Industry* ◆

927. Lew, Alan A. and VanOtten, George A. *Tourism and Gaming on American Indian Lands*. Los Angeles CA: Cognizant, c1998. 252p. $30.00. Examines the rise, role, and effects of reservation gambling on the economic, political, and social environment of the Native American communities. Emphasis is on the tourism dynamics of the gambling movement.

928. Munting, Roger. *An Economic and Social History of Gambling in Britain and the USA*. Manchester ENG: Manchester University, c1996. 272p. $79.95. Comparative study of gambling over the last 200 years. Focuses on the changes that have taken place in the business environment from hostility to a permissive, if not supportive, environment.

929. O'Brien, Timothy L. *Bad Bet: The Inside Story of the Glamour, Glitz, and Danger of America's Gambling Industry*. New York NY: Times Books, c1998. 352p. $25.00. Account of gambling's spread, expansion, and diversity in the US. Emphasis is on legalized gambling and the variety and diversity of the types of gaming which have been tried. Examines the differences between "commercial gambling" and "recreational gambling," the amateur and the professional. Looks at the rule of computerized, online gaming. Views gambling from Las Vegas to hometown USA.

♦ *Market* ♦

930. Davidson, D. Kirk. *Selling Sin: the Marketing of Socially Unacceptable Products*. Westport CT: Quorum Books, c1996. 221p. $29.95. Examines the rise of a whole series of previously banned activities and publications including gambling. Looks as the market for these products, its development, and scope. Includes bibliography and index.

931. Douglas, Andrew. *British Charitable Gambling 1956-1994: Towards a National Lottery*. London ENG: Athlone, c1995. 603p. $80.00. Traces the evolution of lotteries and fund-raising football pools and their impact on the development of the British national lottery. Compares national lotteries and other related gambling activities with the US and Europe. Discusses the role of social acceptance and psychology of charitable gambling and gambling in general. Includes case studies.

932. Minnesota State Lottery. *Gambling in Minnesota*. Roseville MN: Author, 1994. 421p. free. Study of who? what? where? people in Minnesota gamble. Similar studies undertaken in Colorado, Louisiana, New Mexico, Alberta, and other states and provinces.

◆ *Periodicals* ◆

933. *Casino Executive.* New York NY: GEM Communications. Monthly. $48.00. Edited to serve the business information needs of North American casino executives. Features current issues and trends and profiles of industry leaders and companies. Articles on management, marketing, legal matters, non-gambling services, and gambling worldwide.

934. *Casino Journal.* Las Vegas NV: Casino Journal. Monthly. $79.00. e-mail: info@casinocenter.com website: http://www.casinocenter.com Edited for executives and managers. Contains corporate news and profiles, financial and stock analysis, news of gaming technology and trends. Includes interviews with top personnel in the industry.

935. *Gaming Products and Services.* St. Paul MN: RCM Enterprises. Monthly. $36.00. e-mail: rcm@aol.com Edited for managers who purchase, operate, and maintain gaming equipment and facilities. Features articles on new equipment and services, technical innovations, and design trends. Monthly supplement: "Bingo Manager" focus on bingo hall equipment and operations.

936. *International Gaming & Wagering Business Magazine.* New York NY: GEM Communications. Monthly. $113.00. website: http://www.igwb.com Edited for private, public, and Indian gaming establishments in North America. Features news of trends, new products, marketing, finances, legislation, and new venues. Covers established gaming centers in the US, London, and Australia. Specials issues on gaming research and statistics including annual "North American Gaming Report": a compilation of wagering statistics and activities in the US and Canada.

937. *Public Gaming International.* Kirkland WA: Burke. Monthly. $85.00. e-mail: pgrinst@aol.com website: http://www.pgrinstitute.com Edited for the worldwide lottery industry. Features articles on operations, marketing, sales, distribution, security, new games, and technology.

◆ *Databases* ◆

938. *Casino Network.* Las Vegas NV: Casino Network. online. website: http://www.casino-network.com Access to news, casinos, gambling locations, sports gambling, and games. Also includes entertainment, lodging, dining, reservations, merchandise information, and websites.

939. *Gambling.* St. Peter, Channel Islands ENG: Software Centre. online. website: http://www.gambling.com Interactive gambling directory links to casinos, online gambling, blackjack, poker, horse racing, sports betting, lotteries, slots, Las Vegas, bingo, craps, puzzles, and more. Search engine to forum, competitions, prizes, and top gambling sites.

◆ *Biblio/Index* ◆

940. Mirkovich, Thomas R. and Cowgill, Allison A. *Casino Gambling in the United States: A Research Guide.* Lanham MD: Scarecrow, c1997. 401p. $48.00. Sourcebook and directory. Subdivided into seven sections including Indian Casinos, economic development, and crime. Covers monographic and periodical literature. Detailed annotations. Directory of agencies and associations.

941. Thompson, William Norman. *Legalized Gambling: A Reference Book.* Santa Barbara CA: ABC-Clio, c1997. 224p. $45.00. Reference books, articles in periodicals, government reports, and films. Includes review of legislation, editorial opinions, social and religious views, statistics for the US and Canada, and chronology of major gambling events.

◆ *Associations* ◆

942. American Gaming Association. 555 13th St., NW., Suite 430-W Washington DC 20004. phone: (202) 637-6500; fax: (202) 637-6507.

Lobbying representative for private and state lotteries and gambling interests.

943. American Greyhound Track Operators Association. 2000 Seminola Blvd. Casselberry FL 32707. phone: (407) 699-4286; fax: (407) 696-0695. e-mail: info@agto.com website: http://www.agto.com Association of pari-mutuel betting tracks. Purpose is to further the growth of the industry as a sport and business venture through creation of uniform policies and by the exchange of information. Compiles statistics. Publishes newsletter.

944. British Casino Association. 29 Castle St. Reading ENG RG1 57B. phone: 441189589191; fax: 441189590592. website: http://www.british-casino.co.uk Association licensed dealers. Purpose is to provide a unifying force and forum. Lobbys. Publishes newsletter.

945. Harness Tracks of America. 4640 E. Sunrise, Suite 200. Tucson AZ 85718-4576. phone: (520) 529-2525; fax: (520) 259-3235. e-mail: harness@azstarnet.com Association of pari-mutuel betting tracks. Purpose is to promote the growth of racing through research and publicity. Provides legal information and counsel. Compiles statistics. Maintains library. Publishes newsletter, directory, statistics, research.

946. National Association of Casino and Theme Party Operators. 147 SE. 102nd. Portland OR 97216. phone: (503) 252-6827; free phone: (800) 505-1027; fax: (503) 253-9172. website: http://www.casinoparties.com Association of companies that plan and operate gaming parties and special events. Purpose is to promote industry development nationwide. Publishes newsletter, directory.

947. National Association of Off-Track Betting. Park Pl. Pamona NY 10970. phone: (914) 362-0400; fax: (914) 362-0419. Association of legal operations. Purpose is to coordinate actions of members. Lobbys.

948. National Indian Gaming Association. 224 Second St., SE. Washington DC 20003-1943. phone: (202) 546-7711; free phone: (800) 286-6442; fax: (202) 546-1735. e-mail: niga@dgsys.com website: http://www.indiangaming.com Association of tribal establishments. Purpose is to work to maintain the rights of native Americans. Cooperates in the establishment of laws, rules, and regulations applicable to gambling. Lobbys. Conducts educational programs. Sponsors trade show.

949. Thoroughbred Racing Associations. 420 Fair Hill Dr., Suite 1. Elkton MD 21921-2573. phone: (410) 392-9200; fax: (410) 398-1366. e-mail: traoffice@pnet.net website: http://www.traofna.com Association of tracks. Purpose is to promote thoroughbred racing. Compiles statistics. Maintains library. Publishes Directory and Record Book.

25. *The Nightclub Industry*

NAICS 71399, 72241.

DRINKING PLACES, NON-ALCOHOLIC NIGHTCLUBS.

♦ *Directories* ♦

950. *Pubcrawler*. Washington DC: Potomac Interactive. online. website: http://www.pubcrawler.com Listing of websites to 3,500 bars, pubs, and microbreweries in the US and Canada. Access is via type, city, state or province, zip or area code, or name of establishment.

951. *WorldClubs*. Surrey Hills AUT. Kotogaea. online. website: http://www.worldclubs.net Listing of websites to nightclubs, pubs, dance clubs, other similar establishments worldwide. Access is via regional map or country list. Clubs are organized by type, music, and culture.

♦ *Management* ♦

952. Fier, Bruce. *Start and Run a Money-Making Bar*. New York NY: Tab, c1993. 275p. $17.95. Explains basics as well as day-to-day activities essential to "making it." Focuses on location, market, loans, design, records, and personnel. Also gives hints on food service, entertainment, and handling laws and regulations.

953. Marvin, Bill. *Restaurant Basic: Why Guests Don't Come Back...* New York NY: Wiley, c1992. 225p. $50.00. Examines the service aspects of running an establishment. Focuses on the term "good service" from the perspective of training and operational guidelines. Attempts to define what the customer expects of service. Looks at the cost factors.

954. National Restaurant Association. A Guide for Preparing a Restaurant Plan. Washington DC: Author, c1995. 58p. $48.95. Outline elements for writing. Provides examples for each element. Discusses issues unique to restaurant organization, finance, management, personnel, and marketing. Includes list of resources.

955. Sargent, Michael. *Successful Pubs and Inns.* Oxford ENG: Butterworth-Heinemann, c1994. 246p. $34.95. Guide to opening and operating a traditional English pub without rooms. Assumes owners live on premise. Examines laws, finances, markets, and trends and practices.

◆ *Industry* ◆

956. *Restaurant Industry Operations Report.* Washington DC: National Restaurant Association. Annual. $95.75. Accounting format statistical report on US sales, cost of sales, gross profit, average check size, and other income data. A sampling of restaurants in the US. Worksheet for comparative study provided.

957. Haden-Guest, Anthony. *The Last Party: Studio 54, Disco, and the Culture of the Night.* New York NY: Morrow, c1998. 432p. $15.00. A British socialite's observations on the rise and fall of the "Disco Culture." Not so much a business study, but has implications for those planning future nightclub ventures.

958. KPMG Canada. *Canadian Restaurant Industry Operation Report.* Toronto ON: Canadian Restaurant and Foodservices Association. Biennial. $100.00. Statistics collected from records of major restaurants. Provides revenue, and sales data, statistical analysis by type, demographic and geographical prospective, and profit and loss.

959. Lynk, William M. *Dinner Theatre.* Westport CT: Greenwood, c1993. 128p. $59.00. Examines the relatively recent growth of this theatrical phenomena from all of its forms and variations. Intended as a history, reference guide, and manual for practitioners. Includes chapters on food, performance, and the business of operating. Profiles major US dinner theaters. Bibliography and index.

960. National Restaurant Association. *Eating and Drinking Place Figures.* Washington DC: Author, c1998. 5v. $229.95. Statistical analysis based upon Census of Retail Trade. Volumes for Sales and Payroll, Metropolitan and County Areas, Establishment Sales by state and county, Size and Legal Form, and Menu Type.

◆ *Market* ◆

961. Euromonitor. *Alcoholic Drinks Distribution in Europe.* London ENG: Author, c1995. 164p. $990.00. Compiles statistics on on- and off-sale liquor in 15, mostly western, European countries. Provides data on trends generally and by country, sales by product sector and distribution channel, and prices and margins. Includes 132 tables.

962. Marvin, Bill. *Guest-Based Marketing...* New York NY: Wiley, c1997. 200p. $47.00. Examines how to draw upon customer habits to increase sales without increasing significantly your marketing budget. Focuses on loyalty, frequency of visit, word-of-mouth advertising, business customers, groups, the like.

963. National Restaurant Association. *Restaurant Industry Forecast.* Washington DC: Author. Annual. $24.95. Overview of customer trends. Outlook on sales by industry segments. State-by-state projections.

◆ *Periodicals* ◆

964. *Bartender Magazine.* Liberty Corner NJ: Foley. Quarterly. $25.00. website: http://www.bartender.com Edited for full-time dining establishments. Focus on new products, recipes, and drink ideas. Features bar designs, merchandising activities, and marketing ideas.

965. *Chef.* Chicago IL: Talcott. Monthly. $24.00. Edited for food service buyers. Profiles chefs, foods, food services, and trends. Features articles on management, finance, and marketing. Special feature in many issues.

966. *Cooking for Profit.* Fond du Lac WI: C P Publishing. Monthly. $24.00. Edited for food service owners and managers. Features back-of-the-house information. Step-by-step recipe preparation. Provides news, trends and management information. Each month profiles "successful" operation.

967. *Cornell Hotel & Restaurant Administration Quarterly.* Ithaca NY: Cornell University School of Hotel Administration. Quarterly. $50.00. Edited for management. Contains research articles. Reports on research studies and statistical reports. Book reviews.

968. *Culinary Trends.* Long Beach CA: Culinary Publications. Quarterly. $24.00. Edited for chefs, beverage directors, and restaurateurs. Features industry news and events, new products, recipes, a wine column, and people.

969. *El Restaurante Mexicano.* Oak Park IL: Marion Street. Bimonthly. $18.00. Bilingual periodical. Edited for owner/operators of restaurants featuring Mexican cuisine. Features new products, recipes, and profiles of operations.

970. *Equipment Solutions.* Chicago IL: Talcott. Bimonthly. $38.00. Edited for food service operators. Features articles on equipment and facility design and operation. Covers equipment shows, trends, and new technology.

971. *F&B Magazine.* Malibu CA: Miramar. Bimonthly. free. Edited for banquet establishments. Features articles on management, personnel, efficient service operations, and profiles.

972. *Food Arts.* New York NY: M. Shanken. Monthly. free. Edited for fine food establishments. Features news, trends, recipes, and information on equipment.

973. *Food Management.* Cleveland OH: Penton. Monthly. $50.00. Edited primarily for the large scale food service, but many of the articles applicable to nightclub operations. Includes features on personnel management and regulations.

974. *Food Service and Hospitality.* Don Mills ON: Kosluch. Monthly. $60.00. Edited for Canadian food establishments. Focuses on trade shows, market reports, and industry developments. Includes articles on operations, management, equipment, and merchandising.

975. *Hospitality Industry International.* Croydon ENG: BMI Publications. 6 issues. $54.00. Edited for hotels, restaurants, and other food services. Feature articles on management, presentation, service, staff motivation, and marketing. Focus on conventions and exhibitions.

976. *Hospitality Technology.* Randolph NJ: Edgell. Bimonthly. $36.00. Edited for foodservice and lodging professionals. Focus on point-of-sale and back-office electronic systems. Features new hardware and software and on enterprise-wide communications systems.

977. *Nation's Restaurant News.* New York NY: Lebhar-Friedman. Weekly. $34.50. Edited for general, club, and hotel establishments. Focus on news of the industry. Special subject featured in each issue.

978. *Nightclub & Bar.* Oxford MS: Oxford Publishing. Monthly. also online. free. website: http://www.nightclub.com Edited for owners and managers. Features articles on products, equipment, management, marketing, and profiles. Special feature each issue.

979. *Restaurant Business.* New York NY: Restaurant Business. 24 issues. $79.00. website: http://www.restaurantbiz.com Edited for commercial food service organizations. Focus on growth, business opportunities, management, productivity, personnel, and markets. Special feature each issue.

980. *Restaurant Hospitality.* Cleveland OH: Penton. Monthly. $60.00.

Edited for food service professionals. Focus on industry news, trends, and happenings. Features articles on operations, equipment, legislation, labor relations, and strategies. Special feature each issue.

♦ *Databases* ♦

981. *Hospitality Industry Resource Center.* Port Richey FL: Ford Management Services. online. website: http://www.fordmgtsvc.com Website has been created by a nightclub and bar service. Nevertheless, it is primary source for information on nightclubs. Of particular value is "Hello, I'm Blanch," a directory of bar, lounge, and nightclub websites. Free newsletter and links to many other nightclub sites.

982. *Nightclubs.* Longhair Productions. online. website: http://www.nightclubs.com Proposes to link all of the world's nightclub industry information under a single website. Not accomplished, so far, but does list nightclub websites, concert listings, performers and acts, vendors and other services, and bar recipes. Nightclubs are categorized by general, adult, blues, comedy, country, gay, rave, global, and virtual.

983. *RestaurantResults.* Goodyear AZ: Interactive Marketing Technologies. online. website: http://www.restaurantresults.com Another attempt to function as a single Internet resource for the nightclub industry. Its more that 25 categories of information include accessing bar, nightclub, restaurant, and entertainment information and websites worldwide.

♦ *Associations* ♦

984. American Dinner Theatre Institute. P.O. Box 7075. Akron OH 44306. phone: (216) 724-9855. Association of owner/operators. Purpose is to assist in the development of professional, year-around theaters. Provides construction, maintenance, management, and operations advise. Fosters exchange of information on successful productions and profitable food service. Maintains library. Publishes newsletter, directory.

985. British Hospitality Association. 55-56 Lincoln's Inn Fields. London ENG WC2A 3BH. phone: 441714047744; fax: 441714047799. e-mail: info@bha.org.uk website: http://www.bha.org.uk Association of group and individually owned hotel, restaurant, and catering businesses and suppliers. Purpose is to represent members to government. Lobbys. Provides consultation. Publishes periodical.

986. Canadian Restaurant and Foodservices Association. 316 Bloor St., W. Toronto ON M5S 1W5. phone: (416) 923-8416; fax: (416) 923-1450. e-mail: 102477.3104@compuserve.com Association of restaurants, hotels, caterers, and food service corporations and suppliers. Purpose is to represent members before government agencies and general public, certify eating establishments, and provide group buying programs. Lobbys. Conducts research and serves as an information clearing house. Maintains library. Publishes newsletter, reports.

987. Hospitality Association of Northern Ireland. 108-110 Midland Bldg., Whitla St. Belfast NI BT15 1JP. phone: 441232351110; fax: 441232351509. Association of hotels, restaurants, and associated services. Purpose is to represent interests of its members. Lobbys. Provides counsel. Conducts training programs. Publishes newsletter, directory.

988. International Hotel and Restaurant Association. 251, rue de Faubourg, St. Martin. Paris FRE F-75010. phone: 333144893400; fax: 333140367330. e-mail: onfos@ih-ra.com website: http://www.ih-ra.com Association of national and regional organizations in 150 countries involved in all aspects of the hospitality industry from accommodations to food to supplies to reservations. Purpose is to represent the industry before international and national government agencies, raise the level of professionalism worldwide, and encourage the exchange of students and information. Compiles statistics. Conducts research. Publishes periodicals, directories, manuals.

989. National Licensed Beverage Association. 4214 King St., W. Alexandria VA 22302-1507. phone: (703) 671-7575; free phone: (800)

441-9894; fax: (703) 845-0310. e-mail: nlba@mns.com website: http://www.nlba.org Association of on- and off-sale establishments. Purpose is to represent its members, promote positive image of industry, and campaign for safe drinking. Lobbys. Sponsors education programs and National Tavern Month. Compiles statistics. Publishes newsletter, directory, manual. Formerly: National Tavern Association.

990. National Dinner Theatre Association. 8204 Highway 100. Nashville TN 37221. phone: (615) 646-9977; free phone: (800) 282-2276; fax: (615) 622-5439. e-mail: info@dinnertheatre.com website: http://www.webcom.com/ndta/ Association of 40 dinner theaters nationwide. Purpose is to enhance and market their service. Access to each is available via the Internet.

991. National Restaurant Association. 1200 17th St., NW. Washington DC 20036-3097. phone: (202) 331-5900; fax: (202) 331-5971. e-mail: info@dineout.org website: http://www.restaurant.org Association of regular, club, hotel, fast-food, and food service establishments. Purpose is to represent the food serving industry to government, the media, and the general public. Through Education Foundation provides research and training. Publishes periodical, newsletter, directory, numerous research and statistical manuals.

992. Restaurateurs Association of Great Britain. 28 Kingsway. London ENG WC2B 6JR. phone: 441718318727; fax: 441718318703. Association of independently operated establishments. Purpose is to publicize and protect the interests of its members. Lobbys. Publishes periodical.

26. *The Tourist Lodging Industry*

NAICS 7211, 72112, 721191, 721199.

VACATION HOTELS, MOTELS, RESORTS, B&BS, INNS, TIME-SHARES, VACATION RENTALS.

♦ *Directories* ♦

993. *Annual Directory of American and Canadian Bed & Breakfasts.* Boston MA: Rutledge Hill. Annual. $19.95. Listing of over 7,000 B&Bs, country inns, historic houses, farmhomes, etc. Arrangement is by state or province and alphabetical by name under each. For each entry gives description, contact details, and amenities. Maps.

994. *British Bed and Breakfast Annual.* London ENG: American Automobile Association. Annual. $16.95. Listing of more than 3,000 B&Bs and other overnight tourist lodgings in the UK and Ireland. Arrangement is by region and alphabetically by name under each. Address, phone, and description for each entry. Reservation data included.

995. *Hotel and Travel Index.* Secaucus NJ: Cahners. Quarterly. $89.00. (annotation, same as #1468, 1st edition)

996. *Directory of Hotel & Motel Companies.* Washington DC:

American Hotel and Motel Association. Biennial. $82.00. Listing of chain, management, franchise, and referral companies worldwide. Three part directory: part 1— alphabetical listing of companies with name, officers, address, phone, fax, e-mail, website, company properties by name with location; part 2 — companies by state or country; part 3 — companies by rank with number of properties and rooms.

997. *Resort Finder.* Indianapolis IN: Resort Condominium International. online. website: http://www.rci.com Information on over 4,000 timeshare resorts worldwide. Access via regions, city, state, country, accommodations, activities, and amenities. For each entry gives name, location, description, seasons, accommodations, activities, and amenities.

◆ *Management* ◆

998. Davis, Mary. *So-You Want to Be an Innkeeper: The Definitive Guide...* San Francisco CA: Chronicle Books, c1996. 240p. $14.95. Provides information and details on how to start, promote and operate. Extensive charts and worksheets. Recommended by both the ABBA and PAII.

999. Gray, William S. *Hotel and Motel Management and Operations.* Upper Saddle River NJ: Prentice Hall, c1994. 346p. $77.00. Textbook. Covers all aspects of operations including restaurant. Extensive examples, sample forms, and worksheets on finance, management, and marketing.

1000. Jerris, Linda A. *Human Resource Management for Hospitality.* Upper Saddle River NJ: Prentice Hall, c1999. 528p. $64.00. Textbook. Focuses on those aspects of personnel which effect the efficiency and profitability of a business. Reaches beyond the day-to-day operations to examine the industry in the context of a global economy and the role of the employee in successfully competing in this environment. Considers both the "soft" and "hard" skills required.

1001. Lewis, Robert C. *Cases in Hospitality Marketing and Management.* New York NY: Wiley. c1997. 400p. $77.55. Focus is on cases which demonstrate strategies. Each case deals with management situations from more than one perspective. Marketing viewed as an aspect of management. Includes international cases.

1002. Schwanke, Dean. *Resort Development Handbook*. Washington DC: Urban Land Institute, c1997. 300p. $89.95. Handbook outlining the steps involved in planning and executing. Extensive diagrams and examples.

◆ *Industry* ◆

1003. American Resort Development Association. *The United States Timeshare Industry: Overview and Economic Impact Analysis*. Washington DC: Author, c1997. 91p. free. Impact study of regions. Profiles resorts and timeshare owners. Extensive charts and tables based upon surveys.

1004. Kotas, Richard; Teare, Richard; Logie, Jeremy and Bowen, John, eds. *The International Hospitality Industry*. London ENG: Cassell, c1997. 224p. $69.50. Collection of articles by specialists in the field on major aspects of the past and current developments in the industry. Covers the industry worldwide with major emphasis on the growth of mainline hotels and resorts and related restaurant services.

1005. Pannell Kerr Foster PC. *Trends in the Hotel Industry*. New York NY: Author, Annual. $215.00. website: http://www.pkf.com Statistical review incorporating operating and financial data on hotels and motels in the US. Editions also for Canada, Australia, Europe, Middle East, Asia, and the UK.

1006. PKF Consulting. *B&B/Country Inns Industry Study*. Santa Barbara CA: Professional Association of Innkeepers International. Biennial. $99.00. Financial, operating, and marketing analysis based upon accounting data furnished by survey of US establishments. Covers occupancy, amenities, pricing, revenue, expenses, and rate of return. Broken out by geography, size, location, and age of business.

1007. Shaw, Garth and Williams, Allen, eds. *The Rise and Fall of British Coastal Resorts.* New York NY: Pinter, c1996. 325p. $89.50. Economic/cultural articles. Examine the impetus for the rise, the social and cultural patterns that sustained the industry, the role of class, the economic changes after World War II, the attempts at preservation, and the status today. Includes a focus on the "customer." Bibliography and index.

◆ *Market* ◆

1008. Abbey, James R. *Hospitality Sales and Advertising.* Washington DC: American Hotel and Motel Association, c1998. 691p. $71.95. Based upon a study of the lodging consumer. Covers how to attract lodgers, gain customer attention, and motivate your sales team. Checklists and examples included. Profiles successful programs and companies.

1009. Cahill, Denis J. *How Consumers Pick a Hotel: Strategic Segmentation and Target Marketing.* New York NY: Haworth, c1997. 170p. $19.95. Based upon examination of psychological motivation, the author proposes a theoretical model for application to consumer motivation. Lacks the normal practical approach to marketing, but offers an alternative to traditional merchandising.

1010. Morrison, Alastiar M. *Hospitality and Travel Marketing.* Albany NY: Delmar, c1996. 567p. $50.95. Textbook. Examines the market. Looks at aspects of marketing and merchandising. Proposes methods. Emphasizes cooperative efforts between marketers, managers, personnel, and the industry.

1011. Wolosz, Joe. *Hotel & Motel Sales, Marketing & Promotion: Strategies … for Smaller Lodging Properties.* Chicago IL: Infinite Corridor, c1997. 176p. $24.95. Step-by-step practical guide to market in today's changing economy. Guide to the identification of potential and target markets. Examines methods and ideas for "filling rooms." Provides outline for "Marketing Plan."

1012. YBR Marketing. *United States B&B/Inn Guest Study.* Santa

Barbara CA: Professional Association of Innkeepers International, c1997. 4v. $45.00. Published in regional editions for Northeast, South, Midwest, West. Documents what inngoers want in an inn, what they spend, and how to successfully market to them. Guests of all types are identified and surveyed.

♦ *Periodicals* ♦

1013. *Bed & Breakfast.* Phoenix AZ: Virgo. 10 issues. $19.95. website: http://www.vpico.com Edited for owners and operators. Covers all aspects of innkeeping. Emphasizes management. Special feature each issue.

1014. *Bottomline.* Austin TX: Hospitality Financial & Technology Professionals. Bimonthly. $50.00. website: http://www.hftp.org Edited for professionals working in hotels and resorts. Focus is on finance, accounting, and economic trends. Special feature each issue.

1015. *Cornell Hotel & Restaurant Administration Quarterly.* Ithaca NY: Cornell University School of Hotel Administration. Quarterly. $50.00. Edited for management. Contains research articles. Reports on research studies and statistical reports. Book reviews.

1016. *Hospitality Industry International.* Croydon ENG: BMI Publications. 6 issues. $54.00. Edited for hotels, restaurants, and other food services. Feature articles on management, presentation, service, staff motivation, and marketing. Focus is on conventions and exhibitions.

1017. *Hospitality Technology.* Randolph NJ: Edgell. Bimonthly. $36.00. Edited for foodservice and lodging professionals. Focus on point-of-sale and back-office electronic systems. Features new hardware and software and enterprise-wide communications systems.

1018. *Hotel & Motel Management.* Cleveland OH: Advanstar. 21 issues. $35.00. website: http://www.hmmonline.com Edited for owners and managers concerned with latest news of the industry. Features late-breaking news, ideas, and tips. Covers management, finance, marketing, technology, and regulations. Annual "Management Show Daily" published separately.

1019. *Hotel Business*. East Setauket NY: ICD Publications. Bimonthly. $65.00. website: http://www.hotelbusiness.com Provides news analysis, statistics, product information, and financial data. Features technology trends and company profiles.

1020. *Hotels*. Des Plaines IL: Cahners. Monthly. $89.90. website: http://www.hotelsmag.com Official publication of the International Hotel and Restaurant Association. Focuses on trends, hotel design, operations, and technology worldwide. Special feature each issue.

1021. *Innkeeping World*. Seattle WA: Innkeeping World. Monthly. $25.00. Edited for owner/managers of B&Bs and country inns. Focuses on news and technology designed to assist in better and more efficient operations.

1022. *Lodging*. Washington DC: American Hotel and Motel Association. Monthly. $45.00. website: http://www.lodgingmagazine.com Official publication of the American Hotel & Motel Association. Focuses on design, development, amenities, management, finance, marketing, products, and people.

1023. *Lodging Hospitality*. Cleveland OH: Penton. Monthly. $60.00. Edited for management. Focus is on trends, globalization, profitability, and crucial issues facing the industry. Special feature each issue.

1024. *RCI Premier*. Indianapolis IN: Resort Condominiums International. Bimonthly. free. Edited for executives in the timeshare resort industry. Focus is on trends, operations, sales, and legal issues. Includes executive, resort, and company profiles.

◆ *Databases* ◆

1025. *All Hotels on the Web*. Edinburgh SCO: Articulate Solutions. online. website: http://www.all-hotels.com Independent hotel and travel site. Provides worldwide directory, tour, travel, event, and service links, discount information, and a search engine. Map gives access to hotel websites by country.

1026. *Bed & Breakfast Inns Online.* Innkeeper Services. online. website: http://www.bbonline.com Access to websites of 2,000 inns and 22 state innkeeper associations in the US. Includes innkeeper and aspiring innkeeper information. Recipes and cookbooks recommended by practicing innkeepers. Links to B&Bs worldwide.

1027. *Rentalgetaways.* West Orange NJ: Getaways. online. website: http://www.rentalgetaways.com Information on vacation rental homes, condos, and townhouses in North America. Access to listing is by map of US states, Canada, Mexico, and the Caribbean. Links to other rental databases.

1028. *Resorts Online.* New York NY: Resorts Online. online. website: http://www.resortsonline.com Worldwide listing. Access emphasis is on type of activity, e.g., golf, skiing, casino. Resort websites listed under continent and country. Includes listing of amenities. Links to other resort databases provided as well as currency converter.

1029. *Timeshares.* New York NY: Com Marketing. online. website: http://www.timeshares.com Information on buying, renting, and operating in the US. Links to Europe and other timeshare websites.

♦ *Associations* ♦

1030. American Bed and Breakfast Association. P.O. Box 1387. Midlothian VA 23113-1387. phone: (804) 379-2222; free phone: (800) 769-2468; fax: (804) 330-2729. website: http://www.abba.com Association of innkeepers and reservation service agencies. Purpose is to act as an information clearinghouse. Inspects and rates accommodations. Publishes newsletter, directory, guide.

1031. American Historic Inns. P.O. Box 669. Dana Point CA 92629.

phone: (949) 499-8070; free phone: (800) 397-4667; fax: (949) 499-4022. e-mail: ahii@ix.netcom.com website: http://www.homearts.com/affil/ahi Association of bed and breakfast buildings being preserved because of their historical significance. Purpose is to encourage the preservation of historic homes. Publishes directories, guides. Formerly: Association of American Historic Inns.

1032. American Hotel and Motel Association. 1201 New York Ave., NW., Suite 600. Washington DC 20005-3931. phone: (202) 289-3193; fax: (202) 289-3199. e-mail: info@ahma.com website: http://www.ahma.com Federation of state lodging associations. Purpose is to coordinate information and promote business. Compiles statistics. Conducts research. Sponsors education programs. Maintains library. Publishes periodical, newsletter, directories, survey, manuals, brochures.

1033. American Resort Development Association. 1220 L St., NW., Suite 500. Washington DC 20005-4059. phone: (202) 371-6700; fax: (202) 289-8544. e-mail: info@arda.org website: http://www.arda.org Association of developers of timeshare, resort, recreational, residential, and retirement communities and suppliers. Purpose is to publicize and advance the concept of vacation ownership through timeshare. Lobbys. Sponsors seminars. Compiles statistics. Conducts research and surveys. Maintains library. Publishes periodical, directory, reports, surveys, manuals.

1034. American Spa and Health Resort Association. P.O. Box 585. Lake Forest IL 60045. phone: (847) 234-8851; fax: (847) 295-7790. Association of small and diverse fitness enterprises and resorts. Serves as an information exchange and contact with data and statistical resources. Conducts inspections and certifies qualifying facilities. Sets standards.

1035. British Federation of Hotel, Guest House, and Self-Catering Associations. 5 Sandicroft Rd. Blackpool ENG FY1 2RY. phone: 441253352683. Association of small, family-run hotels, guest houses, B&Bs, and self-catering establishments. Purpose is to assist and represent members. Lobbys. Provides consultation. Publishes newsletter.

1036. British Hospitality Association. 55-56 Lincoln's Inn Fields.

London ENG WC2A 3BH. phone: 441714047744; fax: 441714047799. e-mail: info@bha.org.uk website: http://www.bha-online.org.uk Association of group and individually owned hotel, restaurant, and catering businesses and suppliers. Purpose is to represent members to government. Lobbys. Provides consultation. Publishes periodical.

1037. Canadian Resort Development Association. 48 Hayden St. Toronto ON M4Y 1V8. phone: (416) 960-4930; free phone: (800) 646-9205; fax: (416) 923-8348. Association of owners and operators. Purpose is to promote Canada as a vacation destination. Lobbys. Compiles statistics. Conducts research. Sponsors education programs. Provides counsel. Maintains library. Publishes newsletter, brochures. Formerly: Resort Timesharing Council of Canada.

1038. Caribbean Hotel Association. 1000 Ave. Ponce De Leon. San Juan PR 00907. phone: (787) 725-9139; fax: (787) 725-9108. website: http://www.smallhotels.com/cha.htm Association of establishments and organizations in the hospitality industry. Purpose is to promote the area as a travel destination. Provides counsel. Lobbys. Sponsors education and training programs. Maintains library. Publishes newsletter, directory, guide.

1039. Green Hotels Association. P.O. Box 420212. Houston TX 77242-0212. phone: (713) 789-8889; fax: (713) 789-9786. e-mail: info@greenhotels.com website: http://www.greenhotels.com Association of lodging establishments committed to promoting ecological consciousness in the hospitality industry. Publishes newsletter, directory, guide.

1040. Hospitality Association of Northern Ireland. 108-110 Midland Bldg., Whitla St. Belfast NI BT15 1JP. phone: 441232351110; fax: 441232351509. Association of hotels, restaurants, and associated services. Purpose is to represent interests of its members. Lobbys. Provides counsel. Conducts training programs. Publishes newsletter, directory.

1041. Hospitality Sales and Marketing Association International. 1300 L. St., NW., Suite 1020. Washington DC 20005. phone: (202) 789-0089; fax: (202) 789-1725. e-mail: hsmai@aol.com website: http://www.

hsmai.org Association of owners and executives in the industry. Purpose is the education and training of personnel in the industry. Conducts seminars, clinics, workshops. Publishes periodical, directory, manuals.

1042. Independent Innkeepers Association. P.O. Box 150. Marshall MI 49068. phone: (616) 789-0393; free phone: (800) 344-5244; fax: (616) 789-0970. e-mail: smoore@internetl.net website: http://www.innbook.com Association of independent country inns. Purpose is to promote standards and its members. Publishes newsletter, directory.

1043. International Association of Holiday Inns. 3 Ravinia Dr., Suite 2900. Atlanta GA 30346. phone: (770) 604-5555; fax: (770) 604-5684. Association of owners and franchisees. Purpose is to serve as a liaison between owner/operators and the franchiser company. Provides counsel. Sponsors education programs. Publishes newsletter.

1044. International Hotel and Restaurant Association. 251, rue de Faubourg, St. Martin. Paris FRE F-75010. phone: 333144893400; fax: 333140367330. e-mail: onfos@ih-ra.com website: http://www.ih-ra.com Association of national and regional organizations in 150 countries involved in all aspects of the hospitality industry from accommodations to food to supplies to reservations. Purpose is to represent the industry before international and national government agencies, raise the level of professionalism worldwide, and encourage the exchange of students and information. Compiles statistics. Conducts research. Publishes periodicals, directories, manuals.

1045. Irish Hotels Federation. 13 Northbrook Rd. Dublin 6 IRE. phone: 353 1 976459; fax: 353 1 974613. Association of proprietors. Purpose is to represent interests of its members. Lobbys. Provides counsel. Publishes newsletter, guide.

1046. National Bed and Breakfast Association. P.O. Box 332. Norwalk CT 06852. phone: (203) 847-6196; fax: (203) 847-0469. website: http://www.nbba.com Association of small, family-owned inns in the US. Provides counsel. Publishes newsletter, directory.

1047. National Forest Recreation Association. 325 Pennsylvania Ave.,

SE., Suite 271. Washington DC 20003. phone: (202) 546-8527; fax: (202) 546-8528. e-mail: info@nfra.org website: http://www.nfra.com Association of resorts, camps, and other recreational facilities on or adjacent to federal land. Purpose is to serve as the liaison between the members and federal and state government agencies on matters of legislation, regulation, taxation, and other requirements. Lobbys. Provides counsel. Publishes newsletter.

1048. Preferred Hotels and Resorts Worldwide. 311 S. Wacker Dr., Suite 1900. Chicago IL 60606-6618. phone: (312) 913-0400; fax: (312) 913-0444. Association of independent, luxury facilities. Purpose is to unite promotion activities for better competition with the major hotel and resort chains. Establishes standards. Provides counsel. Maintains reservation center. Publishes newsletter, directory.

1049. Professional Association of Innkeepers International. P.O. Box 90710. Santa Barbara CA 93190. phone: (805) 569-1853; fax: (805) 682-1016. e-mail: info@paii.org website: http://www.paii.org Association of bed and breakfast and country inn establishments. Purpose is to promote and support its members. Provides counsel. Conducts research. Conducts education programs. Maintains library. Publishes newsletter, directory, surveys, studies, manuals.

1050. Resort and Commercial Recreation Association. P.O. Box 1998. Tarpon Springs FL 34688-1998. phone: (813) 939-8811. e-mail: rcraone@aol.com Association of suppliers and agents. Purpose is to act as an agency for the interchange of information within the industry and establish a network for professional development and education. Provides counsel. Conducts education programs. Publishes periodical, newsletter, directory.

1051. Small Luxury Hotels of the World. 1716 Bank St. Houston TX 77098-5402. phone: (713) 522-9512; free phone: (800) 525-4800; fax: (713) 524-7412. e-mail: gracie@uetropolis.net website: http://www.slh.com Association of independently owned facilities. Purpose is to act as marketing agency for members and develop an interhotel information network.

1052. Timeshare Council. 23 Buckingham Gate. London ENG SW1E

6LB. phone: 441718218845; fax: 441718280739. Association of developers and associates. Purpose is to promote, develop, represent and regulate the industry. Lobbys. Establishes standards. Provides counsel. Maintains library. Publishes guide.

1053. Tourist House Association of America. Rt.2, Box 355A. Greentown PA 18426. phone: (717) 676-3222; free phone: (888) 888-4068. Association of bed and breakfast proprietors and agents. Purpose is to promote B&B usage and provide information to members. Provides counsel. Publishes guide, manual.

1054. Vacation Rental Managers Association. P.O. Box 1202. Santa Cruz CA 95061-1202. phone: (408) 458-3573; free phone: (800) 871-8762; fax: (408) 450-3637. e-mail: info@vrma.com website: http://www.vrma.com Association of companies. Purpose is to promote the industry and provide for exchange of information among members. Provides counsel. Conducts seminars. Publishes newsletter, directory, guide, manual.

27. The Campground Industry

NAICS 721199, 721211.

CAMPGROUNDS, RV PARKS, HOSTELS.

◆ *Directories* ◆

1055. *Canada Camping Guide.* Lake Forest IL: Woodall. Annual. $5.99. Listing of private and public campgrounds. Arrangement is by province and city and alphabetical by facility name under each. Gives address, phone, fax, e-mail, website, rates, rating, and facilities. Includes how-to-find, sightseeing, and RV service information.

1056. *Hosteling International — Europe.* Welwyn Garden City ENG: International Youth Hostel Federation. Annual. $10.95. Listing of facilities. Arrangement is by country and alphabetical by city under each. Gives address, phone, fax, dates open, hours, information on making reservations, price range, facilities, directions, and map.

1057. *Hosteling Passport to North American.* Washington DC: Hosteling International — American Youth Hostels. Annual. $3.00. Listing of facilities. Arrangement is by province and state and alphabetical by city under each. Gives address, phone, fax, dates open, hours, information on making reservations, price range, facilities, description of hostel, directions for locating, and a map.

1058. *North American Campground Directory*. Lake Forest IL: Woodall. Annual. $21.95. Listing of private and public campgrounds. Arrangement is by state and city and alphabetical by facility name under each. Gives address, phone, fax, e-mail, website, rates, rating, and facilities. Includes how-to-find, sightseeing, and RV service information.

1059. *Where to Stay in Britain*. London ENG: British Tourist Authority. Annual. $10.95. Listing of camping and caravan parks in England, Northern Ireland, Scotland, and Wales. Arrangement is by county and city and alphabetical by facility name. Gives address, phone, fax, e-mail, website, facilities, rates, and location including sightseeing information for area.

♦ *Management* ♦

1060. Canadian Industrial Development Branch. *Planning Canadian Campgrounds*. Ottawa ON: Canadian Office of Tourism, 1980. 118p. op. Directions for campground and recreational vehicle park development and management. Includes information on feasibility studies, planning, design, construction, and all aspects of operation.

1061. Cooper, Rollin B. *Campground Management*. Champaign IL: Sagamore, c1992. 425p. op. Step-by-step guide to establishing and operating. Emphasis on planning, management, and marketing. Statistics, forms, and examples. Bibliography and index.

1062. McEwen, Douglas and Mitchell, Clare. *Fundaments of Recreation Programming for Campgrounds and RV Parks*. Champaign IL: Sagamore, c1991. 212p. op. Proposes types of activities which might be operated in connection with a campground or park. Presents details on planning and operation. Includes bibliography and index.

♦ *Industry* ♦

1063. Williams, Jim. *The Hostel Handbook for the USA and Canada*. New York NY: Author, c1999. 104p. $3.00. Overview of the development of hosteling. Provides a selected directory of over 600 hostels but is much more than that. Written by the operator of two hostels in New York City.

◆ *Market* ◆

1064. Fillman, William. *First Complete Marketing Guide for Campgrounds*. Champaign IL: Sagamore, c1990. 110p. op. Examines the categories of people who frequent campgrounds. Proposes merchandising to these groups. Provides strategies. Includes advertising and marketing forms.

◆ *Periodicals* ◆

1065. *Outdoor Hospitality*. Chicago IL: Imagination. Quarterly. free. website: http://www.imagepub.com Edited for owners and operators. Provides news, product information, technology data, and management information. Special feature each issue.

1066. *Recreation Advisor*. Gonzalez FL: RLT Resource Group. 5 issues. $15.00. Edited for campers and RVers. Valuable for campground owners and operators for the news, current event, legislation, and club information provided. Special feature each issue.

1067. *RV Park & Campground Report*. Vienna VA: National Association of RV Parks and Campgrounds. Monthly. $25.00. Official publication of the National Association of RV Parks and Campgrounds. Provides industry information and news, new products and services, calendar of events, association events, legislative updates, and general data pertinent to the RV industry.

1068. *Woodall's Campground Management*. Lake Forest IL: Woodall. Monthly. $24.95. website: http://www.woodalls.com Edited for operators of RV parks, resorts, and campgrounds. Emphasis on management.

Profiles, trends, and successes. Includes news, new products, and reports from franchise and state organizations. Special feature each issue.

♦ *Databases* ♦

1069. *Camping — USA.* Detroit MI: Camping — USA. online. website: http://www.camping-usa.com Advertises as "your one stop shop for all your camping information." Provides campground directory, access to campground websites, directory of national forest campgrounds, list and web access to camping events, details on sites for sale, checklist of camping item, access to camping books and related materials, and a forum and chat line for "why not" camping.

1070. *Camping & Caravaning UK.* Mansfield ENG: Rothgarth. online. website: http://www.camping.uk-directory.com Comprehensive resource for information on sites, retailers, buying and selling, and links. Access is by website. under each of the categories listed.

1071. *KOA Country.* Billings MT: Kampgrounds of America. online. website: http://www.koacampgrounds.com Primarily a vehicle for presentation of information of KOA facilities; however, is a significant resource for information on camping in the US, Canada, and Mexico. Information on facilities, activities, special resources, and camping and exploring.

1072. *Outdoors — RV Park.* St. Louis MO: Rik Brown. online. website: http://www.travel.com/outdoors/rvp.htm Part of a broader travel website. Provides access to a variety of campground, RV, and travel-related websites.

1073. *RV Camping Magazine.* Raynham Center MA: Campground Online. online. website: http://www.channel1.com/users/brosius/ Online periodical providing current directory, industry, manufacturing, employment, club, resource, publication, and other camp-related information. Provides message board and links to other campground websites.

◆ *Associations* ◆

1074. An Oige, Irish Youth Hostel Association. 61 Mountjoy St. Dublin 7 IRE. phone: 353 1 8304555; fax: 353 1 8305808. e-mail: anoige@iol.ie website: http://www.irelandyha.org Association of private and public hostels in Ireland. Works in partnership with state and local government and other youth organizations. Provides counsel. Maintains reservation service. Publishes guide.

1075. British Holiday and Home Parks Association. 6 Pullman Ct., Great Western Rd. Gloucester ENG GL1 3rd. phone: 441452526911; fax: 441452307266. Association of residential, caravan, chalet, tent, and self-catering parks. Purpose is marketing and promotion, exchange of information, and representation before governmental agencies. Lobbys. Provides counsel. Publishes periodicals.

1076. Holiday Centres Association. 28 Albion St. Chipping Norton ENG OX7 5BJ. phone: 441608644824; fax: 441608644229. Association of facilities. Purpose is to establish and maintain standards. Formerly: National Association of Holiday Centres.

1077. Hosteling International — American Youth Hostels. 733 15th St., SW., Suite 840. Washington DC 20005. phone: (202) 783-6161; fax: (202) 783-6171. e-mail: hiayhser@hiayh.org website: http://www. hiayh.org Association of private and public hostels in the US. Works in partnership with state and local government and other youth organizations. Provides counsel. Maintains reservation service. Publishes directory, handbooks.

1078. Hosteling International — Canada. 205 Catherine St., Suite 400. Ottawa ON K2P 1C3. phone: (613) 237-7884; fax: (613) 237-7868. e-mail: info@hostelingintl.ca website: http://www.hostelingintl.ca Association of private and public hostels in Canada. Works in partnership with state and local government and other youth organizations. Provides counsel. Maintains reservation service. Publishes guide, handbooks.

1079. Hosteling International — Northern Ireland. 22 Donegall Rd.

Belfast NOI BT12 5JN. phone: 441232315435; fax: 441232439699. e-mail: info@hini.org.uk website: http://www.hini.org.uk Association of private and public hostels in Northern Ireland. Works in partnership with local government and other youth organizations. Provides counsel. Maintains reservation service. Publishes guide, handbooks.

1080. International Youth Hostel Federation. 9 Guessens Rd. Welwyn Garden City ENG AL8 6QW. website: http://www.iyhf.org Association of youth hostel associations worldwide. Develops and enforces international standards. Works with international organizations. Supports international reservation service. Publishes newsletter, directories.

1081. KampGround Owners Association. 6201 N. 35th Ave., Suite C2. Phoenix AZ 85017-1413. phone: (602) 973-2889; fax: (602) 973-0270. Association of KOA franchisees. Purpose is to provide for the interchange of information. Conducts seminars. Compiles statistics. Publishes newsletter.

1082. National Association of RV Parks and Campgrounds. 8605 Westwood Center Dr., Suite 201. Vienna VA 22182. phone: (703) 734-3000; fax: (703) 734-3004. e-mail: arvc@erols.com website: http://www.gocampingamerica.com Association of owners, operators, manufacturers, and suppliers. Purpose is to represent members in contacts with producers, government agencies, the media, and general public. Compiles statistics. Conducts research. Sponsors workshops. Provides counsel. Publishes periodical, newsletter, directory, guide, research, manuals, brochures.

1083. National Forest Recreation Association. 325 Pennsylvania Ave., SE., Suite 271. Washington DC 20003. phone: (202) 546-8527; fax: (202) 546-8528. e-mail: info@nfra.org website: http://www.nfra.com Association of resorts, camps, and other recreational facilities on or adjacent to federal land. Purpose is to serve as the liaison between the members and federal and state government agencies on matters of legislation, regulation, taxation, and other requirements. Lobbys. Provides counsel. Publishes newsletter.

1084. Scottish Youth Hostels Association. 7 Glebe Crescent. Stirling

SCO FK8 2JK. phone: 441786891400; fax: 441786891333. e-mail: info@syha.org.uk website: http://www.syha.org.uk Association of private and public hostels in Scotland. Works in partnership with state and local government and other youth organizations. Provides counsel. Maintains reservation service. Publishes guide.

1085. YHA Limited. 8 St. Stephen's Hill. St. Albans ENG AL1 2DY. phone: 441727845047; fax: 441727844126. e-mail: yhacustomerservices@compuserve.com website: http://www.yha.org.uk Association of private and public hostels in England and Wales. Works in partnership with state and local government and other youth organizations. Provides counsel. Maintains reservation service. Publishes guide.

28. The Vacation Camp Industry

NAICS 721214.

PRIVATE CAMPS, DUDE RANCHES.

♦ Directories ♦

1086. *Camp Directors' Purchasing Guide.* Littlerock CA: Klevens. Annual. $65.00. Listing of products and services. Information is organized by type of product and by supplier. Each listing describes the product and offers a sample of product literature.

1087. *Guide to ACA-Accredited Camps.* Martinsville IN: American Camping Association. Annual. $19.95. Listing of only about one quarter of all US, Canadian, and other camps, but all listed meet American Camping Association standards. Arrangement is alphabetical by states then alphabetical by name under each. For each facility gives name, founding date, address, phone, director, description, activities, session, fees, and contact including e-mail and website. Indexing by activity, physical and/or mental challenges, special groups, e.g., gifted, special philosophies, e.g., religion, day camps, Christian camps, and name.

1088. *Kid's Camps.* Boco Raton FL: Kid's Camps. online. website: http://www.kidscamps.com. More comprehensive listing of camps in the US and Canada. Access to websites for residential, day, sports, arts, academic, family, special needs, resort, and tour facilities.

◆ *Management* ◆

1089. Ball, Armand and Ball, Beverly. *Basic Camp Management.* Martinsville IN: American Camping Association, c1995. 284p. $23.95. Introduction to administration. Includes an historic overview, the director, philosophy, programming, staff, marketing, the participant, site, risks, services, evaluation and reporting, finance, and volunteers. Sample job description, governmental, association, and international resources, bibliography, and index.

1090. Bryan, William L. *Sharing Your Home on the Range.* New York NY: Underhill & Wild Wings Foundation, c1991. 130p. op. Handbook for dude ranch and farm hospitality providers. Step-by-step procedures for development and operation.

1091. Ditter, Bob. *In the Trenches.* Martinsville IN: American Camping Association, c1998. 187p. $27.95. Answers by an expert to the toughest problems faced in camping. Focus is on behavioral challenges, but provides guideline for dealing with campers, staff, management, parents, and child abuse. Bibliography and index.

◆ *Industry* ◆

1092. American Camping Association. *Accreditation Standards for Camp Programs and Services.* Martinsville IN: Author. Annual. $42.95. Discusses the Association, purpose and history of the Standards, administration, and guidelines. Lists and outlines current standards. Glossary and explanation of standards included in appendix. Association resources and index.

1093. Flood, Elizabeth Clair. *Old-Time Dude Ranches Out West.* Salt Lake City UT: Gibbs Smith, c1995. 95p. $17.95. Introductory overview of the development of the dude ranch. Currently available along with other of her works. A more complete study, now op is Borne, Lawrence R. DUDE RANCHING: A COMPLETE HISTORY. Albuquerque NM: University of New Mexico, c1983. 322p.

◆ *Market* ◆

1094. Borden, Marian Edelman. *Summer Fun: The Parents' Complete Guide...* New York NY: Facts on File, c1999. 208p. $14.95. Not a true market study, but rather a guide to what the researcher and practitioner views as the criteria for a "good summer camp." Presents a step-by-step outline of what should be looked for and examined.

◆ *Periodicals* ◆

1095. *Camping Magazine.* Martinsville IN: American Camping Association. Bimonthly. $24.95. Edited for camp management. Provides practical information impacting on management. Features articles on construction, maintenance, equipment, staffing, program, and purchasing. Special feature each issue.

1096. *Frost's Summer Camp Sourcebook.* Harrington Park NJ: Frost. Annual. $10.00. website: http://www.frosts.com Edited for owners and directors. Primarily a directory of companies that provide supplies and services, but contains a variety of articles on new trends and products, computerization, support services, and supplier profiles.

◆ *Databases* ◆

1097. *CampPage.* Cedar Mountain NC: CampPage. online. website: http://www.camppage.com Much more than a good directory. Offers information and services for directors, employment opportunities, and equipment data. Good links to other camping resources.

1098. *Ranchweb Travel.* Eureka CA: Kilgore Ranch. online. website: http://www.ranchweb.com Produced by the man who for more than a decade has written the primary guide to dude and other types of ranches. In addition to a major directory of facilities, the database provides access to all the resources involved in running and getting to all type of facilities. Includes current news and links to other websites.

◆ *Associations* ◆

1099. American Camping Association. 5000 State Rd. 67 N. Martinsville IN 46151-7902. phone: (756) 342-8456; fax: (756) 342-2065. e-mail: aca@aca-camps.org website: http://www.aca-camps.org Association of owners, directors, and other resident and daycamp associates. Purpose is to offer programs and guidance in the areas of administration, staffing, activities, child development, promotion, and programming. Develops and enforces standards. Maintains library. Publishes periodical, directory, manuals.

1100. Canadian Camping Association. 1810 Avenue Rd., Suite 303. Toronto ON M5M 3Z2. phone: (416) 781-4717; fax: (416) 781-7875. e-mail: canada@kidscamp.com website: http://www.kidscamp.com/ canadian-camping Association of commercial and non-profit facilities. Purpose is to promote, coordinate, and represent. Develops and enforces standards. Provides counsel. Compiles statistics. Operates bookstore. Publishes newsletter.

1101. Christian Camping International. P.O. Box 62189. Colorado Springs CO 80962-2189. phone: (719) 260-9400; fax: (719) 260-6398. e-mail: info@cciusa.org website: http://www.cciusa.org Association of camps and conference centers. Purpose is to encourage, train and develop, and provide timely resources for operators, directors, and leaders. Publishes periodical, newsletter.

1102. Dude Ranchers' Association. P.O. Box 471. LaPorte CO 80535. phone: (970) 223-8440; fax: (970) 223-0201. e-mail: duderanches@ compuserve.com website: http://www.duderanch.org Association of facilities in the US and Canada. Purpose is to provide a forum for the exchange of ideas, publicize dude ranching as a vacation activity, interact with federal land management agencies, and preserve and protect wildlife, parks, and forests. Publishes directory.

1103. Forest School Camps. 90 Fordwyck Rd., First Fl. London ENG SE24 9HD. phone: 441814521142; fax: 441814521142. Association of educational youth camps in the UK. Purpose is to provide a system of facilities to develop self-esteem and woodcraft skills. Publishes catalog.

1104. National Camp Association. P.O. Box 5371, 610 Fifth Ave. New York NY 10185-5371. phone: (212) 645-0653. e-mail: info@summer-camp.org website: http://www.summercamp.org Advisory service to campers worldwide. Provides assistance to parents in choosing the right camp for their children. Publishes manual.

1105. North American Gamebird Association. 1214 Brooks Ave. Raleigh NC 27607. phone: (919) 782-6758; fax: (919) 782-6758. e-mail: gamebird@naga.org website: http://www.naga.org Association of operators of shooting preserves, breeders, and others associated with commercial gamebird management and propagation. Purpose is to establish standards, monitor legislation and regulations, and develop cooperation and exchange of information among members. Lobbys. Sponsors education programs. Publishes newsletter, directories.

29. *The Tour Industry*

NAICS 48711, 48721, 48799, 56152, 71399.

SCENIC AND SIGHTSEEING TRANSPORTATION, TOUR OPERA-
TORS, GUIDE SERVICES.

♦ *Directories* ♦

1106. *Adventure Holidays.* Oxford ENG: Vacation-Work. Annual.
$45.00. Directory of companies and organizations, primarily British,
which provide unique recreational tours and activities worldwide.
Arrangement is by type of activity and then geographical. For each
business listed gives address information.

1107. *Motorcoach Marketer.* Washington DC: American Bus Association. Annual. $95.00. Listing of tour and charter companies, bus lines,
and bus-related, hospitality companies. Designed to assist in operations management and marketing of tours. Arrangement is by type of
service. Each entry gives address and destinations served.

1108. *National Directory of Guide & Charterboat Services.* Hull GA:
Outdoor Statistical Resources. Semiannual. $75.00. Listing of profes-
sional outdoor service organizations in the US. Arrangement is alphabetical by name. Reference section indexes services geographically, by
body of water, and fishing.

1109. *Official Tour Directory.* New York NY: Thomas. Semiannual.

$100.00. Listing of tours, cruises, and worldwide vacation packages offered by US and Canadian operators. Arrangement is by type of tour. For each gives provider, address, schedule, cost, and contact information.

1110. *Specialty Travel Index.* San Anselmo CA: Alpine Hansen. Semi-annual. $100.00. website: http://www.specialtytravel.com Edited for travel agents who book adventure and special interest travel. Editorial section features articles and description of exotic tours and destinations. Directory section lists tours from archeology to zoology. Listing is indexed by activity and destination.

◆ *Management* ◆

1111. *Specialty Travel and Tours.* Irvine CA: Entrepreneur Magazine. c1992. 200p. $59.50. Focus on new and unique types of tours. Step-by-step guide to the opening, operating, managing, and marketing. Includes bibliographical references and index.

1112. Braidwood, Barbara. *Start and Run a Profitable Tour Guiding Business: ...* New York NY: Self Counsel, c1996. 200p. $14.95. Step-by-step business plan for part-time, full-time, domestic, or foreign ventures. Covers all aspects from formation to marketing. References.

1113. Ecotourism Society. *Ecotourism: A Guide for Planners and Managers.* North Bennington VT: Author, c1997. 2v. $42.00. Textbook as well as practical guide to formation of ecotours. Overview of industry and development. Planning initiatives and organization. Marketing tips and techniques. Lessons and problems. Case studies. References and index.

◆ *Industry* ◆

1114. Cater, Erlet and Lowman, Gwen, eds. *Ecotourism: A Sustainable Option?* New York NY: Wiley, c1994. 230p. $84.95. Collection of articles examining the prospects and the problems from the perspective of guides, guests, hosts, and environmental groups. Diverse geographical, education, and business backgrounds give articles a varied approach to industry.

1115. Cruise Lines International Association. *The Cruise Industry: An Overview.* New York NY: Author, c1998. 43p. free. Examines growth and development of this "new industry" since 1970. Looks at potential. Compares industry statistically with other vacations. Charts consumers, capacity, and embarkations. Comments on cruise-travel agent relationships. References and other resources.

1116. Strandeven, Joy and DeKnop, Paul. *Sports Tourism.* Champaign IL: Human Kinetics, c1998. 285p. $38.00. Overview and study of the recent development of a "touring phenomenon." Examines who, what, where, why, and how. References and an index.

◆ *Market* ◆

1117. Heath, Ernie. *Marketing Tourism Destinations: A Strategic Planning Approach.* New York NY: Wiley, c1992. 240p. $54.95. Provides detailed plans based upon consumer projects for marketing region and community tourism. Examines resource analysis, target marketing, support systems, management, and regional-mix strategies. References and index.

1118. Kinnaird, Vivian and Hall, Derek, eds. *Tourism: A Gender Analysis.* New York NY: Wiley, c1994. 218p. $105.00. Examines the needs, expectations, and demands. Introduces a series of models for consideration. Divided into three sections: overview, detailed analysis, and case studies. References and index.

1119. Swarbrooke, John. *Consumer Behavior in Tourism.* London ENG: Butterworth-Heinemann, c1999. 453p. $36.95. Examination of attitudes of travelers and their actions. Valuable to tour providers as a portrait of what the consumer expects of his or her venture into the outside world for travel and relaxation. References and index.

◆ *Periodicals* ◆

1120. *Bus Tours Magazine.* Polo IL: National Bus Trader. Bimonthly. $10.00. Edited for operators. Features articles on planning, operating, and marketing tours and long-distant charters. Includes reviews of areas, attractions, and hospitality facilities. Contains news, events, and trends. Special annual issue: "Bus Tours Planner's Guide."

1121. *Byways.* Fairfax VA: Patriot Marketing. Bimonthly. free. Edited for motorcoach charter/tour operators and travel agents. Focus is on tourist attractions, events, and facilities. Provides information on destination accessibility by motorcoach.

1122. *Courier.* Lexington KY: National Tour Association. Monthly. $36.00. Official publication of the National Tour Association. Primarily features articles on tour sites. Includes information and discussions on organization, management, and marketing, tourism news, and activities of the association. Special feature each issue.

1123. *Destinations.* Washington DC: American Bus Association. Monthly. membership. Edited for inter-city bus companies, but of value to tour operator and travel agents. Focus is on attractions, events, and access to major US cities. Includes marketing hints. Special feature each issue.

1124. *Group Tour Magazines.* Holland MI: Shoreline Creations. Quarterly. free. Edited for group tour organizers. Issued in five US regional editions. Features articles to assist tour planners. Includes extensive information on destinations.

1125. *Group Travel Leader.* Lexington KY: Group Travel Leader. Monthly. $39.00. website: http://www.grouptravelleader.com Edited for individuals leading senior citizen tours. Primary focus is on destinations, but includes information on the +50 market and hints on marketing to this age group. Special feature each issue.

1126. *Senior Group Travel.* Boca Raton FL: Senior Travel. Quarterly. $18.00. Edited for individuals leading senior citizen tours. Primary focus is on destinations, but includes articles impacting on tour and travel agents marketing to this age group. Special feature each issue.

1127. *Sports Travel.* Marina del Ray CA: Schneider. Monthly. $48.00. Edited for individuals responsible for sports events decision-making and event travel sponsors. Focus is on sports events and destination facilities and amenities. Information and articles indirectly impact on agencies organizing and/or marketing tours and travel for this group of tourists. Special feature each issue.

♦ *Databases* ♦

1128. *Caribbean-On-Line: Tour Operators and Travel Agents.* London ENG: Cartographers. online. website: http://www.caribbean-on-line.com/tour-ops/ Information on tours, airlines, car rentals, cruise lines, sailing, dining, golf, and resorts. Links to websites. Also provides access to weather, travel tips, magazines, and a bulletin board.

1129. *Tour Director.* San Francisco CA: Link Exchange. online. website: http://www.tourdirector.com Online community of travel planners, tourist guides, and tour managers. Directories listing websites for guides, planners, tours, buses, hotels, schools, and associations. Includes weather, currency conversion, reference tools, destination information, and jobs.

1130. *Travel Promotions Directory.* Manchester NH: Promotion Technologies. online. website: http://www.travelpromodirectory.com Designed for travel agents to find the latest information on tours. Restricted access. Probably the most comprehensive source for tour information on the web.

♦ *Associations* ♦

1131. Adventure Travel Society. 6551 S. Revere Pkwy., Suite 160. Englewood CO 80111. phone: (303) 649-9016; fax: (303) 649-9017. e-mail:

ats@adventuretravel.com website: http://www.adventuretravel.com/ats/ Association of tour operators, travel agents, and organizations and persons involved in environmentally sound tourism. Purpose is to promote non-traditional, natural tourism. Provides referral and networking assistance. Sponsors trade expo. Maintains library. Publishes periodical, newsletter.

1132. American Sightseeing International. 490 Post St., Suite 1701. San Francisco CA 94102. phone: (415) 986-2082; free phone: (800) 225-4437; fax: (415) 986-2703. e-mail: info@sightseeing.com website: http://www.sightseeing.com Association of independent companies worldwide. Purpose is to improve image and service. Develops and enforces standards. Conducts cooperative marketing programs. Maintains library. Publishes directory, manual.

1133. Association of Independent Tour Operators. 133 St. Margaret's Rd., Suite A. Twinckenham ENG TW1 1RG. phone: 441817449280; fax: 441817443187. e-mail: aito@martex.co.uk Association of small, specialized companies. Purpose is cooperative marketing, joint purchasing, training, and insurance. Lobbys. Enforces standards. Publishes directories, guides.

1134. Association of Pleasurecraft Operators on Inland Waterways. Portland House, Audvey Ave. Newport ENG TF10 7BX. phone: 441952813572; fax: 441952820363. Association of hireboats, marinas, and other hospitality-related businesses. Purpose is to promote the industry, provide a forum for exchange of information, and monitor laws and regulations.

1135. British Activity Holiday Association. 22 Green Ln., Hersham. Walton-on-Thames ENG KT12 5HD. phone: 441932252994; fax: 441932252994. website: http://www.baha.org.uk Association of organizations which provide holiday activities. Purpose is to promote industry, develop and enforce standards, and advise and represent members. Publishes newsletter, consumer guide.

1136. British Incoming Tour Operators Association. 120 Wilton Rd. London ENG SW1 1JZ. phone: 441719310601; fax: 441718280531. e-mail:

reachus@bitoa.co.uk website: http://www.bitoa.co.uk Association of companies involved in providing tourism services to UK visitors. Purpose is to promote the industry worldwide, lobby the government for support, and cooperate in the securing of goods and services. Publishes directory.

1137. Canadian Association of Tour Operators. 70 University Ave., Suite 250. Toronto ON M5j 2M4. phone: (416) 348-9083; fax: (416) 977-2895. Association of companies. Purpose is to promote growth and development of the industry, facilitate cooperation among members, and develop operation standards.

1138. Canadian Tour Guides Association. Vancouver BC. phone: (604) 669-0851. Association of tour operators and suppliers.

1139. Cruise Lines International Association. 500 Fifth Ave., Suite 1407. New York NY 10110. phone: (212) 921-0066; fax: (212) 921-0549. website: http://www.cruising.org Association of cruise lines and travel agencies. Purpose is to create a united force for the industry, exchange information, and train agents. Conducts educational programs and seminars. Publishes manual.

1140. Ecotourism Society. P.O. Box 755. North Bennington VT 05257-0755. phone: (802) 447-2121; fax: (802) 447-2122. e-mail: ecomail@ecotourism.org website: http://www.ecotourism.org Association of tour operators and other organizations and individuals in tourism interested in making the industry environmentally friendly. Purpose is to develop standards and policies, offer consulting services, and provide educational training. Compiles statistics. Conducts research. Maintains library. Publishes directory and extensive collection of research manuals and guides.

1141. Gray Line Sightseeing Association. 2460 W 26th Ave., Suite C-300. Denver CO 80211. phone: (303) 433-9800; fax: (303) 433-4742. e-mail: info@grayline.com website: http://www.grayline.com Association of independent and autonomous companies licensed to use the "Gray Line" name. Purpose is to exchange information among members. Publishes newsletter, directory, guide.

1142. International Council of Cruise Lines. 1211 Connecticut Ave., NW., Suite 800. Washington DC 20036. Association of companies. Purpose is to enhance the image, safety, and profitability of member lines. Lobbys. Maintains library.

1143. International Federation of Tour Operators. 170 High St. Lewes ENG BN7 1YE. phone: 441273477722; fax: 441273483746. Federation of national associations. Purpose is to provide a voice nationally and internationally for member organizations and to liaison with other tourism agencies worldwide.

1144. National Association of Charterboat Operators. 1600 Duke St., Suite 220. Alexandria VA 22314. phone: (703) 519-1714; free phone: (800) 745-6094; fax: (703) 519-1716. e-mail: naco@charterboat.org website: http://www.charterboat.org Association of companies and captains. Purpose is to provide a forum for the exchange of information and represent members before government agencies. Lobbys. Offers insurance and drug testing. Publishes newsletter.

1145. National Bareboat Charter Association. 6553 46th St., N. Pinellas Park FL 33781-0913. phone: (727) 520-1555; fax: (727) 520-8765. Association of companies and captains. Purpose is to represent members and industry on legislative issues and regulations with government agencies particularly the Coast Guard. Lobbys. Provides counsel. Publishes newsletter.

1146. National Party Boat Owners Alliance. 181 Thames St. Groton CT 06340. phone: (860) 535-2066; fax: (860) 535-8389. Association of owners and operators of passenger carrying vessels used for charter and sightseeing. Purpose is to monitor operating and safety rules and regulations. Lobbys. Provides counsel. Publishes newsletter.

1147. National Tour Association. P.O. Box 3071, 546 E. Main St. Lexington KY 40596-3071. phone: (606) 226-4444; free phone: (800) 682-8886; fax: (606) 226-4404. e-mail: ntahci@aol.com website: http://www.ntaonline.com Association of operators, packaged travel companies and tourism-related businesses in the US and Canada. Purpose is to develop and enforce standards and represent members before government agencies. Lobbys. Provides counsel. Publishes periodical, newsletter.

1148. Passenger Shipping Association. 288-300 Regent St., 4th Fl. London ENG WR1 5HE. phone: 441714362449; fax: 441716369206. Association of cruise lines and ferry operators in the UK. Purpose is to compile and provide market information and to represent members before government agencies. Compiles statistics. Conducts research. Provides counsel.

1149. Passenger Vessel Association. 1600 Wilson Blvd., Suite 1000-A. Arlington VA 22209. phone: (703) 807-0100; fax: (703) 807-0103. e-mail: pasvessel@msn.com Association of owners, operators, and suppliers of US and Canadian flagged passenger, dinner, private charter, tour, gambling, and excursion boats. Purpose is to monitor and disseminate information of legislation and regulation of the industry. Lobbys. Publishes newsletter, directory.

1150. Tourist Railway Association. P.O. Box 28007. Denver CO 80228. phone: (303) 988-7764; free phone: (800) 678-7246; fax: (303) 989-2192. Association of shortline, scenic railroads, museum, excursion operators, and suppliers. Purpose is to inform members of laws, regulations, and other governmental actions related to operations and service, to provide a forum for the exchange of management and technical information, and to establish safety and other standards. Lobbys governments and AMTRAK. Maintains insurance program. Publishes periodical, directory, manuals.

1151. United States Tour Operators Association. 342 Madison Ave., Suite 1522. New York NY 10173. phone: (212) 599-6599; fax: (212) 599-6744. e-mail: ustoa@aol.com website: http://www.ustoa.com Association of wholesale tour operators and tour-related agencies and suppliers. Purpose is to develop the interests and financial security of the industry worldwide and to interact with other elements of the travel industry, government, and the general public. Lobbys. Publishes directory, guide.

1152. World Federation of Tourist Guide Associations. Guild House,

Borough High St., Suite 52D. London ENG SE1 1XN. website: http://www.wftga.org Federation of national associations. Purpose is to maintain contact among national bodies, to represent these associations internationally and protect their interests, and to promote high standards of training and service. Conducts training courses. Publishes manuals, guides.

1153. Yacht Charter Association. Building 2, Shamrock Quay, Northam. Southampton ENG SO14 5QL. phone: 441703338400; fax: 441703338480. website: http://www.yca.co.uk Association of companies and operators in the UK. Purpose is to provide forum for the exchange of information. Develops and enforces standards. Lobbys. Provides counsel. Maintains library. Publishes manual, guide.

30. *The Travel Agency Industry*

NAICS 56151, 561599.

TRAVEL AGENCIES, TICKET AGENCIES.

♦ *Directories* ♦

1154. *Travel Agents — UK* London ENG: Lifestyle Internet. online. website: http://www.lifestyle.com/ada.htm Website access to 400 agency and related resources. Each entry is described briefly.

1155. *Travel Data Links.* Marlborough MA: Travel Data. online. website: http://www.traveldata.com Currently providing access to websites of B&Bs worldwide, but also contains other travel sites. Expected to expand its coverage in the future.

1156. *Travel Trade Personnel Guide and Booking Directory.* New York NY: Travel Trade. Annual. $150.00. Listing of tour, travel, and hospitality companies worldwide. Arrangement is by category. Gives address, type of service offered, and key personnel for each company listed.

1157. *Travel World.* London ENG: Travel World. online. website: http://www.travel.world.co.uk Website access to European travel agents, national tourism agencies, and agency, and other travel associations. Links to all forms of tours and holidays worldwide. Also information on airlines, hotel chains, and other resources useful to agents and travelers. Searching by specific subject provided.

1158. *World Wide Travel Source.* San Diego CA: Travel Source. online. website: http://www.travelsource.com Website access to accommodations, airlines, arts, aviation, destinations, dining, entertainment, exchange rates, ground transportation, locations worldwide, malls, outdoor sites, passports/visa, sea travel, tours, weather, and other travel information and services.

◆ *Management* ◆

1159. Gee, Chuck Y.; Boberg, Kevin B.; Makens, James G. and Choy, Dexter J. L. *Professional Travel Agency Management.* Upper Saddle River NJ: Prentice Hall, c1990. 220p. $57.00. Advanced textbook. Emphasizes management aspects of operations, finance, personnel, legal issues, automation, and marketing. Discusses the industry, trends, and future issues. References and index.

1160. Howell, David W. *Principles & Methods of Scheduling Reservations.* Upper Saddle River NJ: Prentice Hall, c1992. 300p. $68.80. Covers domestic and international ticketing and fare rules and regulations, classes, and rates. Includes examples of forms connected with the ticketing process. Vital data, references, and index.

1161. Ogg, Joanie and Ogg, Tom. *How to Start a Home Based Travel Agency.* Tom Ogg & Associates, c1997. 318p. $29.95. Step-by-step guide. Based upon authors' experiences. Covers all aspects from planning to customer satisfaction.

1162. Semen-Yurzycki, Jeanne and Purzycki, Robert. *Sail for Profit: A Complete Guide to Selling and Booking Cruise Travel.* Upper Saddle River NJ: Prentice Hall, c1999. 208p. $46.00. Interactive textbook. Covers all aspects of selling cruise vacations from basic terminology to shipboard life, world itineraries, and agent resources. Examines various types of cruises. Presents passenger demographics. Gives organization and marketing tips. References and index.

1163. Syratt, Gwenda. *Manual of Travel Agency Practice.* Oxford ENG: Butterworth-Heinemann, c1995. 259p. $34.95. Emphasis is on how an agent operates rather than how to operate an agency. Discusses day-to-day activities, interaction with tourism and hospitality business, and customer relations.

◆ *Industry* ◆

1164. *World Travel and Tourism Review.* Wallingford ENG. CAB International. Biennial. $200.00. Contains statistical data and charts on all aspects of travel and tourism, forecasts, market segmentation, surveys of key sectors, and an overview. Provides facts to assist in mapping strategies, pinpointing emerging markets, and identifying key sector developments.

1165. Edgell, David L. *World Tourism at the Millennium.* Washington DC: United States Travel and Tourism Administration, 1993. 97p. $12.00. Discusses changes and trends. Proposes an agenda for industry, education, and government. Bibliographic references.

1166. Sinclair, M. T. and Stabler, M. J. The Tourist Industry: An International Analysis. Wallingford ENG. CAB International, c1991. 244p. $60.00. Overview and study of the interrelationship of the industry, tourists, and products. Analysis of the framework for tourism. Impact of new technology. Tour operators and strategies. Sports tourism. Guest-host perceptions.

1167. Sorensen, Halle. *International Travel and Tourism.* Albany NY: Delmar, c1997. 432p. $59.95. Introduction to the world of the travel agent and agency. Covers background and all aspects of traveling abroad and servicing travelers. Includes common and "off-beat" travel.

1168. Travel Industry Association of America. *Economic Review of Travel in America.* Washington DC: Author, c1996. 120p. $125.00. References consumer and industry trends, regional patterns, pricing, energy supply and travel, and employment. Discusses the economic impact of travel. Includes an executive summary, charts, tables, maps, and historic data.

◆ *Market* ◆

1169. *American Travel Survey.* Washington DC: United States Bureau of Transportation Statistics. online. website: http://www.bts. gov/ats/ Survey of the travel habits of Americans. Examines types, mode, purpose, frequency, size of party, long- or short-haul, length of stay and season. Demographics include age, sex, race, income, type of household, and education level.

1170. *Travel and Tourism: The International Market.* London ENG: Euromonitor, c1994. 302p. $3,190.00. Examines the changes in consumer attitudes in length, type, and destination. Provides statistics and charts on accommodations, tours, and transportation. Includes 277 tables. Loose-leaf.

1171. Butter, John P. *Travel Industry Marketing.* Wellesly MA: Institute of Certified Travel Agents, c1990. 405p. op. Textbook and study guide. Collection of articles and case studies illustrating various aspects of planning, advertising, and merchandising. References and index.

1172. Hilton, Howard J. *Tracking the Group Sales Trail for Profit.* Chicago IL: Transportation Trails, c1995. 120p. $13.00. Examines what it takes to successfully participate in the growing field of group travel. Describes types of groups, how to identify and market, and what types of activities are most in demand.

1173. Travel Industry Association of America. *Outlook for Travel and Tourism.* Washington DC: Author. Annual. $175.00. Collection of presentations by experts at the annual conference forecasting trends in consumer demand and demographic outlook for the coming year. Studies include US, Canada, Asia, Europe, and Latin America.

◆ *Periodicals* ◆

1174. *AL DIA/Travel Agent Update.* Heathrow FL: Pepperdine. Bimonthly. free. Edited for Latin America travel agents. Written in Spanish with bilingual English section. Focus is on news, special reports, and destination data. Contains operations and technical articles. Lists package, conference, and tour opportunities.

1175. *ASTA Agency Management.* New York NY: Miller Freeman. Monthly. membership. Official publication of the American Society of Travel Agents. Analyzes the Business of Travel. Focuses on achieving profitable agency operations. Reports on news, trends, and association activities.

1176. *Canadian Travel Press.* Toronto ON: Baxter. 47 issues. website: http://www.travelpress.com Edited for travel agents and tourism industry professionals. Features articles on agency operations, management, and marketing. Includes information on industry leaders, tours, hospitality, and trends. Reports US travel activities. Special issues and features focus on places, events, and activities worldwide.

1177. *Cruise and Vacation News.* Morristown NJ: Orban Communications. Bimonthly. free. Edited for travel agents. Focuses on sales and marketing. Features articles on education and training of personnel. Special features on vacation locations each issue.

1178. *Cruise Trade.* New York NY: Travel Trade. Monthly. website: http://www.traveltrade.com Edited for cruise-focused travel agents. Focuses on sales and marketing. Features articles on operations and management. Special cruise article featured each issue.

1179. *Destinations.* Washington DC: American Bus Association. Monthly. membership. Edited for inter-city bus companies, but of value to tour operator and travel agents. Focus is on attractions, events, and access to major US cities. Includes marketing hints. Special feature each issue.

1180. *Group Travel Leader.* Lexington KY: Group Travel Leader.

Monthly. $39.00. website: http://www.grouptravelleader.com Edited for individuals leading senior citizen tours. Primary focus is on destinations, but includes information on the +50 market and hints on marketing to this age group. Special feature each issue.

1181. *Group Travel Organizer.* London ENG: London Travel. 10 issues. $24.00. Edited for agents who arrange and schedule for the UK and overseas. Contains articles on specialized travel, events, and entertainment. World Travel Market report each October. Special country feature each issue.

1182. *Incentive.* New York NY: Bill Communications. Monthly. $48.00. website: http://www.incentivemag.com Edited primarily for persons involved in performance improvement through the offering of travel incentives. Of value to travel agents for its information on potential business market. Information on use of travel incentives may help to identify potential clients. Special feature each issue.

1183. *Jax Fax Travel Marketing Magazine.* Darien CT: Jet Airtransport Exchange. Monthly. $12.00. website: http://www.jaxfax.com Edited reservations and sales managers of retail travel agencies. Focus is on air flight and tour schedules and information worldwide. Features articles on travel services and operations. Profiles agencies and suppliers. Country featured each issue.

1184. *Leisure Travel News/TTG North America.* New York NY: Miller Freeman. 48 issues. website: http://www.ttgweb.com Newspaper of the US and Canadian retail travel industry. Features news. Focuses on sales, marketing, and promotion. Includes information on packages, tours, cruises, and destination information.

1185. *Outbound Traveler.* Marblehead MA: Travel Review. Monthly. website: http://www.outboundtrav.com Edited for up market retail travel agents. Focuses on exceptional international destinations. Special type of holiday activity featured each issue.

1186. *Recommend Magazine.* Miami Lakes FL: Worth International. Monthly. website: http://www.gotravel.com Edited for retail travel agents. Features articles on destination product information and selling tools. Focuses on accommodations, programs, and events.

1187. *Scottish Travel Agent News.* Bridge of Allen SCO: S&G Publishing. Weekly. $45.00. Edited for local travel agents. Focuses on news and information and events which affect business and the industry.

1188. *Seatrade Cruise Review.* Colchester ENG: Seatrade. Quarterly. $25.00. Edited for cruise-focused travel agents. Focus is on news, packages, and destination information. Contains articles on product positioning, operating costs, financing, market trends, and industry profiles. Industry statistical. Digest each issue.

1189. *Selling Long-Haul.* Croydon ENG: BMI Publications. Monthly. free. Edited for long-distance travel agents in the UK. Provides news and destination information. Section devoted to linking retailers with wholesalers. Special US section.

1190. *Selling Short Breaks & Holidays.* Croydon ENG: BMI Publications. 6 issues. free. Edited for UK travel agents. Focuses on weekend, city, winter, and theme breaks in the UK and in Europe. Contains information on holiday marketing. Provides news and information packages and sites.

1191. *Senior Group Travel.* Boca Raton FL: Senior Travel. Quarterly. $18.00. Edited for individuals leading senior citizen tours. Primary focus is on destinations, but includes articles impacting on tour and travel agents marketing to this age group. Special feature each issue.

1192. *Sports Travel.* Marina del Ray CA: Schneider. Monthly. $48.00. Edited for individuals responsible for sports events decision-making and event travel sponsors. Focus is on sports events and destination facilities and amenities. Information and articles indirectly impact on agencies organizing and/or marketing tours and travel for this group of tourists. Special feature each issue.

1193. *Travel Agent.* New York NY: Universal Media. Weekly. $250.00. Edited for travel agents and travel professionals in the US and Canada.

Features news. Focuses on travel and destinations. Includes articles on agency operations and travel programs.

1194. *Travel Courier.* Toronto ON: Baxter. Weekly. website: http://www.baxter.net Edited for travel agents in Canada. Features articles on product, pricing, destinations, industry events, and issues. Special feature each issue.

1195. *Travel Digest.* Fort Lauderdale FL: Transatlantic. Monthly. $24.00. Edited for travel agents focusing on worldwide travel. Focuses on sales news under nine categories from air to tours. Each issue features data on several destinations.

1196. *Travel Trade.* New York NY: Travel Trade. Weekly. $10.00. website: http://www.traveltrade.com Edited for travel agents and other travel professionals. Published in a newspaper and a magazine edition. Newspaper features news and analysis. Certain issues focus on activities and destinations. Magazine features sales and operations information.

1197. *Travel Weekly.* Secaucus NJ: Cahners. Semiweekly. $26.00. website: http://www.traveler.net Edited for travel agents and suppliers. Features articles on travel services, tour packages, and destinations. Includes news, reports on trends, and a biennial market survey for the US. Special supplements in many issues.

1198. *Travel Weekly (UK).* Sutton ENG: Cahners. Weekly. $26.00. UK equivalent of the US edition. Emphasizes UK and European interests.

1199. *Travel World News.* South Norwalk CT: Travel Industry Network. Monthly. free. Edited for travel agents. Focuses on short news reports and lengthy articles. Features special promotions, unique destinations, travel products, industry trends, and profiles. Special destination features in many issues.

1200. *TravelAge.* Secaucus NJ: Reed. Weekly. free. Edited for US travel agents in three regional editions. Features news. Focuses on agency operations. Lists special programs and seminars.

1201. *TravelWeek.* Toronto ON: Concepts Travel. Weekly. $85.00. Edited for Canadian travel agents. Focuses on news and developments. Includes extensive coverage of travel and tour activities. Special feature each issue on either type of travel or destination.

◆ *Databases* ◆

1202. *Canada Tourism.* Ottawa ON: Canada Tourism Commission. online. website: http://www.canadatourism.com Website access to travel and tourism businesses, Canadian travel destinations, and tourism business partners. Specific subject access also provided.

1203. *Information Britain.* London ENG: Crawbar. online. website: http://www.information-britain.co.uk Website access to hospitality facilities, tourist areas and attractions, tours, golf, and links to other travel and tourism sites.

1204. *Travel and Tourism Research.* Boise ID: Travel and Tourism Research Association. online. website: http://www.ttra.com Information on current research, publications, newsletters, conferences, jobs, promotions, and a calendar.

1205. *Travel Industry Association of America.* Washington DC: U.S. Travel Data Center/Travel Industry Association of America. online. website: http://www.tia.org News, government affairs, meetings and education, councils, research and statistics, publications, tourism, destinations, and links. Restricted access to some areas.

1206. *World Tourism.* Madrid SPA: World Tourism Organization. online. website: http://www.world-tourism.org Information Center provides current information on activities of the association, a statistical service, a listing of WTO publications and services, and calendar of upcoming meetings.

◆ *Biblio/Index* ◆

1207. McElhaney, David R. and Jarema, Frank E. *National Travel Surveys.* Washington DC: United States Bureau of Transportation Statistics.

online. website: http://www.bts.gov/smart/cat.surveys.html Review and listing of country travel surveys worldwide. Background, contents, and limited critique of surveying activities of each country.

♦ *Associations* ♦

1208. Adventure Travel Society. 6551 S. Revere Pkwy., Suite 160. Englewood CO 80111. phone: (303) 649-9016; fax: (303) 649-9017. e-mail: ats@adventuretravel.com website: http://www.adventuretravel.com/ats/ Association of tour operators, travel agents, and organizations and persons involved in environmentally sound tourism. Purpose is to promote non-traditional, natural tourism. Provides referral and networking assistance. Sponsors trade expo. Maintains library. Publishes periodical, newsletter.

1209. Africa Travel Association. 347 Fifth Ave., Suite 610. New York NY 10016. phone: (212) 447-1926; fax: (212) 725-8253. e-mail: africa-trvl@aol.com website: http://www.atatrav.org Association of agencies in the US marketing travel to Africa. Conducts trade shows. Maintains library. Publishes periodical, directory. Formerly: American Federation of Representatives of International Companies in Africa.

1210. Alliance of Independent Travel Agents. Herlington, Orton Malborne. Peterborough ENG PE2 5PR. phone: 441733390900; fax: 441733390997. Association of agencies. Purpose is joint marketing of services and representation of members' interests. Lobbys. Publishes newsletter.

1211. American Society of Travel Agents. 1101 King St., Suite 200. Alexandria VA 22314. phone: (703) 739-2782; free phone: (800) 275-2782; fax: (703) 684-8319. website: http://www.astanet.com Association of agents. Purpose is to enhance the professionalism and profitability of members through effective representation in industry and government affairs, education and training, and by identifying and meeting the needs of the traveling public. Lobbys. Conducts research. Sponsors education program, seminars, trade show. Publishes periodical, newsletter, directories, manuals, pamphlets. Formerly: American Steamship and Tourist Agents Association.

1212. Association of British Travel Agents. 68-71 Newman St. London ENG W1P 4AH. phone: 441716372444; fax: 441716370713. website: http://www.abtanet.com Association of agents. Purpose is to create a favorable business climate and maintain high standards of service. Lobbys. Provides complaint service. Publishes newsletter, handbook, brochures.

1213. Association of Canadian Travel Agents. 1729 Bank St., Suite 201. Ottawa ON K1V 7Z5. phone: (613) 521-0474; fax: (613) 521-0805. e-mail: acts.ntl@sympatico.ca website: http://www.acta.net Association of agencies, tour operators, and travel wholesalers. Purpose is to promote the development of the industry, represent its members before governmental agencies and to businesses. Develops and enforces standards. Publishes newsletter.

1214. Association of Retail Travel Agents. 501 Derby Creek Rd., Suite 47. Lexington KY 40509-1604. phone: (606) 263-1194; free phone: (800) 969-6069; fax: (606) 264-0368. e-mail: artahdq@aol.com website: http://www.artaonline.com Association of agents in North America. Purpose is to promote the interests of members in government and industry. Lobbys. Conducts marketing, education, and work study programs. Publishes newsletter.

1215. Bed & Breakfast Reservation Services World-Wide. P.O. Box 61402. San Angelo TX 76906-1402. phone: (915) 947-3506; fax: (915) 949-9493. website: http://www.bandbworldwide.org Association of servicers and hosts. Purpose is to provide service, update members on government laws and regulations worldwide, and promote the industry. Compiles statistics. Conducts education programs. Publishes directory.

1216. Cruise Lines International Association. 500 Fifth Ave., Suite 1407. New York NY 10110. phone: (212) 921-0066; fax: (212) 921-0549. website: http://www.cruising.org Association of travel agencies and cruise lines. Purpose is to create a united force for the industry, exchange information, and train agents. Conducts educational programs and seminars. Publishes manual.

1217. Greater Independent Association of National Travel Services. 2 Park Ave., Suite 2205. New York NY 10016. phone: (212) 545-7460; free phone: (800) 442-6871; fax: (212) 545-7428. Association of retail agencies in the US. Purpose is to establish a marketing cooperative. Conducts workshops and trade show. Publishes newsletters.

1218. Inter-America Travel Agents Society. 4518 City Ave., 3rd Fl. Philadelphia PA 19131. phone: (215) 743-1775; fax: (215) 743-1902. Association of black-owned agencies. Purpose is to present a unified voice, to increase market share, and offer travel opportunities geared to black travelers. Provides counsel. Develops and enforces standards. Publishes newsletter, directory.

1219. International Federation of Women's Travel Organizations. 13901 N. 73rd St., Suite 210-B. Scottsdale AZ 85260-3125. phone: (480) 596-6640; fax: (480) 596-6638. e-mail: ifwtohq@primenet.com website: http://www.ifwto.org Federation of organizations worldwide. Purpose is to promote international goodwill and understanding, to enhance educational growth and leadership development, and to actively participate in the planning and development of travel industry affairs. Conducts education programs and workshops. Publishes newsletter, directory.

1220. International Ticketing Association. 250 W. 57th St., Suite 722. New York NY 10107. phone: (212) 581-0600; fax: (212) 581-0885. e-mail: info@intix.org website: http://www.intix.org Association of companies involved in selling, marketing, and manufacturing tickets worldwide for performances and sports events. Purpose is to unify the industry, exchange information, and monitor technological advances. Compiles statistics. Provides counsel. Publishes newsletter, directories, surveys, manuals. Formerly: Box Office Management International.

1221. Marketing Alliance for Retail Travel. website: http://www. mart.org Consortium of agents selling vacation travel. Purpose is cooperative marketing, networking, and training. Conducts workshops.

1222. National Association for Independent Contractors in Travel. 1340 U.S. Highway One, Suite 102. Jupiter FL 33469. phone: (561) 743-1900; fax: (561) 575-4371. website: http://www.ossn.com Association of agents in the US and Canada. Purpose is to network, market, and educate. Provides Outside Sales Support Network Index.

1223. National Association of Cruise Oriented Agencies. 7600 Red Rd., Suite 128. Miami FL 33143. phone: (305) 663-5626; fax: (305) 663-5625. Association of agencies. Provides education and training programs. Offers insurance. Publishes newsletter.

1224. Receptive Services Association. 236 Rte. 38, W., Suite 100. Moorestown NJ 08057. phone: (609) 231-8500; fax: (609) 231-4664. Association of agencies who provide wholesale tour and travel services in the US to overseas and foreign members of the travel industry. Purpose is to publicize the role of the receptive service company within the travel industry. Conduct seminars and education programs. Maintains phone referral service. Publishes newsletter, directory.

1225. Universal Federation of Travel Agents' Association. 1, Avenue des Castelans, Entree H. Monaco MON MC-98000. phone: 37792052829; fax: 37792052987. e-mail: uttaamc@sunnyworld.mc website: http://www.utaa.com Federation of organizations in 104 countries. Purpose is to recommend a unified international approach to common travel problems, formulate general technical procedures, negotiates with other travel and hospitality associations, and establishes relations with government. Lobbys. Provides counsel and legal assistance. Sponsors training. Maintains library. Publishes newsletter, directory, handbooks.

1226. World Association of Travel Agencies. 14, rue Ferrier. Geneva SWI CH-1202. phone: 41227314760; fax: 41227328161. e-mail: watahq@prolink.ch website: http://www.watanetwork.co.uk Association of independent agencies in 84 countries. Purpose is to promote and protect the economic interests of members. Publishes directory.

Appendix

Basic Reference Sources

♦ Directories ♦

1227. Dervaes, Claudine. *The Travel Dictionary.* Tampa FL: Solitaire, c1994. 326p. $14.95. Professionally oriented definition for people in the industry. Arrangement is in typical dictionary fashion as are the definitions. Numerous abbreviations and acronyms are included in the main body. Associations and other travel organizations appendixed.

1228. Medlik, S. *Dictionary of Travel, Tourism and Hospitality.* Oxford ENG: Butterworth-Heinemann, c1996. 332p. $32.95. Defines and explains usage of over 2000 terms and abbreviations. Listing of over 500 British and international travel organizations. Key data on 200 countries. British orientation.

1229. Smith, Stephen L. J. *Dictionary of Concepts in Recreation and Leisure Studies.* Westport CT: Greenwood, c1990. 220p. $69.50. Different type of dictionary. Primer on approximately 100 major concepts. Arrangement is alphabetical by concept. Under each is a description, the origin of the concept, bibliographic references, sources, and other resources.

♦ Management ♦

1230. *Progress in Tourism, Recreation and Hospitality Management.* New York NY: Wiley. Annual. $150.00. Collection of articles, some original, others published in another format, by prominent people in the industry. Extensive references, numerous tables and diagrams in each volume.

1231. Catherwood, Dwight W.; VanKirk, Richard L. and Ernst, G. Young. *The Complete Guide to Special Event Management...* New York NY: Wiley, c1992. 306p. $29.95. Business insights, financial advice, and successful strategies from persons who were consultants to the PGA, the Olympics, and other tournaments. Practical management and marketing advice. Presented also are a series of interviews with successful event promoters.

1232. Ecotourism Society. *Ecotourism: A Guide for Planners and Managers.* North Bennington VT: Author, c1997. 2v. $42.00. Textbook as well as practical guide to formation on ecotours. Overview of industry and development. Planning initiatives and organization. Marketing tips and techniques. Lessons and problems. Case studies. References and index.

1233. Graham, Stedman and Goldblatt, Joe Jeff. *The Ultimate Guide to Sports Event Management and Marketing.* Chicago IL: Irwin Professional, c1995. 383p. $32.50. Covers both management and marketing. Examines the relationship between sponsorship, products, and public interest and attendance. Provides step-by-step procedures. Forms for agreements, contracts, and publicity included. Glossary and bibliography.

1234. International Health, Racquet and Sports Association. *Ultimate Source.* Boston MA: Author. Series. $10-$25 each. An extensive and frequently updated series of publications relevant to the daily operations of a club. Covers all aspects of management, purchasing, training, marketing, and public relations.

◆ *Industry* ◆

1235. *Producer's Masterguide.* New York NY: Producer's Masterguide. Annual. $125.00. Reference guide to the industry. Includes information on contracts, finance, licensing, regulations, work guidelines, festivals, markets, and a listing by categories of over 30,000 production companies, services, and professionals.

1236. *World Travel and Tourism Review.* Wallingford ENG. CAB International. Biennial. $200.00. Contains statistical data and charts on all aspects of travel and tourism, forecasts, market segmentation, surveys of key sectors, and an overview. Provides facts to assist in mapping strategies, pinpointing emerging markets, and identifying key sector developments.

1237. Adams, Judith A. *The American Amusement Park Industry: A History of Technology and Thrills.* Boston MA: Twayne, c1991. 225p. op. Traces the development of the industry from its show-oriented 19th century roots through the introduction of "rides" to today's focus on the spectacular. Emphasizes the role of the US in today's thrills, technology, and trends. Examines economic, social, and cultural factors.

1238. Bowling, Inc. *Bowlers Encyclopedia.* Greendale WI: Author. c1998. 225p. $7.95. Statistics, records, honors, competition and data on organizations involved in the bowling industry in the United States.

1239. Cruise Lines International Association. *The Cruise Industry: An Overview.* New York NY: Author, c1998. 43p. free. Examines growth and development of this "new industry" since 1970. Looks at potential. Compares industry statistically with other vacations. Charts consumers, capacity, and embarkations. Comments on cruise-travel agent relationships. References and other resources.

1240. Duboff, Leonard D. *The Performing Arts Business Encyclopedia.* New York NY: Allworth, c1996. 256p. $19.95. Listing of business and legal terms and definitions of other practical issues relating to theatre, dance, opera, music, screen, and television. Written for the layman but essential for all performance arts executives.

1241. Gorman, Jerry and Calhoun, Kirk. *The Name of the Game: The Business of Sports.* New York NY: Wiley, c1994. 278p. $19.95. Examines the growth of the industry. Focuses on the impact of television and salaries on the change in the business approach. Looks at the increasingly important role that state-of-the-art facilities and ancillary sources of income have on franchise operations.

1242. Greeting Card Association. *Greeting Card Industry Directory.* Washington DC: Author. Annual. $95.00. Listing of publishers and suppliers. Arrangement is alphabetical by company name. List is cross referenced by geographical location, type of product, and brand name. For each company gives address, phone, key personnel, list of products and brands, and types and areas of distribution. Available on CD-ROM.

1243. Hobby Industry Association. *Annual Size of Industry Report.* Elmwood NJ: Author. Annual. Membership. (annotation, same as #468, 1st edition, add) In each case, these studies stand alone as the only substantive industry data publicly available.

1244. International Health, Racquet and Sports Association. *State of the Health Club Industry.* Boston MA: Author. Annual. $275.00. Presents charts and graphs that chronicle the growth of the exercise industry. Examines internal and external factors that shape the industry and influence the prospects of growth. A directory of major fitness club companies and a compendium of cutting-edge club programs is included.

1245. Kotas, Richard; Teare, Richard; Logie, Jeremy and Bowen, John, eds. *The International Hospitality Industry.* London ENG: Cassell, c1997. 224p. $69.50. Collection of articles by specialists in the field on major aspects of the past and current developments in the industry. Covers the industry worldwide with major emphasis on the growth of mainline hotels and resorts and related restaurant services.

1246. Martec Group. *Study of Trends in the Marine Industry.* Chicago IL: National Marine Manufacturers Association, c1995. 65p. $125.00. Five-year analysis involving over 275 discussions with all segments of the industry. Predicts new directions and trends and prospects for consolidation.

1247. Munting, Roger. *An Economic and Social History of Gambling in Britain and the USA.* Manchester ENG: Manchester University, c1996.

272p. $79.95. Comparative study of gambling over the last 200 years. Focuses on the changes that have taken place in the business environment from hostility to a permissive, if not supportive, environment.

1248. NAMM International Music Products Association. *Music USA.* Carlsbad CA: Author. Annual. $45.00. Statistical review of the music products industry. Contains data on over 20 instrument and accessory categories shipped from manufacturers to retailers. Includes economic and social indicators affecting the industry.

1249. National Golf Foundation. *Operating and Financial Performance Profiles of Golf Facilities in the US.* Jupiter FL. Author. Annual. $150.00 each. Separate reports on "Daily Fee," "Municipal," and "Private" 18- and 9-hole courses. Operating data, revenues, merchandise, food, and beverage sales, expenses, net income, capital investment, rounds played, and much more nation-wide and by region.

1250. National Music Publishers' Association. *International Survey of Music Publishing Revenues.* New York NY: Author. Annual. $450.00. Data from over 50 countries on music publishing revenues. Income results for performance, reproduction, and distribution. Includes royalties and exchange rates. Statistics on one featured country in each issue.

1251. National Restaurant Association. *Eating and Drinking Place Figures.* Washington DC: Author, c1998. 5v. $229.95. Statistical analysis based upon Census of Retail Trade. Volumes for Sales and Payroll, Metropolitan and County Areas, Establishment Sales by state and county, Size and Legal Form, and Menu Type.

1252. National Ski Areas Association. *Economic Analysis of United States Ski Areas.* Lakewood CO: Author. Annual. $200.00. Annual review of financial data and ski area characteristics, e.g., size, days of operation, capacity, skiers, and ticket prices. Includes economic ratios, probability, and regional variation factors.

1253. Pannell Kerr Foster PC. *Clubs in Town and Country.* New York NY: Author. Annual. $50.00. Statistical review incorporating operating and financial data on private clubs in the US.

1254. Photo Marketing Association International. *Industry Trends.* Jackson MI: Author. Biennial. $125.00 each. A two work set, US and international, covering 25 countries worldwide. Analyzes and presents extensive statistics on the consumer and professional markets and channels of distribution.

1255. Press, Skip. *Writer's Guide to Hollywood Producers, Directors, and Screenwriter's Agents.* Rocklin CA: Prima, c1998. 454p. $23.00. Compendium of agent listings. Way to proceed in choice of successful road to Hollywood career. Overview of the role of agents in this quest.

1256. Recreational Vehicle Industry Association. *Recreation Vehicle & Conversion Vehicle Market Reports.* Reston VA: Author, c1998. 21p. membership. Graphs and charts reflecting, delivery and retail sales of specific types of vehicles in 1997 by month.

1257. Sinclair, M. T. and Stabler, M. J. *The Tourist Industry: An International Analysis.* Wallingford ENG. CAB International, c1991. 244p. $60.00. Overview and study of the interrelationship of the industry, tourists, and products. Analysis of the framework for tourism. Impact of new technology. Tour operators and strategies. Sports tourism. Guest-host perceptions.

1258. Sporting Goods Manufacturers Association. *Industrial Financial Study.* North Palm Beach FL: Author. Annual. $300.00. Compendium of company sales and financial records. Based upon actual sales. Presents 26 key financial ratios including margins, productivity, and profitability. Organized for ease of comparison.

1259. Travel Industry Association of America. *Economic Review of Travel in America.* Washington DC: Author, c1996. 120p. $125.00. References consumer and industry trends, regional patterns, pricing, energy supply and travel, and employment. Discusses the economic impact of travel. Includes an executive summary, charts, tables, maps, and historic data.

1260. Vogel, Harold L. *Entertainment Industry Economics.* New York NY: Cambridge University, c1998. 472p. $39.95. Study of the business economics of all forms of personal and group entertainment. Provides a guide to the financing, production, and marketing of each. Focus is on the US but the scope is worldwide. References and index.

◆ *Market* ◆

1261. American Travel Survey. Washington DC: United States Bureau of Transportation Statistics, online. http://www.bts.gov/ats/ Survey of the travel habits of Americans. Examines types, mode, purpose, frequency, size of party, long- or short-haul, length of stay and season. Demographics include age, sex, race, income, type of household, and education level.

1262. *Video Marketing Surveys and Forecasts.* Hollywood CA: VidmaR. Monthly. $4500.00. Tracking service for products, markets, and technologies. Latest statistics and developments. Detailed data on product, sales, and usage. Loose-leaf format.

1263. American Music Conference. *Music USA.* Chicago IL: Author. Annual. $45.00. Survey of amateur music participation.

1264. Audits & Surveys Worldwide. *National Survey of American Tennis Players.* North Palm Beach FL: Tennis Industry Association. Periodically. $450.00. Study of players in the United States by age, sex, demographics, and level of participation, and frequency. About 1000 persons who participate more then four times each year are interviewed.

1265. Canadian Ski Council. *Canadian Skier/Snowboard Survey.* Mississauga ON: Author, c1998. $100.00. Most extensive regional and national study of demographics and consumer patterns ever completed. Interviewed 12,800 people. Complemented by Market Segmentation Research Report" ($120.00) compiled from 1,154 questionnaires collected at eight Canadian ski areas.

1266. Hobby Industry Association. *Nationwide Craft/Hobby Consumer Study.* Elmwood Park NJ: Author, c1997. $400.00. Examines attitudes and behavior of consumers towards crafts and hobbies. Presents statistics nationwide, by demographics and region, and by type of interest. Includes comparative data from earlier studies. Executive summary free from association.

1267. Minnesota State Lottery. *Gambling in Minnesota.* Roseville MN: Author, 1994. 421p. free. Study of who? what? where? people in Minnesota gamble. Similar studies undertaken in Colorado, Louisiana, New Mexico, Alberta, and other states and provinces.

1268. National Golf Foundation. *Golf Participation in the United States.* Jupiter FL: Author. Annual. $250.00. Ongoing national survey. Surveys households in the categories of core, occasional, junior, senior, beginning, private, and public. Measurement is by age, gender, income, education, and occupation. Provides statistics on rounds played, frequency of play, national and state participation rate, and total number of players nationally and regionally.

1269. National Marine Manufacturers Association. *Boating Registration Statistics.* Chicago IL: Author. Annual. $50.00. A detailed, state-by-state analysis of registrations by hull type, length, materials, and other factors.

1270. National Restaurant Association. *Restaurant Industry Forecast.* Washington DC: Author. Annual. $24.95. Overview of customer trends. Outlook on sales by industry segments. State-by-state projections.

1271. National Sporting Goods Association. *Sporting Goods Market.* Mount Prospect IL: Author. Annual. $225.00. Survey of 100,000 households on purchases of equipment and apparel. Provides unit and price point information, sales by channel of distribution, and demographics of purchasers.

1272. Photo Marketing Association International. *Consumer Photographic Survey.* Jackson MI: Author. Biennial. $125.00 each. Surveys are currently conducted for the US, Canada, the UK, and France. Surveys camera ownership and usage, types of cameras owned, photo activities, and expenditures on equipment, supplies, and services. Charts delineate demographic and regional characteristics.

1273. Recording Industry Association of America. *RIAA Statistics.* Washington DC: Author. online. website: http://www.riaa.com/ stats.htm Demographic survey and consumer profiles of music buyers. Manufacturer, shipment, and value statistics. Data on anti-piracy activities and Hispanic music. Updated annually.

1274. Recreational Vehicle Industry Association. *Recreation Vehicle & Conversion Vehicle Market Reports.* Reston VA: Author, c1998. 21p. membership. Graphs and charts reflecting, delivery and retail sales of specific types of vehicles in 1997 by month.

1275. Wellner, Alison S. *Americans at Play: Demographics of Outdoor Recreation and Travel.* Ithaca NY: New Strategist, c1997. 367p. $89.95. Information on participation in 60 activities. Statistics are broken down by age, sex, race, income, education, and household type and size. Similar to many studies which have utilized data collected by the Forest Service and the Census Bureau. Publication valuable for its organization.

1276. YBR Marketing. *United States B&B/Inn Guest Study.* Santa Barbara CA: Professional Association of Innkeepers International, c1997. 4v. $45.00. Published in regional editions for Northeast, South, Midwest, West. Documents what inngoers want in an inn, what they spend, and how to successfully market to them. Guests of all types are identified and surveyed.

◆ *Periodicals* ◆

1277. *Amusement Business.* Nashville TN: BPI Communications. Weekly. $129.00. website: http://www.amusementbusiness.com Edited for owners and managers of public amusement facilities and their suppliers. Covers the spectrum of the international live entertainment amusement enterprises. Provides news, attendance, revenue, financial, and operational data and box scores on top concerts. Special directory for amusement parks, festivals, expositions, and trade shows. Indexed in Business Index, Trade & Industry Index.

1278. *ASTA Agency Management.* New York NY: Miller Freeman. Monthly. membership. Official publication of the American Society of Travel Agents. Analyzes the Business of Travel." Focuses on achieving profitable agency operations. Reports on news, trends, and association activities.

1279. *Back Stage.* New York NY: BPI Communications. Weekly. $75.00. website: http://www.backstage.com Theatre trade newspaper edited for all types of involved professionals. Focuses on auditions, notices, industry news, and service features. Includes regional news. Indexed in Trade & Industry Index.

1280. *Billboard.* New York NY: BPI Communications. Weekly. $279.00. website: http://www.billboard.com Edited for the music and video industries worldwide. Reports on news, events, people and companies that impact on sales and marketing. Features statistics, charts, and analysis. Emphasis is on the music and recording industries. Indexed in Trade & Industry Index.

1281. *Boating Industry.* Latham NY: National Trade. Monthly. $38.00. website: http://www.boatbiz.com Edited for manufacturers, distributors, and retailers. Features articles on management, merchandising, selling, marketing, and industry trends. Annual Buyers' Guide issued separately. Indexed in Business Index, Trade & Industry Index.

1282. *Bowling Proprietor.* Arlington TX: Bowling Proprietors' Association of America. Monthly. $30.00. Edited for center owners. Covers business practices, equipment, marketing and promotions, and general industry news.

1283. *Box-office.* Chicago IL: RLD Communications. Monthly. $30.00. website: http://www.boxoffice.com Edited for the motion picture theatre industry. Focus on management, operations, trends, production events, and distribution of films. Reviews and charts new releases. Film exposition or topic featured each issue. Indexed in Film Literature Index.

1284. *Camping Magazine.* Martinsville IN: American Camping Association. Bimonthly. $24.95. Edited for camp management. Provides practical information impacting on management. Features articles on construction, maintenance, equipment, staffing, programs, and purchasing. Special feature each issue. Indexed in Readers' Guide to Periodical Literature, Sports Periodical Index.

1285. *Canadian Travel Press.* Toronto ON: Baxter. 47 issues. website: http://www.travelpress.com Edited for travel agents and tourism industry professionals. Features articles on agency operations, management, and marketing. Includes information on industry leaders, tours, hospitality, and trends. Reports US travel activities. Special issues and features focus on places, events, and activities worldwide.

1286. *Club Industry.* Atlanta GA: Primedata Intertec. Monthly. $68.00. Edited for owners and operators of fitness and health facilities as well as other membership clubs. Features news, opinions, program design, financial and operational statistics, and industry products and trends. Indexed in Lodging, Restaurant and Tourism Index.

1287. *Cornell Hotel & Restaurant Administration Quarterly.* Ithaca NY: Cornell University School of Hotel Administration. Quarterly. $50.00. Edited for management. Contains research articles. Reports on research studies and statistical reports. Book reviews. Indexed in Business Periodicals Index, Lodging, Restaurant and Tourism Index, Trade & Industry Index, and many others.

1288. *Courier.* Lexington KY: National Tour Association. Monthly. $36.00. Official publication of the National Tour Association. Primarily features articles on tour sites. Includes information and discussions on organization, management, and marketing, tourism news, and activities of the association. Special feature each issue.

1289. *Daily Variety.* Los Angeles CA: Cashners Business Information. Daily. $187.00. website: http://www.cashners.com/mainmag/dvar.htm Major source for breaking news in the industry worldwide. Tracks the entire scope of Hollywood and world film activities. Contains reviews and statistics.

1290. *Dealernews.* Santa Ana CA: Advanstar Communications. Monthly. $25.00. Edited for motorcycle and powersports dealers. Features news, industry trends, marketing, merchandising, and sales techniques, and profiles of successful retailers. Indexed in Business Index, Trade & Industry Index.

1291. *Funworld.* Alexandria VA: International Association of Amusement Parks and Attractions. Monthly. $35.00. Trade magazine for executives.

1292. *Gift & Stationery Business.* New York NY: Miller Freeman. Monthly. free. website: http://www.giftline.com Edited for retailers. Contains original market research reports. Profiles major retailers.

1293. *Giftware News UK.* Chicago IL: Talcott Communications. Quarterly. $195.00. website: http://www.giftwarenews.net Edited for the English market. Features news, trends, new products, and events worldwide.

1294. *Golf Club Management.* Weston-super-Mare, ENG: Association of Golf Club Secretaries. Monthly. membership. Official publication of the Association of Club Secretaries. Features articles on the operation of British courses, trends, and news.

1295. *Golf Course Management.* Lawrence KS: Golf Course Superintendents Association of America. Monthly. $48.00. Contains long articles on turf management, course design, construction, and maintenance, and products. Special "Show" issue in January.

1296. *Harpers Sports and Leisure.* Watford ENG: Harpers. 19 issues. $80.00. website: http://www.harpub.co.uk Edited for UK manufacturers, distributors, and retailers. Features product news and updates, statistical data, and trade show information. Various sports industries featured each month, e.g., golf in December issue. Indexed in Articles in Hospitality & Tourism.

1297. *Hospitality Industry International.* Croydon ENG: BMI Publications. 6 issues. $54.00. Edited for hotels, restaurants, and other food services. Feature articles on management, presentation, service, staff motivation, and marketing. Focus on conventions and exhibitions. Indexed in Articles in Hospitality & Tourism.

1298. *IDEA Health & Fitness Source.* Boston MA: IDEA: The International Association for Fitness Professionals. 10 issues. membership. Primarily a publication for users but is essential resource for owners and operators because of extensive coverage new trends and products, motivational guidelines and fitness research.

1299. *International Gaming & Wagering Business Magazine.* New York NY: GEM Communications. Monthly. $113.00. website: http://www.igwb.com Edited for private, public, and Indian gaming establishments in North America. Features news of trends, new products, marketing, finances, legislation, and new venues. Covers established gaming centers in the US, London, and Australia. Specials issues on gaming research and statistics including annual "North American Gaming Report,: a compilation of wagering statistics and activities in the US and Canada." Indexed in Lodging, Restaurant and Tourism Index.

1300. *ISI Edge.* Dallas TX: Ice Skating Institute of America. Bimonthly. membership. Geared to ISI members involved in day-to-day rink operations. Features articles on operations, maintenance, marketing, and successful customer programming. Calendar of ISI events and competitions.

1301. *Leisure Management.* Hitchin ENG: Leisure Media. Monthly. $120.00. website: http://www.leisuremedia.co.uk Edited for companies in the international recreation and entertainment fields. Focuses on news, market reports, and profiles. Features articles on theme parks, attractions, sports, play, and tourism. Indexed in Articles in Hospitality & Tourism.

1302. *Leisure Travel News/TTG North America.* New York NY: Miller Freeman. 48 issues. $95.00. website: http://www.ttgweb.com Newspaper of the US and Canadian retail travel industry. Features news. Focuses on sales, marketing, and promotion. Includes information on packages, tours, cruises, and destination information.

1303. *Mix.* Emeryville CA: Primedia Intertec. Monthly. $46.00. website: http://www.mixonline.com Edited for the world of professional recording, sound, and music production. Features articles on all aspects of recording production. Includes new and information on new products and technology. Profiles successful people and operations. Special feature in each issue.

1304. *Music Trades Magazine.* Englewood NJ: Music Trades. Monthly. $16.00. Edited for retailers and wholesalers of musical instruments and accessories. Features articles on management, success stories, merchandising, and selling. Includes news, new products, personnel changes, stock quotations, and forecasts.

1305. *PGA Magazine.* Troy MI: Quarton Group. Monthly. $23.95. Official publication of the Professional Golfers Association of America. Focus is on articles for members. Includes data and statistics on the PGA Tour. Features on Tour sites.

1306. *Photo Marketing.* Jackson MI: Photo Marketing Association International. Monthly. $30.00. Official publication of the Photo Marketing Association International. Edited for the photographic industry. Features news, profiles of industry leaders, products and production techniques. Special feature each issue.

1307. *Playthings.* New York NY: Cahners. Monthly. $29.00. Principal industry magazine for merchandisers of toys, hobbies, and crafts. Features articles on sales and promotional techniques, "what's selling," profitable operations, and analysis of industry trends. Special feature each issue. Special issues: "New Products Showcase" in February, April, August, and November; "Licensing Scope" in February and June. Separate "Buyers Guide" issued annually. Indexed in Business Index, Trade & Industry Index.

1308. *Powersports Business.* Minnetonka MN: Ehlert Publishing Group. 16 issues. free. Edited for dealers, distributors, suppliers and manufacturers of all-terrain vehicles, motorcycles, snowmobiles, and personal watercraft. Designed to facilitate communication between manufacturer and dealer. Features news, product information, product launchings, legislation and regulation, market analysis, and retail trends.

1309. *Roller Skating Business.* Indianapolis IN. Roller Skating Association International. Bimonthly. $30.00. Edited for rink operators. Features articles on management, operations, maintenance, marketing, and safety.

1310. *RV News.* Tempe AZ: D&S Media. Monthly. $36.00. http://www.rvamerica.com/rvnews/ Reports on developments, new products, trends, events, and the future. Features include monthly shipment figures, production forecasts, trade show data, legislative happenings, and spotlighted events. Regional editions.

1311. *Screen International.* London ENG: EMAP Business. Weekly. $195.00. Edited for the film, TV, and video industry. Features news, information, statistics, and analysis. Includes articles on production, distribution, and marketing.

1312. *Selling Long-Haul.* Croydon ENG: BMI Publications. Monthly. free. Edited for long-distance travel agents in the UK. Provides news and destination information. Section devoted to linking retailers with wholesalers. Special US section.

1313. *Ski Area Management.* Woodbury CT: Beardsley. Bimonthly. $32.00. website: http://www.saminfo.com Edited for managers of North American ski resorts. Articles on operations, technology, products, construction, and maintenance. Specials issues: "Product and Suppliers Directory;" "Lift Construction Index."

1314. *Sporting Goods Business.* New York NY: Miller Freeman. 18 issues. $65.00. website: http://www.sgblink.com Edited for a cross section of the sports industry including manufacturers and distributors. Focus is on trends and their potential effect on retail sales. Articles include industry statistics, market research, and profiles of top producers. Special focus feature in each issue. Indexed in Business Index, Trade & Industry Index.

1315. *Symphony-*. Washington DC: American Symphony Orchestra League. Bimonthly. $35.00. Official publication of the American Symphony Orchestra League. Emphasis on issues facing orchestras today. Directed towards management personnel.

1316. *Tableware International*. Redhill ENG: dmg Business Media. 11 issues. $181.79. http://www.dmg.co.uk/tableware/ Provides updates of the latest news and views in the international tabletop, gifts, and home market. Coverage emphasis is Europe, the US, and Japan. Separate European Tableware Buyers Guide issued annually.

1317. *Tennis Industry*. New York NY: Tennis Industry. Bimonthly. $18.00. http://www.tennisindustry.com. Provides information on equipment and retailing with emphasis on merchandising. Special columns on new products and court construction.

1318. *Travel Agent*. New York NY: Universal Media. Weekly $250.00. Edited for travel agents and travel professionals in the US and Canada. Features news. Focuses on travel and destinations. Includes articles on agency operations and travel programs. Indexed in Trade & Industry Index.

1319. *Variety*. Los Angeles CA: Cahners Business Information. Weekly. $167.00. website: http://www.cashners.com/mainmag/var.htm Edited for the global entertainment industry. Features news, reviews, and box office statistics. Focus on companies, performance, finance, and marketing.

1320. *Video Store*. Santa Ana CA: Advanstar. Weekly. $48.00. Edited for the retailer. Primary resource for new product information. Includes articles on the industry trends, product development, and market analysis. Special issues survey retailers and consumers.

1321. *Woodall's Campground Management*. Lake Forest IL: Woodall. Monthly. $24.95. website: http://www.woodalls.com Edited for operators of RV parks, resorts, and campgrounds. Emphasis on management. Profiles, trends, and successes. Includes news, new products, and reports from franchise and state organizations. Special feature each issue.

♦ Biblio/Index ♦

1322. *Articles in Hospitality and Tourism.* Guildford ENG: George Edwards Library, University of Surrey. Quarterly. £107. Index to articles in periodicals and books. Also available online.

1323. *Leisure, Recreation and Tourism Abstracts.* London ENG: CAB International. Quarterly. $171.00. Coverage is worldwide. Organized by major category. Arrangement under each is alphabetical by author. Author, subject, and geographical indexes.

1324. *Lodging, Restaurant and Tourism Index.* West Layfayette IN: Purdue University. Quarterly. $225.00. Index to articles in periodicals and books. Also available in CD-ROM format.

1325. Herron, Nancy L., ed. *The Leisure Literature: A Guide to Sources in Leisure Studies, Fitness, Sports, and Travel.* Englewood CO: Libraries Unlimited, c1992. 181p. $28.50. Organized under four major categories. Each proceeded by an essay. Sources cited include reference works, directories, periodicals, proceedings, statistical reports, and research studies. List of associations and education programs included in appendix.

1326. Shoebridge, Michele, ed. *Information Sources in Sports and Leisure.* London ENG: K. G. Saur, c1992. 345p. $95.00. Extensive listing of sources compiled by individual contributors. Focus is on British and European materials.

Index

A & E 450
Abbey, James R. 1008
Abdilla, Brenda 14
Aboard Boats and Yachts Market 357
ActorSource 642
Adams, Judith A. 871, 1237
Adult Video Association 647
Adventure Holidays 1106
Adventure Travel Society 1131, 1208
AFFA 28
Africa Travel Association 1209
Agents 540
Agents' Association (Great Britain) 554
AL DIA/Travel Agent Update 1174
Albrecht, Ernest 872
All Hotels on the Web 1025
Alliance of Independent Travel Agents 1210
Alliance of Motion Picture and Television Producers 648
AMA Pro Racing 804
American Amusement Machine Association 890
American Association of Community Theatres 582
American Bed and Breakfast Association 1030
American Bicyclist 300
American Boat and Yacht Council 361
American Boat Builders and Repairers Association 343, 362
American Camping Association 1092, 1099
American Casino Guide 919
American Dinner Theatre Institute 583, 984
American Film Marketing Association 649

American Firearms Industry 219
American Fitness Magazine 21
American Gaming Association 942
American Greyhound Track Operators Association 805, 943
American Historic Inns 1031
American Hockey League 765
American Horse Shows Association 836
American Hotel and Motel Association 1032
American League of Professional Baseball Clubs 766
American Music Conference 498, 702, 1263
American Music Festival Association 891
American Platform Tennis Association 133
American Power Boat Association 806
American Pyrotechnics Association 892
American Resort Development Association 1003, 1033
American Sail Training Association 527
American Sightseeing International 1132
American Society of Golf Course Architects 171
American Society of Theater Consultants 893
American Society of Travel Agents 1211
American Spa and Health Resort Association 32, 1034
American Specialty Toy Retailing Association 416
American Sportfishing Association 212
American Sportfishing Members Locator 204
American Sports Data 15, 16

American Sports Fishing Association 255
American Stamp Dealers Association 417
American Symphony Orchestra League 707
American Travel Survey 1169, 1261
AmericanTheatre Web Listings 561
Amusement and Music Operators Association 894
Amusement Business 876, 1277
Amusement Industry Manufacturers and Suppliers International 895
An Oige, Irish Youth Hostel Association 1074
Andreasen, Alan R. 572
Annesi, James J. 17
Annual Directory of American and Canadian Bed & Breakfasts 993
Annual Guide to Full Line Retailing 445
Archery Business 220
Archery Manufacturers and Merchants Organization 256
Archery Range and Retailers Organization 257
Arena Football League 767
Arenas & Rinks 68
Articles in Hospitality and Tourism 1322
ASCAP Resource Guide 703
ASR Trade Expo Show Guide 221
Association for Independent Music 708
Association for the International Collective Management of Audiovisual Works 650
Association of British Orchestras 709
Association of British Riding Schools 528
Association of British Sailmakers 363
Association of British Travel Agents 1212
Association of Canadian Travel Agents 1213
Association of Cinema and Video Laboratories 651
Association of Crafts and Creative Industries 418
Association of Cycle Traders 318
Association of Golf Merchandisers 258
Association of Importers-Manufacturers for Muzzleloading 259

Association of Independent Tour Operators 1133
Association of Independent Video and Filmmakers 652
Association of Pleasurecraft Operators on Inland Waterways 1134
Association of Professional Bridge Players 837
Association of Professional Recording Studios 710
Association of Retail Travel Agents 1214
Association of Scottish Games and Festivals 896
Association of Ski Schools in Great Britain 529
Association of Surfing Professionals 838
Association of Talent Agents 555
ASTA Agency Management 1175, 1278
ATP Tour 839
Audits & Surveys Worldwide 123, 1264
AV Market Place: The Complete Business Directory... 601, 676
Awards & Recognition Association 465
Awards and Recognition Association 443, 447

Back Stage 575, 1279
Ball, Armand 1089
Ball, Beverly 1089
Bartender Magazine 964
BASI 522
Beard, James B. 143
Bed & Breakfast 1013
Bed & Breakfast Inns Online 1026
Bed & Breakfast Reservation Services World-Wide 1215
Benson, Martin E. 144
BFI Film & Television Handbook 611
Bicycle Association of Great Britain 319
Bicycle Dealer Strategies 301
Bicycle Manufacturers Association of America 320
Bicycle Product Suppliers Association 321
Bicycle Retailer & Industry News 302
Bicycle Trade Association of Canada 322
Bicycle/Moped Store 293
Bike Shops 288
Bikelinks 313
Billboard 621, 696, 1280

Billboard International Buyer's Guide 677
Billboard International Talent & Touring Directory 562
Billiard and Bowling Institute of America 260
Black Filmmaker Foundation 653
Blue Book of European Ski Areas 39
Blumenthal, Howard J. 613
BMX Business News 303
Boat & Motor Dealer 351
Boat Racing 784
Boatbuilders 335
Boatbuilding Community 358
Boating Industry 352, 1281
Boating-USA 359
Boberg, Kevin B 1159
Borden, Marian Edelman 1094
Bottomline 1014
Bowen, John, ed. 1004, 1245
Bowlers Journal 98, 222
Bowling Alleys Around the World 87
Bowling and Billiard Buyers Guide 223
Bowling Center 91
Bowling Center Listings 88
Bowling Center Management 99
Bowling Headquarters 102
Bowling Industry, International 100
Bowling Proprietor 101, 1282
Bowling Proprietors' Association of America 96, 108
Bowling Proprietors' Association of Canada 109
Bowling, Inc. 95, 1238
Boxing Ring 831
Box-office 622, 1283
BPAC Member Centres 89
Brabec, Jeffrey 686
Brabec, Todd 686
Braidwood, Barbara 1112
Brandon Associates 793
Brennan, Stephen J. 762
Brian Mclean's Canadian Bowling 103
British Activity Holiday Association 1135
British Artistic Roller Skating 80
British Arts Festivals Association 897
British Association of Leisure Parks, Piers, and Attractions 898
British Association of Symphonic Bands and Wind Ensembles 711

British Association of Toy Retailers 419
British Bed and Breakfast Annual 994
British Casino Association 944
British Country Music 703
British Federation of Hotel, Guest House, and Self-Catering Associations 1035
British Film Institute 643
British Holiday and Home Parks Association 1075
British Hospitality Association 985, 1036
British Incoming Tour Operators Association 1136
British Marine Industries Federation 364
British National Ice Hockey League 768
British Numismatic Trade Association 420
British Phonographic Industry 712
British Photographic Importers' Association 487
British RidingSchools 514
British Sports and Allied Industries Federation 261
British Toy and Hobby Manufacturers Association 421
British Toy Importers and Distributors Association 422
British Video Association 654
Brooks, Christine M. 18, 750
Brown, Allen E. 794
Bryan, William L. 1090
Burke Market Research, Inc. 297
Burnett, Robert 687
Bus Tours Magazine 1120
Business Pages: Hobby Industry Directory 378
Business Trend Analysis 392
Butter, John P. 1171
Byl, John 822
Byways 1121

Cahill, Denis J. 1009
Calhoun, Kirk 747, 1241
Cameron, David Kerr 873
Camp Directors' Purchasing Guide 1086
Camping—USA 1069
Camping & Caravaning UK 1070

Camping and Outdoor Leisure Association 262
Camping Magazine 1095, 1284
CampPage 1097
Canada Camping Guide 1055
Canada Tourism 1202
Canadian Association of Film Distributors and Exporters 655
Canadian Association of Professional Dance Organizations 584
Canadian Association of Tour Operators 1137
Canadian Camping Association 1100
Canadian Country Music Association 713
Canadian Football League 769
Canadian Gift and Tableware Association 466
Canadian Independent Film Caucus 656
Canadian Independent Record Production Association 714
Canadian Industrial Development Branch 1060
Canadian In-Line and Roller Skating Association 263
Canadian Popular Theatre Alliance 585
Canadian Professional Rodeo Association 840
Canadian Recording Industry Association 715
Canadian Recreational Vehicle Association 323
Canadian Resort Development Association 1037
Canadian Restaurant and Foodservices Association 986
Canadian Ski Council 52, 64, 1265
Canadian Society of Club Managers 196
Canadian Sporting Arms and Ammunition Association 264
Canadian Sporting Goods Association 265
Canadian Tour Guides Association 1138
Canadian Toy Association 423
Canadian Travel Press 1176, 1285
Cantor, George 923
Caputo, Kathryn 867
Card Trade 396
Caribbean Hotel Association 1038

Caribbean-On-Line: Tour Operators and Travel Agents 1128
Carter, David M. 752
Casino Executive 933
Casino Journal 934
Casino Network 938
CasinoLinks 920
Cater, Erlet, ed. 1114
Catherwood, Dwight W. 823, 1231
Cavalcade of Acts and Attractions 563, 860
CCSAA's Nordic, Cross Country & Snowshoeing Information Center 59
Celentano, Suzanne Carmack, and Kevin Marshall 566
Cerver, Francisco Asensio 874
Chamber Music America 716
Championship Auto Racing Teams 807
Chef 965
Choy, Dexter J.L. 1159
Christian Camping International 1101
CIMTA Inc., Travel Guide 379
Cinemedia 602
Circuits International 808
CircusWeb: Circuses Past and Present 884
City Clubs 179
Cleve, Bastian 606
Club Director 192
Club Industry 22, 193, 1286
Club Management 194
Club Managers Association of America 181, 182, 190
ClubCorp International 201
ClubNet 197
CNN Sports Illustrated 756
Collins, Bill 121
Comics Retailer 397
Complete Bowlingindex 104
Complete Wrestling Page 832
Conference of Drama Schools 530
Connellan, Thomas K. 868
Continental Basketball Association 770
Cooking for Profit 966
Cooper, Rollin B. 1061
Cornell Hotel & Restaurant Administration Quarterly 967, 1015, 1287
Cottage Industry Miniatures Trade Association 424
Council of Film Organizations 657

Country Music Association 717
Country Music Association (UK) 718
Courier 1122, 1288
Cowgill, Allison A. 940
Craft & Needlework Age 398
Craftrends 399
Crafts Report 451
Crittenden Golfinc 157
Cross Country Ski and Nordic Center 41
Cross Country Ski Areas of America
 44, 46, 65
Cruise and Vacation News 1177
Cruise Lines International Association
 1115, 1139, 1216, 1239
Cruise Trade 1178
Culinary Trends 968
Curtin, Richard T. 297
Cusic, Don 691
Cyber Cyclery 314
Cycle Dealers County List 289
Cycle Parts and Accessories Association
 324
CycleSource 315

Daily Variety 623, 1289
Dance Teachers Now 520
Dance/USA 573
Danielson, Michael N. 753
Davidson, D. Kirk 930
Davis, Mary 998
Dealernews 304, 1290
DeKnop, Paul 1116
Dell, Donald L. 552
Dervaes, Claudine 1227
Destinations 1123, 1179
Directory of British Entertainment
 Agents 541
Directory of Funparks & Attractions 862
Directory of Hotel & Motel Companies
 996
Directory of North American Fairs Fes-
 tivals and Expositions 863
Ditter, Bob 1091
Diving Equipment and Marketing Asso-
 ciation 266
Douglas, Andrew 931
Drama Schools UK 515
Drum Business 499
Duboff, Leonard D. 570, 1240
Duckpin Bowling Pages 105

Duckpin Bowling Proprietors of America
 90, 110
Dude Ranchers' Association 1102
Dyer, Kathleen M. 382

Eade, Vincent H. 924
Ecotourism Society 1113, 1140, 1232
Edgell, David L. 1165
Edplay 400
Entertainment Services and Technology
 Association 586
Equipment Solutions 970
Ernst, G. Young 822, 1231
ESPN 757
Euchner, Charles C. 746
Euro Gambling 921
Euromonitor 393, 692, 961
European Festivals Association 899
European Fishing Tackle Trade Associa-
 tion 267
European Tableware Buyers Guide 441
Event Solutions 877
Events Business News 878
Everest, Frederick Alton 681

F&B Magazine 971
The Fair 887
Farber, Donald C. 567
Festivals 885
Fier, Bruce 952
Fillman, William 1064
Film & Video 624
Film & Video News 625
Film Journal International 626
Film Producers, Studios, Agents & Cast-
 ing Directors 603
Filmmaker Magazine 627
Find an RV Manufacturer 290
Find/SVP 216, 295, 448, 618
Fishing Tackle Retailer 224
Fishing Tackle Trade News 225
Fitclubs 29
Fitlinxx 19
Fitness Industry Association 33
Fitness Management 23
Fitness Products News 24
5-Pin Bowling: A Real Canadian Sport
 106
Flood, Elizabeth Clair 1093
Florence, Rich 97

Index

Food Arts 972
Food Management 973
Food Service and Hospitality 974
Forest School Camps 1103
Fort, Rodney D. 750
4 Hobbies 411
4 Musicians 503
Fox, Jim 925
Frascogna, Xavier M. 546
Fredriksson, Kristine 825
Frost & Sullivan 478
Frost's Summer Camp Sourcebook 1096
Funworld 879, 1291

Gambling 939
Gamers Central 412
Games Retailer 401
Gaming Products and Services 935
Gee, Chuck Y. 1159
Geller, Mark 685
Gerson, Richard F. 20
Gift & Stationery Business 452, 1292
Gift Association of America 467
Gift Packaging and Greeting Card Association of Canada 468
GiftBusiness 462
Giftline 463
Gifts & Decorative Accessories 453
Giftware Association 469
Giftware News 454
Giftware News UK 455, 1293
Gimmy, Arthur E. 11, 122, 144
Giordano, Frank S. 3
Goldblatt, Joe Jeff 827, 869, 1233
Golf Business 158
Golf Club Management 159, 1294
Golf Club Secretaries 164
Golf Course Builders Association of America 172
Golf Course Management 160, 1295
Golf Course News 161
Golf Courses of the World 136
Golf Index 137
Golf Manufacturers and Distributors Association 268
Golf Pro 226
Golf Product News 227
Golf Range & Recreation Report 162
Golf Range and Recreation Association of America 173

Golf Range Times 163
Golf Shop Operations 228
Golf Source Magazine 229
Golf UK and Ireland 138
Golf Com 165
Golfersweb 166
Golfweb 167
Goodenaugh, Oliver R. 613
Gorman, Jerry 747, 1241
Gospel Music Association 719
Graham, Stedman 827, 1233
Grantham, William C. 6
Gray Line Sightseeing Association 1141
Gray, William S. 999
Great Skiing and Snowboarding in Canada 60
Greater Independent Association of National Travel Services 1217
Green Hotels Association 1039
Greenberg, Gary 688
Greeting Card Association 444, 470, 1242
Greetings Today 456
Greyhound Starting Box 799
Greyhound Tracks in North America 785
Group Tour Magazines 1124
Group Travel Leader 1125, 1180
Group Travel Organizer 1181
Guide to ACA-Accredited Camps 1087
Guitar and Accessories Marketing Association 505
Gyms Locator 1

Haden-Guest, Anthony 957
Hagstrom, Robert G. 795
Hall, Derek, ed. 1118
Hardy, Stephen 828
Harmon, Renee 607
Harness Tracks of America 809, 945
Harpers Sports and Leisure 230, 1296
Health Clubs 2
Heath, Ernie 1117
Herron, Nancy L., ed. 1325
Hetherington, H. Lee 546
Hilger Flick & Co. 188
Hilton, Howard J. 1172
Hobby Industries of America 383, 426
Hobby Industry Association 388, 389, 394, 1243, 1266
Hobby Merchandiser 402
Hobby Store Search 380

Hockey Business News 231
Holiday Centres Association 1076
Hollander, Zander 121
Hollywood Reporter 628
Home Sewing Association 427
Horse Racing 800
Hospitality Association of Northern Ireland 987, 1040
Hospitality Industry International 975, 1016, 1297
Hospitality Industry Resource Center 981
Hospitality Sales and Marketing Association International 1041
Hospitality Technology 976, 1017
Hosteling International — American Youth Hostels 1077
Hosteling International — Canada 1078
Hosteling International — Europe 1056
Hosteling International — Northern Ireland 1079
Hosteling Passport to North American 1057
Hotel & Motel Management 1018
Hotel and Travel Index 995
Hotel Business 1019
Hotels 1020
Houseboat Association of America 365
Howell, David W. 1160
Huls, Mary Ellen 84
Hurdzan, Michael J. 145

Ice Skating Institute of America 71, 73, 85
IDEA Fitness Manager 25
IDEA Health & Fitness Source 26, 1298
IDEA: The Health and Fitness Source 30
Incentive 1182
Independent Feature Project 658
Independent Film and Video Alliance 659
Independent Film Distributors' Association 660
Independent Innkeepers Association 1042
Independent Music Association
Independent Music Retailers Association 721
Independent Theatre Council 587
Indian Casinos 922

Indoor Professional Football League 771
Industry Insights, Inc. 210
Indy Racing League 810
Information Britain 1203
Inline Retailer & Industry News 76, 232
Innkeeping World 1021
Inter-America Travel Agents Society 1218
International Amusement Industry Buyers Guide 864
International Association for Sports and Leisure Facilities 900
International Association of Amusement Parks and Attractions 901
International Association of Electronic Keyboard Manufacturers 506
International Association of Fairs and Expositions 902
International Association of Family Entertainment Centers 903
International Association of Holiday Inns 1043
International Bluegrass Music Association 722
International Brotherhood of Magicians 588
International Council of Air Shows 904
International Council of Cruise Lines 1142
International Council of Folklore Festival Organizations and Folk Art 905
International Council of Marine Industry Associations 347
International Council of Toy Industries 428
International Documentary Association 661
International Federation of Associations of Film Distributors 662
International Federation of Festival Organizations 906
International Federation of Stamp Dealers' Association 429
International Federation of the Phonographic Industry 723
International Federation of Tour Operators 1143
International Federation of Women's Travel Organizations 1219

International Festivals and Events Association 907
International Gaming & Wagering Business Magazine 936, 1299
International Group of Agencies and Bureaus 556
International Group of Agents and Bureaus
International Health, Racquet and Sports Association 4, 7, 8, 9, 12, 13, 34, 115, 117, 118, 119, 134, 180, 183, 184, 202, 1234, 1244
International Hockey League 772
International Hot Rod Association 811
International Hotel and Restaurant Association 988, 1044
International Inline Skating Association 269
International League of Professional Baseball Clubs 773
International Marina Institute 344, 345, 366
International MIDI Association 724
International Minilab Association 488
International Motion Picture and Lecturers Association 663
International Offshore Team Association 812
International Physical Fitness Association 35
International Professional Rodeo Association 841
International Recording Media Association 725
International Sailing Federation 518
International Sailing Schools Associations 531
International Snowmobile Manufacturers Association 325
International Society for the Performing Arts 589
International Spa and Fitness Association 36
International Sports Show Producers Association 908
International Table Tennis Federation 842
International Theatre Equipment Association 590
International Ticketing Association 1220

International Youth Hostel Federation 1080
Irish Hotels Federation 1045
ISI Edge 77, 1300
ISPA 578
ITF—Tennis on Line 126
ITI-Worldwide 579
IUMA: Internet Underground Music Archive 705

Jarema, Frank E. 1207
Jax Fax Travel Marketing Magazine 1183
Jerris, Linda A. 1000
Johnson, Arthur T. 748

KampGround Owners Association 1081
Kart Marketing International 305, 796
Kashif 688
Kid's Camps 1088
Kilby, Jim 925
Kinnaird, Vivian, ed. 1118
Kite Trade Association International 430
Klinkowitz, Jerome 741
KOA Country 1071
Kotas, Richard, ed. 1004, 1245
Kotler, Philip 574
KPMG Canada 958
Krasilovsky, M. William 689
Krause, Jerry V. 762

Ladenson, Sydney 390
Ladies Professional Golf Association 843
Langley, Stephen 568
Laventhol and Horwath 45
Lawn Bowls 107
Lawrence, Jim 607
League of American Theatres and Producers 591
League of Historic American Theatres 592
League of Resident Theatres 593
Leisure Management 1301
Leisure Travel News/TTG North America 1184, 1302
Leisure Trends Group 53
Leisure, Recreation and Tourism Abstracts 1323

Lew, Alan A. 927
Lewis, Robert C. 1001
Lichstein, Larry 92
Light Aircraft Manufacturers Association 326
Lightweight Cycle Manufacturers' Association 327
Litwak, Mark 547
Location Update 629
Locations 630
Lodging 1022
Lodging Hospitality 1023
Lodging, Restaurant and Tourism Index 1324
Logie, Jeremy, ed. 1004, 1245
Lowman, Gwen, ed. 1114
Lukk, Tiiu 619
Lynk, William M. 959

Major League Roller Hockey 774
Major League Soccer 775
Makin' Stamps 403
Makens, James G. 1159
Marina/Dock Age 352
Marinas 336
Marine Retailers Association of America 367
MarineData Internet 360
Markee 631
Market Tracking International 449
Marketing Alliance for Retail Travel 1221
Martec Group 348, 1246
Martinez, Ruben 926
Marvin, Bill 953, 962
Massachusetts Port Authority Trade Development Unit 395
Material Matters 233
McCormick, Mark H. 826
McCurry, William 475
McElhaney, David R. 1207
McEwen, Douglas 1062
MDi Boating Industry Classified Index: Marina and Moorings Search 337
MDi Boating Industry Classified Index: Market Search 338
Medlik, S. 1228
Miniature Golf Development of America 146, 174
Miniatures Industry Association of America 431

Minnesota State Lottery 932, 1267
Mirkovich, Thomas R. 940
Mitchell, Clare 1062
Mix 697, 1303
Model Railroad Industry Association 432
Model Retailer 385, 404
Model Search Magazine Worldwide Model & Talent Agency Guide 542
Morales, Leslie Anderson 63
Morgan, Jon 742
Morrison, Alastiar M. 1010
Motion Picture Association 664
Motion Picture Association of America 665
Motor Sports Race Tracks 786
Motorcoach Marketer 1107
Motorcycle Industry Council 296, 328
Motorcycle Industry Magazine 306
Motorcycle Product News 307
Muirhead, Desmond 150
Muller, Peter 682
Mullin, Bernard James 828
Munting, Roger 928, 1247
Music & Sound Retailer 500
Music Connection 698
Music Distributors Association 726
Music Film and Video Producers' Association 666
Music Inc. 699
Music Industries Association — England 496, 507
Music Industries Association of Canada 508, 727
Music Publishers Association 728
Music Publishers Association of the United States 729
Music Trades Magazine 501, 1304
Music Yellow Pages 504, 678
Music Yellow Pages Business Directory 494
Musical America International Directory of the Performing Arts 679
Musical Merchandise Review 502
MusicSearch 706

Nafzger, Carl F. 789
NAKMAS Journal 521
NAMM International Music Products Association 497, 509, 730, 1248

National Alliance for Musical Theatre 594

National Association for Independent Contractors in Travel 1222

National Association for Stock Car Auto Racing 813

National Association of Band Instrument Manufacturers 510

National Association of Casino and Theme Party Operators 909, 946

National Association of Charterboat Operators 1144

National Association of Cruise Oriented Agencies 1223

National Association of Doll and Stuffed Toy Manufacturers 433

National Association of Federally Licensed Firearms Dealers 270

National Association of Golf Tournament Directors 844

National Association of Independent Resurfacers 111

National Association of Karate and Martial Arts Schools 532

National Association of Off-Track Betting 947

National Association of Performing Arts Managers and Agents 557

National Association of Professional Baseball Leagues 776

National Association of Quick Printers 489

National Association of Recording Merchandisers 731

National Association of RV Parks and Campgrounds 1082

National Association of Sailing Instructors and Sailing Schools 533

National Association of School Music Dealers 732

National Association of Sporting Goods Wholesalers 271

National Association of Television Program Executives 667

National Association of Theater Owners 668

National Association of Video Distributors 669

National Ballroom and Entertainment Association 910

National Bareboat Charter Association 1145

National Basketball Association 777

National Bed and Breakfast Association 1046

National Bicycle Dealers Association 294, 329

National Bowling Pro Shop and Instructors Association 534

National Camp Association 1104

National Caravan Council 330

National Caves Association 911

National Club Association 191, 203

National Conference of Personal Managers 558

National Council of Music Importers and Exporters 511

National Dinner Theatre Association 595, 990

National Directory of Guide & Charterboat Services 1108

National Federation of Sea Schools 535

National Fitness Trade Journal 27

National Football League Europe 779

National Football League 778

National Forest Recreation Association 1047, 1083

National Golf Car Manufacturers Association 331

National Golf Course Owners Association 175

National Golf Foundation 142, 147, 151, 152, 153, 154, 155, 156, 157, 185, 519, 824, 1249, 1268

National Health Club Association 37

National Hockey League 780

National Indian Gaming Association 948

National League of Professional Baseball Clubs 781

National Licensed Beverage Association 989

National Marine Distributors Association 368

National Marine Manufacturers Association 349, 350, 369, 1269

National Marine Representative's Association 346, 370

National Movement Theatre Association 596

National Music Publishers' Association 690, 733, 1250

National Needlework Association 386, 434

National Party Boat Owners Alliance 1146

National Plastercraft Association 435

National Professional Soccer League 782

National Restaurant Association 954, 960, 963, 991, 1251, 1270

National Retail Hobby Stores Association 387, 436

National School Sailing Association 536

National Shooting Sports Foundation 211, 272

National Showmen's Association 912

National Ski and Snowboard Retailers Association 273

National Ski Areas Association 42, 47, 48, 66, 1252

National Snow Industries Association 274

National Sporting Goods Association 217, 218, 275, 1271

National Swim and Recreation Association 38

National Swim School Association 537

National Tabletop and Giftware Association 471

National Thoroughbred Racing Association 814

National Tour Association 1147

National Tractor Pullers Association 845

Nation's Restaurant News 977

NCA Resource Center 198

Needlecraft Showcase 413

Needlework Retailer 405

NFL Players 758

NGF 168

NHL Players 759

Nightclub & Bar 978

Nightclubs 982

Noll, Roger G., ed. 749

Non-Powder Gun Products Association 437

North American Campground Directory 1058

North American Gamebird Association 1105

North American Paddlesports Association 371

North American Race Tracks 787

NSAA/OITAF National International Trade Show 61

NSGA Buying Guide 205

O'Brien, Timothy L. 929

Official British Theatre Directory 564

Official Country Music Directory 680

Official International Toy Center Directory 381

Official Tour Directory 1109

Ogg, Joanie 1161

Ogg, Tom 1161

Opera America 597, 734

Orchestras Canada 735

Organization of Professional Acting Coaches and Teachers 538

Outbound Traveler 1185

Outdoor Amusement Business Association 913

Outdoor Hospitality 1065

Outdoor Press 234

Outdoor Retailer 235

Outdoors — RV Park 1072

Outfitter Magazine 236

Paddle Dealer 354

Paddlesports Industry Resource — Retailers 339

PADI 523

Pannell Kerr Foster PC 148, 186, 189, 1005, 1253

Party & Paper Retailer 457, 456

Party & Paper Retailer Source Book 442

Party Goods/Gift Store 446

Passenger Shipping Association 1148

Passenger Vessel Association 1149

Passman, Donald S. 683

Patton, Robert W. 10

PCMA 199

Perdue, Joe 187

Performance Racing Industry 797

Personal Managers 545

Personal Managers' Association 559

PGA Magazine 830, 1305

PGA Tour Tournaments Association 846

Phillips, Dennis J. 132

Photo Imaging Entrepreneur 480
Photo Industry Reporter 481
Photo Lab Management 482
Photo Marketing 483, 1306
Photo Marketing Association International 476, 477, 479, 486, 492, 1254, 1272
Photo Trade News 484
Photographic and Imaging Manufacturers Association 491
Photographic Manufacturers and Distributors Association 493
Photographic Processing 485
Physical Fitness Center 5
Piano Manufacturers Association International 512
Piano Trade Suppliers Association 513
Picchietti, Remo N. 93, 94
Pitts, Brenda G., ed. 829
PKF Consulting 1006
Platform Tennis News 124
Playbill-on-Line 580
Playthings 406, 1307
Point of View 632
Pollstar Magazine 700, 880
Post 633
Powerboat Index 801
Powersports Business 237, 308, 355, 1308
PPA Directory 340
Preferred Hotels and Resorts Worldwide 1048
Press, Skip 548, 1255
Private Clubs 195
Private Golf Courses 139
Producers Alliance for Cinema and Television 670
Producer's Masterguide 612, 1235
Production Companies 604
Professional Archers Association 847
Professional Association of Canadian Theatres 598
Professional Association of Innkeepers International 1049
Professional Audiovideo Retailers Association 736
Professional Boatbuilder Magazine 356
Professional Bowlers Association of America 848
Professional Clubmakers Society 276
Professional Cycling Association 849

Professional Golf Club Repairman's Association 277
Professional Golfers' Association 850
Professional Golfers' Association of America 851
Professional NASCAR Garage 798
Professional Numismatics Guild 438
Professional Paddlesports Association 372
Professional Putters Association 852
Professional Rodeo Cowboys Association 853
Professional RV Technician 309
Professional Ski Instructors of America 539
Professional Squash Association 854
Professional Tennis 833
Professional Travelogue Sponsors 671
Professional Women's Bowling Association 855
Progress in Tourism, Recreation and Hospitality Management 1230
Pubcrawler 950
Public Gaming International 937
Public Golf Courses 140
Purchaser's Guide to the Music Industries 495
Purzycki, Robert 1162

Quirk, James P 743, 750

Racecourse Association 815
Racepages 802
Racetracks of Canada 816
Racing Links 788
Racquetball Club 116
Radio Control Hobby Trade Association 439
Ranchweb Travel 1098
Rando, Guy L. 150
RCI Premier 1024
Rebori, Stephen Joseph 889
Receptive Services Association 1224
Recognition Review 458
Recommend Magazine 1186
Recording Industry Association of America 694, 737, 1273
Recreation Advisor 1066
Recreation Vehicle Dealers Association of North America 332

Recreation Vehicle Industry Association
299, 333, 1256, 1274
Recreation Vehicle Rental Association
334
Reed, William F. 790
Regional Film Theatres 605
Reid, Roger A. 608
Rentalgetaways 1027
Resnik, Gail 609
Resort and Commercial Recreation
Association 1050
Resort Finder 997
Resort Golf Courses 141
Resorts Online 1028
Restaurant Business 979
Restaurant Hospitality 980
Restaurant Industry Operations Report
956
El Restaurante Mexicano 969
RestaurantResults 983
Restaurateurs Association of Great
Britain 992
Retail Focus 238
Retail Print Music Dealers Association
738
Roller Coaster Database 886
Roller Skating Association International
72, 74, 86
Roller Skating Business 78, 1309
Roller Skating Resources 81
Rollerjam 834
Rose, Frank 550
Rothman, Howard 744
Rubber Stampin' Retailer 407
Ruxin, Robert H. 548
RV Business 310
RV Camping Magazine 1073
RV Dealer Search 291
RV News 311, 1310
RV Park & Campground Report 1067
RV Rental Dealer Locator 292
RV Trade Digest 312
RVUSA 316

S.H.O.T. Business 239
Sailing Schools 516
Sailors Choice 524
Sanders, Don 614
Sanders, Susan 614
Sargent, Michael 955

Scheff, Joan 574
Schlossberg, Howard 754
Schoenhaus, Ted 390
Schwanke, Dean 1002
Scottish Travel Agent News 1187
Scottish Youth Hostels Association
1084
Screaming in the Celluloid Jungle 644
Screen 634
Screen International 635, 1311
Scuba Retailers Association 278
Scully, Gerald W. 755
Seatrade Cruise Review 1188
Selling Christmas Decorations 459
Selling Long-Haul 1189, 1312
Selling Short Breaks & Holidays 1190
Semen-Yurzycki, Jeanne 1162
Senior Group Travel 1126, 1191
Shagan, Rena Road Show 569
Shaw, Garth, ed. 1007
ShawGuides 517
Shemal, Sidney 689
Sherman, Eric 620
Ship and Boat Builders National Federa-
tion 373
Shoebridge, Michele, ed. 1326
Shooting Industry 240
Shooting Sports Retailer 241
Showman's Directory 865
Showmen's Guild of Great Britain 914
Showmen's League of America 915
Sierra Nevada College 49
Simon, Ron 553
Sinclair, M. T. 1166, 1257
Singular, Stephen 551
Skateboarding Business 79, 242
Skateparks 69
SkateWeb: The Figure Skating Page 82
Ski Area Management 54, 67, 1313
Ski Tech 55, 243
Skiing Trade News Buyers Guide 56,
244
Small Independent Record Manufactur-
ers Association 739
Small Luxury Hotels of the World 1051
Smith, Jim 695
Smith, Myron J., comp. 763, 764
Smith, Stephen L. J. 1229
SNOW PRO 525
Snow Sports Industries America 279

Snowboarding Business 57, 245
Snowlink 206
Snowmobiling 317
SnowSports Industries America 50
Soccer Industry Council of America 280
Society of British Theatre Designers 599
Society of Film Distributors 672
Society of Professional Audio Recording Services 740
Society of Small Craft Designers 374
Society of Theatre Consultants 916
Sorensen, Halle 1167
The Source 474
Souvenir and Novelty Trade Association 472
Souvenirs, Gifts & Novelties 460
Special Events 881
Specialty Retailer 408
Specialty Travel and Tours 1111
Specialty Travel Index 1110
Sporting & Recreational Goods 254
Sporting Goods Agents Association 281
Sporting Goods Business 246, 1314
Sporting Goods Dealer 247
Sporting Goods Manufacturers Association 213, 214, 215, 282, 1258
Sporting News 760
Sporting-Goods Store 209
Sportlink 207
Sports Agents Directory 543
Sports Lawyers Association 560
Sports Marketing Research Group 75
Sports Travel 1127, 1192
Sports Trends 248
Sportstyle 249
Squite, James E., ed. 615
Stabler, M. J. 1166, 1257
Stamp Wholesaler 409
Stein, Gil 745
Stim, Richard 684
Strandeven, Joy 1116
Stringer's Assistant 250
Strode, William 790
Sutton, William A. 828
Swarbrooke, John 870, 1119
Sweeney, Tim 685
Symphony 701, 1315
Syratt, Gwenda 1163

Tableware Distributors Association 473
Tableware International 461, 1316
Tackle and Shooting Sports Agents Association 283
TCI Magazine 5765
Teare, Richard, ed. 1004, 1245
Telefilm Canada 645
Television Industry Tracking Study 616
Tennis Buyers Guide 251
Tennis Clubs 112
Tennis Industry 125, 252, 1317
Tennis Industry Association 284
Tennis Org UK 127
TennisCountry 128
TennisCountry Travel & Camps 113
TennisOne 129
Theater Equipment Association 673
Theatre Journal 577
Theatre List 565
Themed Entertainment Association 917
Thompson, William Norman 941
Thoroughbred Racing Associations 817, 949
Throgmorton, Todd H. 875
Tim Melago's Directory of Amusement Parks and Roller Coaster Links 888
Timeshare Council 1052
Timeshares 1029
Tour Director 1129
Tourist Attractions and Parks 882
Tourist House Association of America 1053
Tourist Railway Association 1150
Toy Book 410
Toy Directory 414
Toy Manufacturers of America 391, 1318
ToyLinks 415
Transworld Skateboarding 83
Travel Agent 1193, 1318
Travel Agents — UK 1154
Travel and Tourism Research 1204
Travel and Tourism: The International Market 1170
Travel Courier 1194
Travel Data Links 1155
Travel Digest 1195
Travel Industry Association of America 1168, 1173, 1205, 1259
Travel Promotions Directory 1130

Travel Trade 1196
Travel Trade Personnel Guide and
　Booking Directory 1156
Travel Weekly 1197
Travel Weekly (UK) 1198
Travel World 1157
Travel World News 1199
TravelAge 1200
TravelWeek 1201
Trost, Scott 609
TSN 761
TV Talent Agents 544

U.S. Professional Cycling Federation
　856
UK Roller Skate Rink Directory 70
UK Theatre Web 581
UKFitlinks 31
Union Internationale Motonautique
　818
United Golfers' Association 177
United States Auto Club 819
United States Professional Racquetball
　Association 857
United States Racquet Stringers Associ-
　ation 285
United States Tour Operators Associa-
　tion 1151
United States Trotting Association 820
Universal Federation of Travel Agents'
　Association 1225
University of Colorado Business
　Research Division 51
Unlimited Hydroplane Racing Associa-
　tion 821
US Tennis Court and Track Builders
　Association 120, 135
US Tennis Information 114
USGA 169
USITT: The American Association of
　Design and Production Professionals
　600
USTA 130
USTC&TBA 131

Vacation Rental Managers Association
　1054
VanKirk, Richard L. 823, 1231
VanOtten, George A. 927
Variety 636, 1319

Video Age International 637
Video Arcade 866
Video Business 638
Video Marketing Surveys and Forecasts
　617, 1262
Video Software Dealers Association 674
Video Store 639, 1320
Video Systems 640
Videography 641
VideoRetailer 646
Virtual Club 200
Vogel, Harold L. 1260
Volleyball Professionals 835

Waite, Andrew J. 791
Water Sports Industry Association 286
Wedding and Event Videographers
　Association International 675
Wellner, Alison S. 1275
What's New for Family Fun 883
Where to Shoot 208
Where to Stay in Britain 1059
White Book of Ski Areas US & Canada
　40
Wiese, Michael 610
Williams, Allen, ed. 1007
Williams, Debra L. 149
Williams, Jim 1063
Williams, Peter 790
Wintersports Business 58, 253
Wolf, Jim F. 608
Wolosz, Joe 1011
Women's National Basketball Associa-
　tion 783
Women's Professional Billiard Associa-
　tion 858
Women's Professional Rodeo Associa-
　tion 859
Woodall's Campground Management
　1068, 1321
Woodworth Brian B. 11, 122
World Association of Travel Agencies
　1226
World Federation of the Sporting Goods
　Industry 287
World Federation of Tourist Guide
　Associations 1152
World Golf 170
World Ski and Public Snowboard Asso-
　ciations 62

Index

World Ski Association 43
World Tourism 1206
World Travel and Tourism Review
    1164, 1236
World Waterpark Association 918
World Wide Travel Source 1158
WorldClubs 951
World's Best Golf Schools 526
WTA Tour 860

Yacht Architects and Brokers Associa-
    tion 375
Yacht Brokers, Designers and Surveyors
    Association 376

Yacht Charter Association 1153
Yachting Clubs 342
Yacht Clubs ... on the World Wide Web
    341
YBR Marketing 1012, 1276
YHA Limited 1085
Youngson, Mark C. 792
Your Guide to Everything Motorsports
    in Britain 803

Zietz, Karyl Lynn 571
Zimbalist, Andrew, ed. 749